WRITTEN EXPRESSION IN THE LANGUAGE ARTS
ideas and skills

SECOND EDITION

Dorothy Grant Hennings
Professor, Kean College of New Jersey

Barbara Moll Grant
Professor, William Paterson College

Teachers College, Columbia University
New York and London 1981

to George, who encourages

Published by Teachers College Press, 1234 Amsterdam Avenue, New York, N.Y. 10027

First edition, entitled *Content and Craft: Written Expression in the Elementary School*, published by Prentice-Hall, Inc.

Copyright © 1981 by Teachers College, Columbia University

Line drawings by George Hennings

Library of Congress Cataloging in Publication Data

Hennings, Dorothy Grant.
    Written expression in the language arts.

    Previous ed. published in 1973 under title: Content and craft: written expression in the elementary school.
    Includes bibliographies and index.
    1. Language arts (Elementary) I. Grant, Barbara Moll, joint author. II. Title.
LB1576.H335   1981   372.6   80-25532

ISBN 0-8077-2604-4 (pbk)
ISBN 0-8077-2653-2 (cloth)

Manufactured in the United States of America

86 85 84 83 82 81   1 2 3 4 5 6

CONTENTS

FOREWORD

I am pleased to welcome into print *Written Expression in the Language Arts: Ideas and Skills.* This excellent text on the teaching of writing in the elementary grades is sorely needed, not only to educate us to the goals and methods of a writing program for children, but also to build our confidence and enthusiasm for the task. Writing, real writing—not just handwriting and spelling—has been crowded out of the elementary school curriculum. As teachers, we have had little commitment to the significance of writing for producing facility in language and clarity in thinking; we have had little understanding of appropriate methods for stimulating interest in writing and revision among children of diverse experiences and abilities.

I can attest that *Content and Craft: Written Expression in the Elementary School,* the title under which the first edition of this text was published, did stimulate many teachers to value writing. It provided practical methods for organizing and maintaining a growing writing curriculum in classrooms. These qualities are expanded and deepened in this new edition. Increased attention is given to the experiences and oral compositions that form foundations for written expression for both children and adults. Creative questioning strategies are suggested throughout the text to guide teachers in helping children probe their thoughts, feelings, insights, and vocabulary for unique ideas—and the language to express them.

I am pleased to see a new chapter in this edition on the beginning writer, the very young child. When children have had few books read to them, they may have little interest in learning to read; when they have had few exhilarating opportunities to see their own ideas and words captured on paper, they may have little interest in learning to write. Kindergarten and primary teachers truly are teaching the basics of writing when they take dictation from children and when they encourage them to participate in the writing process using their own invented spellings. Chapter 3 of *Written Expression in the Language Arts* gives the teacher of beginning writers practical methods for organizing instruction so that frequent dictation from each child is manageable in the busy classroom schedule.

On a firm foundation of confidence, young writers go on to explore the realms of prose and poetry. The authors of this text guide teachers at all grade levels toward possible topics and forms that appeal to children, liberally documenting these with samples of children's writing.

Hennings and Grant are knowledgeable teachers and capable writers; their text is both useful and interesting, practical and challenging. They state in the Introduction to this new edition that current knowledge of the process of learning to write is in an embryonic stage, and it surely is, but these authors have done a masterful job of bringing together up-to-date information on why and how children can gain enthusiasm and skill in writing.

—Sheila Mary Fitzgerald
Associate Professor
Michigan State University

ACKNOWLEDGMENTS

To some extent every author is indebted to others who contributed ideas or rendered assistance in the writing or production of his or her book. This is particularly true when a book includes instructional strategies developed and tested in actual classroom situations. Because *Written Expression in the Language Arts: Ideas and Skills* emphasizes classroom practices, its authors owe a debt of gratitude to all those teachers who have willingly shared their experiences in teaching children to write. Specific thanks are extended to Grace Wiggins, Madeline Bruhn, Stephanie Nowel, and Mary Ellen Dobryznski. The authors extend thanks also to the children who have allowed observers to look over their shoulders and read what they have written and rewritten.

The authors express appreciation to Professor Sheila Fitzgerald and her graduate students at Michigan State University, who analyzed the first edition of this book published under the title *Content and Craft: Written Expression in the Elementary School* (New York: Prentice-Hall, 1973) and rendered suggestions as to the style and direction the second edition should maintain. Mary Allison, former senior editor at Teachers College Press, was helpful too in making suggestions as the manuscript developed; and Marianthi Lazos of the Press contributed through her careful editing of the final manuscript. Louise Craft, managing editor at the Press, helped through her efficient handling of the details associated with publishing a book. George Hennings provided detailed reading and criticism of the manuscript and galleys. To all of these, the authors say a heartfelt "Thank you!"

INTRODUCTION

Nulla dies sine linea.
Not a day without a line.
Apelles, PLINY THE ELDER

The term *language arts* refers to five basic communication processes taught in elementary and middle schools: thinking, listening,
speaking, reading, and writing. *Written Expression in the Language
Arts: Ideas and Skills* focuses on one of these arts—writing—as it occurs
within the language arts program and, indeed, within the total elementary curriculum. Writing is a way of making thoughts stand still so they
can be examined and weighed. It is oral language translated into a more
permanent and at times more structured form. To write requires the
ability to listen, speak, read, and think in a variety of creative and logical
patterns.

When writing is perceived as one means of communicating and as
highly interrelated with the other language arts, then listening, speaking,
dramatizing, nonverbal activity, pictorializing, reading, and thinking
quite naturally become elements within a writing program. A fundamental point stressed in *Written Expression in the Language Arts: Ideas and
Skills* is that each of the arts is not a discrete area to be taught for its own
sake; rather, the relationships between the other language arts and written expression are used in designing a total writing program. Reading,
speaking, working with linguistic concepts, listening, dramatizing, and
creating artistically are all important within an ongoing writing program.

As its title hints, the book also stresses both the substance of
writing—the ideas to be expressed—and the process of writing—the skills
necessary for ideas to be communicated with clarity and style. Children

learn to write by learning to build significant idea-content: an opinion on an issue, a feeling about something special, a sequence of events that teases the imagination. In addition, children learn to write by learning to handle words on paper, that is, by acquiring the skill to translate ideas into the words, lines, stanzas, sentences, and paragraphs characteristic of written material. Without a successful translation, a significant idea can be irretrievably lost. This premise about the importance of both ideas and skills in writing provides the book's overall organizing structure. Part I centers on the ideas for writing, Part II focuses on the skills for writing, while Part III merges ideas and skills by describing ways of making poetry and prose experiences a part of the writing program.

These two major themes of the book are developed inductively. In the first chapter, one element basic to a writing program is considered—firsthand experience as a base for thinking activity. In successive chapters, other elements are added so that the construct proposed expands chapter by chapter. As a result, no one chapter stands completely alone; ideas expressed in one must be interpreted in terms of what has gone before and what will come after. For the reader to take specific teaching suggestions out of context is to defeat the overall direction proposed. To take ideas randomly from the book and design these into isolated lessons is to overlook the importance of a continuous and integrated program in which parts intertwine and skills build one upon another. Each activity must be conceived as part of a meaningful, well-balanced program.

Most readers of a book such as this are looking for practical suggestions and supporting theory that are relevant in their own classrooms. Because readers crave relevancy, only those research studies that bear directly on teaching practices have been cited. For the same reason, many specific examples have been included to show how research and theory translate into classroom activity. All suggestions, of course, are not relevant for all readers. Those who teach in rural areas will find suggestions about visits to airports and excursions along city streets impractical. Conversely, city teachers will find rural activities inappropriate. Similarly, teachers of various grade levels must adapt examples to meet the needs of the group of children they are teaching. There is obviously no such thing as a third grade or kindergarten activity.

In describing specific teaching strategies, the authors risk the charge of being too structured. A reader can rightly question, ''Isn't there a place for completely open writing, motivated by children's inner needs for self-expression?'' The answer is an obvious yes. Yet some structure, or teacher guidance, is needed, especially as children get started writing.

Recently, one of the authors attended a conference-session led by a gifted poet. A member of the audience related that he offered his high school students an opportunity to write every week on topics of their own choosing. After just a few weeks, students began to feel uncomfortable with the assignment, complaining that they did not know what to write about. Their compositions became shorter and shorter. The questioner remarked that he had always believed that completely open assignments were necessary if individual creativity was to emerge. The poet, who had worked with children as poet-in-residence-in-the-schools, reminded the questioner that creativity favors the prepared mind. It is the job of the teacher to help children and youth prepare for writing. This preparation takes the form of teacher-guided group writing, small group writing activities, and structured assignments. In sum, openness must blend with structure; as students gain confidence in their ability to express themselves on paper and acquire the necessary thinking and language skills, structure gives way to openness, allowing them to venture into original areas of expression.

In describing specific teaching strategies, the authors also risk the question, "What evidence is there that supports your prescription?" Three kinds of evidence were used in developing ideas for teaching. The first of these is research and theory. In such areas as revision and skill development, considerable evidence exists that suggests directions that practice should take. Where research studies do exist, they have been cited so that a reader may investigate the primary sources if he or she so desires.

A second kind of evidence is the manner in which writers of the past have pursued their art. Where appropriate, anecdotes or quotations about writing based on the lives of successful writers are included—Wordsworth, Coleridge, Irving. Samples of American and English prose and poetry are included too. These are not intended to be shared with children, but rather to give the reader a clue as to how real writers go about their work. Based on this evidence, we can make hypotheses about ways to help children write.

A third type of evidence is successful practices the authors have seen in classrooms they have visited. In developing an integrated, language arts approach to teaching written expression and an idea/skills orientation, the authors have drawn heavily upon learning experiences they have observed and upon samples of written work produced by children.

Although the ideas proposed in this book are based on the evidence offered by research on writing, by the musings of actual writers on the way they ply their art, and by successful classroom practices, the authors must caution that what educators know about the writing process is still in an embryonic stage. In this respect, the book represents a beginning rather than an end, an exploration into a land in which much more exploring remains to be done.

D. G. H.
B. M. G.

Part I

IDEAS FOR WRITING

Thus great with child to speak and
   helpless in my throes.
Biting my truant pen, beating myself
   for spite:
"Fool," said my Muse to me, "look in
   thy heart and write!"

Sir Philip Sidney, ASTROPHEL AND STELLA

1

LET CHILDREN CULTIVATE IDEAS ◀▶ experiencing and thinking

Sudden a thought came like a full-blown rose,
Flushing his brow.

John Keats, "The Eve of St. Agnes"

Frustrated by problems he was experiencing with English spellings, Rusty took pen in hand and wrote:

GOOFY

Once there was a boy named Goofy. The reason Goofy was named Goofy was because he always goofed.

Like the day Goofy had a spelling test. He spelled "ate" "aet," and he spelled "cat" "kat." Goofy marked his paper right. But the teacher didn't! Goofy could never figure teachers out.

Reacting to a power failure, a teenager wrote:

POWERLESS

the giant city
roars and grinds, slowing to halt:
a total darkness

Writing a science report, yet another student proposed that chemical equations can be solved by using the mathematics of simultaneous equations. Each of these individuals—the third grader named Rusty, the teenager, and the science student—was able to produce an effective written piece because each had an idea to communicate.

3

The sowing, growing, and plucking of an idea are first requisites for effective writing. An idea in its simplest form is an insight that is unique for a person as he or she reacts to a multitude of stimuli from the world around and from the inner self. Studying his or her personal perceptions and restructuring both knowledge and feelings, the thinker forms an original product—an idea. Without an idea to express, a writer can hardly begin to compose, for *ideas are the substance of writing.* This is as true for the poet who produces an imaginative, feeling-laden communication as it is for the mathematician who writes a professional treatise and for the student who composes in response to a classroom activity. The writer must put together an idea before the piece can be written well.

SATURATING THE MIND WITH EXPERIENCES

Ideas do not sprout out of nothingness; they favor the prepared ground. Consider one of the greatest nature poets of the English language, William Wordsworth. Wordsworth was a wanderer amid the hills and rills of the English Lake District. There he felt the power of nature all around him and the stillness and beauty of the English countryside. The results were his nature poems and sonnets, his youthful "Prelude," "Tintern Abbey," and "My Heart Leaps Up." The content of his poetry was the content of his experiences in the Lake District. A London-bound Wordsworth could never have written as the wandering Wordsworth did.

Consider, too, one of the giants of American prose, Washington Irving. The environment that provided the firsthand experiences for Irving's *Tales of Alhambra* was the Alhambra itself; Irving wrote the *Tales* in a little room high in the Moorish palace at Granada, a room overlooking the lush gardens with their magnificent fountains.

Young writers also need the raw material of real experiences to create ideas. How can a third grader write of spelling frustrations without having experienced them directly? How can a teenager write about darkness without firsthand knowledge of a complete blackout? How can the science student propose a relationship between two kinds of equations unless both are within his or her knowledge bank?

Direct experiences with their world should be part of children's activity in schools. Experiences serve as seeds out of which ideas sprout. Children can go to zoos, farms, and aquariums to discover the wide variety of living things. They can take nature walks and walks on city streets. They can tramp through newly fallen snow and leave angel prints behind them. They can stand and watch water trickle in rivulets down a windowpane. They can dig into the earth and find all sorts of things. They can run as fast as they can against the wind. They can walk in soft sand on a beach and feel themselves sink deeply in. They can play tag and ghost and hopscotch. They can peer at the stars and the moon through the lens of a telescope and at skin and blood, algae and paramecia, under the lens of a microscope. They can experience the difficulty of understanding fractions, equations, spelling inconsistencies, and even people. They can watch spontaneous combustion, melting and freezing, and chemical combinations occur on the laboratory table. They can watch a colony of ants make an anthill, a hermit crab navigate its borrowed house, and a spider spin its web.

Children can bake marble cake and swirl chocolate through the batter. They can watch swirls of pollution spiral from a smokestack. They can grow plants from seeds and follow each day's growth. They can rub fat on the bark of trees and observe woodpeckers feed on it. They can simply lie in the grass and watch clouds make pictures overhead. They can get excited over the inequities of life and take positive action. They can look into someone's eyes. They can play with their reflections in concave, convex, and flat mirrors. They can shout as loud as they can shout, throw as far as they can throw, and jump as high as they can jump. They can hammer nails and turn screws. They can watch 747s climb into the sky at a nearby airport. They can eat apple butter, comb honey, and bagels. The experiences we can provide for children are limited only by our imaginations and the available resources.

Experiencing with All the Senses

The person who can gain the most from an experience is one who is primed to receive impressions through all the senses. Impressions come through smell. We smell the rain, the odor of fresh-baked cake, the heavy odor of stale cigarette smoke. Impressions come through sound. We hear the crashing of breaking glass, the chirruping of crickets on a hot evening, and the even roar of an airplane. Our sense of sight brings perceptions of lightness and darkness, reds and roses, greens and blue-greens. Sight allows judgment of distance, the size and shape of objects, motion, and relative motion. Other impressions are tactile: we feel heat and cold, react to pressure, and receive sensations of pain and pleasure. Still other impressions bombard our taste buds. The taste of salted, buttered new corn brings a smile to our faces, whereas the taste of bitter orange rind triggers a frown.

Teachers must prime children to react with all the senses—sound, sight, taste, smell, and touch. They must help children see and feel the concrete, help them become more keenly aware of odors, and encourage children to listen for unusual sounds. Here are some experiences with the senses that can sow lots of idea-seeds.

Sound

1. Ask children to close their eyes and listen. Do this in different situations—in quiet woods, on a busy city street corner, at the airport, on the bank of a stream, on a windy day.
2. Ask children to listen to a record or tape with the volume turned down, then with it turned way up; with the speaker placed at a distance, then placed nearby.
3. Take children for a walk in the woods or park on a fall day. Encourage them to listen to the leaves crackling beneath their feet, the wind rustling through the trees, the birds singing, the dogs barking.
4. Listen to a musical composition and try to distinguish instruments. As a preliminary exercise, have children listen for the precise sound of rhythm band instruments. Students can close their eyes while the teacher demonstrates the sound of each instrument.
5. Listen to records that are filled with sounds such as Disney's *Sounds of a Haunted House.*
6. Take a street walk, note pad in hand, to record sounds heard.
7. Make a tape with the children entitled "Sounds Around Us." Take the recorder outside and tape sounds of lawn mowers, sanitation trucks, fire engines, running water, pneumatic drills, foghorns, and insects singing—whatever sounds make up the local environment.
8. On a city walk, run a stick along a metal fence; try it in different ways to see if sounds of different pitch and amplitude can be produced.
9. Have children vibrate rulers over the edges of their desks. Experiment to determine how sounds can be changed.
10. Listen to and contrast the sounds of motorized vehicles—cars, motorcycles, trucks. Think about differences both in pitch and amplitude.

Sight—Color

1. Play with watercolors. One child has only red, orange, and yellow with which to work; another only yellow, blue, and green; another only orange, blue, and violet. They draw their world in these hues and compare the effects achieved.
2. Make a fluorescent world. Children can draw their world using crayons that fluoresce when held under a black light. Later they talk

about their world made spectacularly colorful as they hold their drawings illuminated only by the black light.
3. On a nature walk, collect greens and compare the different shades of
   green produced by nature.
4. Have a red day when all children should try to wear something red to
   school. Compare shades during talk-time.
5. Observe eye colors of children in the class and describe them.
6. Study the colors of rock samples and describe the pinks, grays,
   greens, and golds found in nature.
7. Play with a prism or a crystal. Make dancing rainbows on the ceiling
   and describe the effect.

Sight—Motion
1. Watch cars moving along the street. Describe how fast they are going.
2. Watch people walking along the street and describe their gait.
3. Observe the relative speeds and kinds of locomotion of different
   animals: the hermit crab, the grasshopper, the toad, the turtle, the
   bird. (A follow-up on this might be a reading of the well-known
   Aesop fable, "The Tortoise and the Hare.")

Sight—Size and Shape
1. At an airport, study the relative sizes and shapes of airplanes.
2. On a street, study the relative sizes and shapes of cars.
3. Study the clouds and imagine what pictures can be "seen" in
   the clouds.
4. Look at buildings. Find rectangles, squares, circles, parallelograms,
   and other geometric shapes in their structures.
5. Study a seashell and then sketch its shape. Make sketches that show
   the shell half its size, double its size, giant size. Do the same with
   other objects.
6. On a large sheet of brown paper have children trace the outlines of
   their hands and feet. Then describe the shapes produced and compare sizes.
7. Bring in a collection of work tools, kitchen gadgets, fruits, or bottles.
   Look at them and describe the shapes.
8. Study the shape of smoke as it comes from smokestacks.

Smell
1. Smell sliced lemon, chocolate, mint, onion, and ammonia. Express
   the smells in words.
2. Visit the cafeteria or the nurse's office and notice the odors there.
3. On a nature walk, break leaves of wintergreen, mint, bayberry,

sassafras, skunk cabbage, and spice bush. Talk about their scents.
4. Take an "air-pollution excursion." Stand on a crowded corner and distinguish the smells. In an industrial area, sniff odors of cookies, perfume, or whatever is being produced.
5. Burn bread, paper, sulfur, and tobacco. Distinguish the odors produced.
6. Stand near a barn and talk about farm smells—cows, chickens, hay.
7. Talk about odors on a trip to the zoo.
8. Whiff different spices: thyme, oregano, bay, nutmeg, cinnamon. Talk about their aromas.
9. Read any of the number of "scratch and sniff" books on the market today. As the story unfolds, share the scents with listeners.

Taste
1. Taste different spices and condiments—salt, pepper, thyme, nutmeg, chocolate. Describe their tastes.
2. Conduct tasting tests of a common product, tasting different brands to note differences.
3. Conduct tasting tests between butter and margarines. See if differences can be noted and described.
4. Conduct tasting tests with canned, frozen, and fresh samples of a commodity: orange, pineapple, or grapefruit juices. See if differences can be noted and described.
5. Taste a strip of PTC test paper. See who can taste it and who cannot. (PTC paper tastes bitter to some and is tasteless to others. Ability to taste is an inherited characteristic. Paper can be purchased from Carolina Biological Supply, Burlington, N.C.)
6. Compare the tastes of natural products—orange rind (bitter), lemon (sour), sugar (sweet), salt (salty). Attach labels to the tastes.

Touch
1. Feel sandpaper, cotton, wood, a mirror, fur, a piece of carpet, a piece of textured wallpaper with eyes closed. Use adjectives to describe the impressions.
2. Put the left hand into water of one temperature. Have other dishes with water at different temperatures. Put the right hand successively in these dishes, and judge the relative temperatures of each. This could be carried out as an "impressions lab." The teacher has large buckets of water at different temperatures on a counter. Children ladle samples into small containers (plastic ice-cream containers) to analyze back at their desks. They set up categories labeled with different adjectives to describe the comparative temperatures.

3. Have children "feel" a cloud by taking them for a walk on a foggy day and having them feel mist brushing their faces.

4. Have children "feel" sunshine by taking them for a walk on a bright, hot, sunny day and having them stand still to let the sun warm their skin. Have them "feel" cold by taking them for a brisk walk on a very cold day. In each case, follow "walk" with "talk" so that children begin to verbalize their sense impressions.

5. Have children "feel" snow by picking up a handful of newly fallen snow, of closely packed snow, and of dirty, melting snow. Ask them to decide how each makes them feel inside.

6. Have children "feel" wind. Go outside and stand facing the wind as it blows all around. Ask children to imagine riding on the wind.

7. Have children feel grass, feathers, tree bark, leaves. Ask them to think of some other material that has the same texture or feel.

8. Have children walk on different surfaces—sand, grass, concrete, and wood—and describe the differences.

9. Have children touch woolen tweeds, silk, cotton, wash-and-wear, linen, and knits. Have them talk about the differences.

10. Conduct consumer tests of products, for example, blankets, sandpaper, and pillows. Decide which is the best for the job it has to do.

Experiencing Through Reading and Listening

A walk in the woods, a visit to a castle, a view of an eclipse—firsthand experiences such as these can blossom into ideas to be expressed in writing. But the reading of a thought that someone else has composed in story or verse form can inspire as well. In the prefatory note to "Kubla Khan" Samuel Coleridge explained that these lines from "Purchas's Pilgrimage"—"Here the Khan Kubla commanded a palace to be built, and a stately garden thereunto. And thus ten miles of fertile ground were inclosed with a wall"—were what inspired him to begin:

KUBLA KHAN
In Xanadu did Kubla Khan
  A stately pleasure-dome decree:
Where Alph, the sacred river, ran
Through caverns measureless to man
  Down to a sunless sea.
So twice five miles of fertile ground
With walls and towers were girdled round:
And here were gardens bright with sinuous rills,
Where blossomed many an incense-bearing tree,
And here were forests ancient as the hills,
Enfolding sunny spots of greenery.

Werner Beyer, an authority on Coleridge, has suggested that Coleridge was also inspired by C. M. Wieland's *Oberon*. Coleridge translated *Oberon,* and Beyer believes that the numerous impressions Coleridge gleaned from it and recorded in his *Notebooks* found their way into "Kubla Khan" and supplied important detail. In short, Coleridge's mind, a storehouse of impressions gathered through reading, was ripe for invention of ideas.

Starting in nursery school, teachers can sow idea-seeds by sharing stories and poems as well as informational material with children. Later, as children become independent readers, their personal reading can generate ideas. In school writing programs, ideas for writing can develop out of actual content heard or read, from themes embodied in literature, and from structures encountered in books, stories, and poems.

Take, for example, Taro Yashimo's old but still popular story of a youth's search for acceptance, *Crow Boy* (Viking Press, 1955). Children in Grace Wiggins's third grade listened intently to the story, talked about Crow Boy's feelings, and "translated" the story into poetry.

CHIBI, THE CROW BOY

Chibi,
a small Japanese boy, was always sad.
He did unusual things—
　　　staring at ceilings,
　　　crossing his eyes.
Chibi was always sad.

Classmates called him names.
Classmates never let him play their games.
But Chibi changed—
　　　He imitated the baby crow.
　　　He imitated the mother and father crows.
Chibi, the Crow Boy.

Grace Wiggins's third grade class

In this instance, a story supplied the content and even the vocabulary for writing.

An upper-grade class listened to their teacher share the first chapter of Mildred Taylor's *Roll of Thunder, Hear My Cry* (Dial, 1976). Later youngsters went in groups to the Listen-here Center to hear a taped rendition of the rest of the book or individually to the Reading Corner to read copies placed there. Throughout the two-week period when youngsters were completing *Roll of Thunder,* they were talking together and writing about how Cassie and her brothers must have felt growing up in an environment where discrimination took violent forms. Their writing activity was varied: diary accounts of a story happening told as if one were Cassie, Little Man, or T. J.; newspaper reports of a striking story event; free verses expressing feelings; reports of other instances of discrimination children had experienced firsthand; character portraits of story people. In this case, the reading-listening supplied the theme or overall topic for writing.

Reading and listening can also provide a writing structure or pattern. Students who have found writing difficult often find it rather easy to compose following the same structure of a repeating piece such as "This Is the House That Jack Built." One older group produced this sample after listening to and chorusing the original version:

THIS IS THE NEST THAT BIRDS BUILT

This is the nest that birds built.
This is the egg that lay in the nest that birds built.
This is the insect that landed on the egg that lay in the
nest that birds built.
This is the butterfly that came out of the insect that landed
on the egg that lay in the nest that birds built.
This is the girl who saw the butterfly that came out of the
insect that landed on the egg that lay in the nest that
birds built.
This is the mosquito that bit the girl who saw the butterfly
that came out of the insect that landed on the egg that
lay in the nest that birds built.
This is the hand that slapped the mosquito that bit the girl
who saw the butterfly that came out of the insect that
landed on the egg that lay in the nest that birds built.
This is the young bird, all newly hatched, that landed on the
hand that slapped the mosquito that bit the girl who saw
the butterfly that came out of the insect that landed on
the egg that lay in the nest that birds built.

A similar piece by a second grader is shown in figure 1.1.

As these examples indicate, experiences with the written word as it is composed in books, stories, and poems can "seed" ideas to be expressed. Such experiences are as important as firsthand encounters with the real world; for the way writers put words together on paper is a bit different from the way speakers do it. For that reason, reading and listening to a wealth of words must be an integral part of any writing program.

Figure 1.1.   A second grader's piece modeled after "This Is The House That Jack Built"

OPERATING ON THE SEEDS OF EXPERIENCE

Although ideas are the substance of all written expression, the kinds of ideas embodied therein are varied. Some written pieces are simply a reflection of the world as perceived by the observer. The observer describes what was viewed, reports on happenings, itemizes procedures, retells something heard, or summarizes perceptions of events. Other pieces of writing suggest relationships: the writer notes similarities or differences, identifies sequences and patterns, relates evidence, or expresses cause-and-effect relationships. In still other pieces, a writer projects explanatory schemes or designs, constructs hypotheses or generalizations, or devises a procedure, a classification scheme, or a taxonomy.

Written content may also be an expression of feeling. The writer "pours out" on paper personal reactions to an event, a person, or an object. He or she may express happiness or sadness, love or hate, envy or satisfaction, anticipation or fear, contentment or anxiety.

Related kinds of written content are those in which the writer expresses a preference for one item over another, an opinion or ideas regarding the value of an object, an event, an individual, or even another written communication. The writer suggests why he or she likes one object but not another, why one event is more important than a second, why a particular technique is more effective than another, why one action is more justifiable than another, why one communication is more consistent than a second. In these cases, the writer is either rendering a judgment or stating preferences or opinions.

Some written pieces are sheer invention. The writer creates a character, an event, and even a place, manipulating characters and action as necessary for story development and designing relationships between characters. In so doing, the writer moves freely from reality into fantasy, describing events or things that could exist in the real world but have not existed exactly as projected. The raw material of such invention may be people, things, or events in the real world, but in the end the creator produces a unique combination of circumstances.

In handling ideas in any of the ways just described, the writer is essentially a thinker, operating intellectually on the seeds of his or her previous experiences with the world and with words. These thinking operations as they apply to writing are of five interrelated kinds—reflecting, relating, projecting, personalizing, and inventing—as shown in the categorization of thinking-writing operations given below:

Thinking-Writing Operations

A. **Reflecting on the world:**   thinking that requires the writer to represent with a high degree of accuracy what has been observed, heard, or read
   1. *Describing:* enumerating the characteristics of an object, material, or person, including such properties as color, shape, size, smell, taste, motion, temperature, texture, quality, weight, purpose
   2. *Reporting on a happening:* recounting an event by telling who was involved, when it happened, where it happened, what happened, under what conditions it happened, what materials were associated with the happening, and/or how long it lasted
   3. *Telling how:* telling how to do something, how to act, or how to go somewhere

4. *Retelling something heard or read:* retelling in one's own words ideas expressed by someone else
5. *Summarizing:* retelling or reviewing in shortened form by highlighting key points or events

B. **Relating phenomena existing in the world:** thinking that requires the writer to identify relationships among items or instances
   1. *Comparing:* identifying ways two or more items are the same
   2. *Contrasting:* identifying ways that two or more items differ
   3. *Classifying:* grouping together items that share a common property
   4. *Analyzing qualitatively:* indicating which items are in a higher or lower position in a hierarchy, are more complex than others, are closer or farther away, or are bigger or smaller
   5. *Analyzing sequentially:* indicating which items sequentially or chronologically come first, second, third, and so forth
   6. *Explaining:* indicating why something happened
      a. Explaining in terms of cause-and-effect, or connecting two events, one of which caused the other
      b. Explaining by referring to known principles, or indicating that certain data are supported by a particular principle
      c. Explaining in terms of rational intent, or suggesting the purpose served by an act or event

C. **Projecting hypotheses, theories, and designs:** thinking that requires the writer to propose ideas that go beyond observable data but are consonant with them
   1. *Hypothesizing:* predicting or guessing based on study of data and leading to future action
   2. *Generalizing:* proposing conceptual schemes, or generalizations, that are founded on analysis of several related events and can be used to explain related events; theorizing
   3. *Designing:* setting forth a scheme for classifying data, taking action, or putting things together; planning
      a. Planning for action: developing an original way of doing something
      b. Creating construction plans: designing plans for an original device
      c. Devising a classification scheme: designing a system for categorizing a number of items
      d. Devising a taxonomy: designing a system for categorizing items that share a hierarchical relationship

D. **Personalizing:**   thinking that requires the writer to express personal feelings, preferences, beliefs, or judgments
 1. *Expressing feelings:* reacting emotionally—either positively or negatively—to an event, person, or object
 2. *Expressing preferences:* stating a liking or disliking for someone or something, with or without supplying reasons
 3. *Expressing opinions:* stating a personal belief or point of view not necessarily in accord with fact
 4. *Expressing judgments:* rendering a judgment about the effectiveness, justifiability, consistency, importance, and overall worth of something and supporting that judgment by referring to clearly defined criteria

E. **Inventing:**   thinking that requires the writer to go beyond real and/or actual occurrences to create descriptions, dialogue, persons, and/or plots
 1. *Creating descriptions:* describing that departs from fact
 2. *Creating dialogue:* inventing conversations or speeches that do not purport to be a record of actual communication that has taken place
 3. *Creating characters:* inventing characters based not completely on individuals who exist or who have existed
 4. *Creating plot:* putting together a sequence of concocted events

THINKING AND WRITING

To define written expression in terms of the mental operations that produce it is not to suggest that one piece of written expression requires only one kind of thought. Indeed, a single piece may require the writer to reflect, to relate, to project, to personalize, and to invent. It does suggest, however, that different kinds of written content demand different kinds and even levels of thinking—that is, to write different kinds of content, *one must be able to manipulate ideas in varying ways.*

To write descriptive content, for example, one must understand the qualities that materials can have and know how to apply that understanding to the study of new material. To write a set of procedures, one must be able to devise a logical framework that gives an orderly sequence to events. To summarize, one must be able to identify what is most significant and discard less relevant points. To write conceptual content, one must be able to identify key elements and see possible relationships existing among the parts. To personalize, one must become emotionally involved and allow one's most personal thoughts to surface for others to see. To invent requires one to put elements together in new and sometimes fanciful patterns.

Pursuing this point to its logical conclusion, the authors propose that *to teach children to write is first to help them operate intellectually on the raw material of experiences they have had and are having with the real and imaginary worlds.* In short, it is to teach them to think in a variety of ways. But to help children think is too general a goal to attack. We must break down the thinking-writing process into its component tasks if we are to know what we are seeking and if we are to reach our objective—a new generation of young people who can handle ideas on paper. To do this, let us return to the categorization of thinking-writing operations on pages 13 to 15, considering what is required to produce each kind of writing.

Reflecting on the World

To write material that is a reflection of the world, the thinker must translate his or her impressions of objects, events, and people into verbal pictures that are faithful representations of that world out there. (See fig. 1.2 for a sample of this kind of writing.) In so doing, of course, a person is limited by his or her ability to perceive accurately, which in turn is determined by his or her background of knowledge, past experiences, present interests, and the ideas already formulated. In the words of Goethe, "We see only what we know."

In *The Art of Scientific Investigation,* W. I. B. Beveridge recounts an anecdote about Darwin's failure to observe unexpected phenomena when he and a colleague were exploring a valley. Darwin stated that

> neither of us saw a trace of the wonderful glacial phenomena all around us; we did not notice plainly scored rocks, the perched boulders, the lateral and terminal moraines.

Beveridge suggests that these "things were not observed" by the great Darwin "because they were not expected or not specifically looked for."

That people observe what they expect and see what they are looking for was personally brought home to one of the authors on a nature outing. Walking along the edge of a pond in an Audubon Society Refuge on Cape Cod, she heard a plop but thought nothing of it. A companion, who was a biologist, stopped in midstep, turned toward the direction of the plop, and pulled aside the undergrowth. The writer still saw nothing until the biologist pointed to the fat green bullfrog, well-camouflaged in the grasses of the pond. After that, she saw many other frogs. She now knew what to listen for and she knew where to look. In teaching children to write reflective content, perhaps we need first to teach them things to expect and things to look for.

To begin to do this, the teacher can set up observational sites—posts from which children can view happenings directly. A site might be a post overlooking a bird-feeding station just outside the classroom window, a post that overlooks a busy street outside, a stool set near a demonstration table where experimentation is carried on in the classroom. Children can take turns observing from the lookout post and recording what they perceive. The teacher can tie a clipboard with a yellow pad and a pencil to the observational post. Children can note their observations on paper, to be shared later with classmates.

Figure 1.2. A child's composition based on her observations

Describing. To describe what they see, thinker-writers must perceive the individual elements of the world around and select the most significant ones to communicate. But before being able to look at a specific situation and perceive elements to describe, students need some understanding about the characteristics, or attributes, things generally have. This understanding guides observations; it gives observers things to expect and things to look for. For example, knowledge that trees have girth, height, motion, bark pattern, and leaf pattern may lead a writer to see those elements in a particular scene and write: "The towering tree swayed menacingly as each new gust caught up its fragile branches and threw them higher into the air. The thick blue-green leaves appeared almost to shiver in the wind and the gray, mottled bark to tighten in protection against the cold." To write this description, the observer must see the action of the wind against the trees and consider the less obvious characteristics—the blue-greenness of the leaves and the mottled texture of the bark.

How can the teacher help children describe fully? One beginning is to set up opportunities for children to describe in terms of Attribute Guides—charts that ask for descriptive words and phrases about objects, places, or people. Figures 1.3, 1.4, and 1.5 provide examples of guides

Figure 1.3. A guide for studying objects

DESCRIBING AN OBJECT

Object to Be Described: _____ Name of Observer: _____
List as many words as you can to describe these qualities of your object.

1. Color: _____

2. Shape: _____

3. Size (how tall, how broad): _____

4. Weight: _____

5. Texture (how rough, how smooth): _____

6. Temperature (how hot, how cold): _____

7. State of motion (how fast, how slow, how even, how jerky): _____

   _____

8. Aroma: _____

9. Taste: _____

Figure 1.4. A guide for studying places

DESCRIBING A PLACE

Place to Be Described: _____ Name of Observer: _____
List as many words as you can to describe these qualities of the place.

1. Important things living there: _____

2. Objects there: _____

3. Arrangement of objects and things (use words such as "by, with, above,
   under, opposite, next to, across from"): _____

   _____

4. Main colors and shapes there: _____

5. Temperature and/or wetness of the place: _____

6. Feeling you get there: _____

---

that help children study objects, places, and people they want to
describe. Children on observational excursions in the out-of-doors can
project descriptive words using this type of observational guide. Objects—leaves, feathers, rocks, pieces of bark, pieces of cloth—can be
brought back to the classroom, placed in descriptive grab bags, and
described with the aid of a guide. Primary graders can go to a Writing
Station to select an object to describe. In the station the teacher can
cluster pictures and reproductions of art to be used in the same way.
Older children can go a step further and indicate which qualities of an
object appear to be the most significant. Photographs of people can be
placed in the station too along with a collection of Guides for Describing
People. (See fig. 1.5.) Later young writers can share completed guides to
see if listeners can figure out which picture they were describing. By pursuing activities such as these, children are learning to think descriptively
as part of everyday classroom work.

Reporting on a Happening. Reporting on a happening, a writer
employs similar thinking skills. He or she considers what happened, who
was involved, when it happened, where it happened, the conditions
under which it occurred, and why it happened. Working with this information, the writer puts together—or as Benjamin Bloom would say,
"synthesizes"—a design through which to report the event.

A Reporting Guide similar to those just discussed will start children

Figure 1.5. A guide for studying people

DESCRIBING A PERSON
Person to Be Described: _____ Name of Observer: _____
1. Size (how tall): _____
2. Weight (how heavy): _____
3. Facial features
a. Hair color and style:_____
b. Eye color and shape: _____
c. Complexion:_____
d. Nose shape:_____
e. Glasses: _____
f. Overall facial shape: _____
4. Clothing
a. General style and fit: _____
b. Color: _____
5. Body features
a. Legs:_____
b. Arms: _____
c. Overall stance: _____
6. Activity level (quiet, in motion): _____

thinking in reportorial terms. (See fig. 1.6 for an example.) Using their Reporting Guides, children can be encouraged to report on classroom, school, community, and televised happenings by jotting down words and phrases. Completed guides can be posted on the bulletin board as a local news roundup—the news in brief—and can be used as notes for sharing during current events discussions. Based on data compiled on the guides, children can work together to write paragraphs about the event.

Telling How. Telling how requires one to think in terms of sequences of action. First, one must see the sequential parts that occur

Figure 1.6. Reporting on an event

A REPORTING GUIDE

Event: _____ Reporter: _____
Next to each question, write a sentence or two that answers it.
1. What action took place?

2. Who was there?

3. What did each person do?

4. When did this happen?

5. Where did it occur?

6. Under what conditions did it happen?

7. Why did this happen?

---

within a happening or that are necessary to achieve a result. For example, explaining how to perform an experiment or bake a cake, one must be aware that there is a systematic sequence of steps to carry out—that *a* is done first, *b* second, *c* next. Explaining how to go from point *x* to point *y*, one must again be aware of sequences: "*Start* out by following Main Street until it intersects with Front Street. *There* turn left and *continue* . . . ; *finally*. . . ." One must also be able to figure out basic steps in the procedure and be able to say to oneself, "Here is the first step, another step, still another." Procedures, after all, are comprised of rather discrete steps; to tell how, the writer must be able to distinguish one step from the next and place them in appropriate order.

A flowchart in which steps are schematically shown with boxes, arrows, and lines is one way to introduce youngsters to telling how. For example, given the problem of telling how to plant tulip bulbs—a procedure they have just carried out—students can plot the sequence of steps diagrammatically as shown in figure 1.7. This type of diagram can be constructed as a group project in which those involved in a procedure go on to design the flowchart on large sheets of brown paper and show the direction of action with colored felt pens. Flowcharts once devised become notes to use in composing paragraphs that tell how to do it.

Figure 1.7. A flowchart to help children understand logical sequences

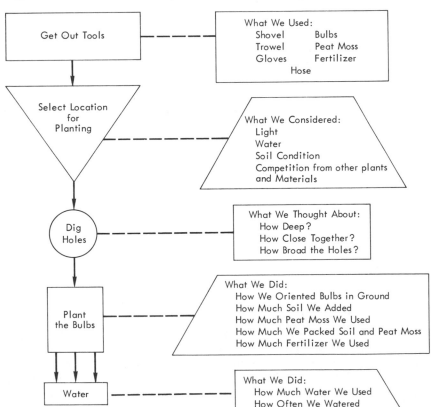

Most classroom procedures are open to analysis of this type: making papier-mâché, mixing paints, performing an experiment, baking bread, lining up to go to the assembly, evacuating the building during fire drills. Although children are not writing in strict prose form as they construct flowcharts, they are involved in sequential thinking, the same kind of thinking that is basic in writing paragraphs that tell how.

Retelling. In the now classic *Taxonomy of Educational Objectives: The Classification of Educational Goals, Cognitive Domain* (New York: Longmans and Green, 1956), Benjamin Bloom defined "translation" as the process of paraphrasing or recounting a communication in one's own words. To be judged a successful translation, a recounting must be faithful to the details of the original communication. When we teach children to retell, therefore, we are helping them acquire the skill of accurate reproduction. Implicit is the ability to understand written and oral communication, for without ability to comprehend what one has read or heard, one can hardly translate it faithfully.

There are numerous opportunities in classrooms to encourage children to build retelling skills. Perhaps one of the best is story retelling, in which each youngster who has read or listened to a tale contributes a sentence or two to a cooperative retelling. In this context some teachers have found a story ladder most helpful as a means of organizing ideas, especially with primary youngsters. Each participant records on a strip of paper a sentence telling one story event. Youngsters staple their strips between two longer strips in the manner of rungs of a ladder. Read from bottom to top, the story ladder retells the tale. Mary Ellen Dobryznski has found that her second graders get particularly excited about retelling stories in this way if each "rung" is shaped to represent a story character or happening. For example, retelling the old story of *Noodle* by Munro Leaf, each participant in the story-retelling group writes his or her contributing sentence on a rung that looks just like that hotdog-shaped pooch called Noodle.

In addition, children who alone have read a story can be asked to tell an interesting part. Others can recount something heard on television. Similarly, they can listen to tapes of stories and tell them to friends during a story-sharing session, or they can record on tape a story they have read, relying on memories for words and sequences. Although these experiences are oral rather than written, they involve children with the cognitive processes that are basic to retelling. In this respect, they lay the foundation for many writing activities that will require the same kind of thinking.

Summarizing. In producing written summaries, a writer draws upon his or her skill to interpret. According to Bloom (in *Taxonomy of Educational Objectives*), interpreting involves a rearrangement, a reordering, or a new view of material, without necessarily relating it to other materials. In the case of summarizing, the thinker must identify those points that are necessary if key ideas are to be communicated. The new view of the material is a shortened version that contains these key points with less significant ones deleted.

Again, classroom activity provides endless opportunity for developing summarizing skills. For example, after Ms. Dobryznski has had her youngsters write out sentences that retell a story in sequence and has had them staple their story strips as ladder rungs, she goes on to ask, "What is the message, or great big idea, this story is trying to tell us?" When children decide, they compose a summary sentence that they record along the side posts of their story ladder, as shown in figure 1.8. The same question can be asked after youngsters have read or listened to a news article reporting an event, have participated in a general discussion, or have viewed a film or filmstrip. Again, such oral experiences with identifying key points build thinking skills needed for writing.

Relating Phenomena

In describing, reporting, telling how, retelling, and summarizing, the writer is primarily concerned with painting an accurate picture of the world around. In contrast, when handling conceptual content, he or she must go beyond what is directly perceived to figure out relationships and ask: How are these events, materials, people, ideas, or feelings related to one another? This task is a more difficult and complex one than simply reflecting on what has been observed or heard.

Comparing and Contrasting. To handle statements of comparison and contrast, the writer must be able to determine how two materials, ideas, or feelings are similar, how they differ. Faced with Idea A that incorporates a particular element, the writer asks: Can I find this same element in Idea B? If the answer is yes, a statement of comparison may be the outcome of the deliberation; if the answer is no, a statement of contrast may result.

Youngsters can be asked to propose similarities and differences that will later form the content of their written expression. To move them up the thinking ladder and encourage them to analyze their experiences with the world and with words, we must give them opportunity to search for common features within groups of materials and eventually within

Figure 1.8. A story ladder for retelling and summarizing

"The Three Wishes" retold by
M. Jean Craig

A woodcutter went to work and met a tree fairy. She granted him three wishes for not cutting down her tree.

The woodcutter went home and told his wife. She was pleased. They talked about their wishes. Then the woodcutter got hungry.

Without thinking, he wished for a sausage. He got his wish. This got his wife very angry. She called him a fool.

The cutter couldn't stand to hear his wife complain. He wished the sausage was stuck to her nose. His wish was granted.

The wife became sad. The woodcutter used his last wish to get the sausage off her nose. They ate the sausage for dinner.

MAIN IDEA: THINK BEFORE YOU ACT.

groups of ideas and feelings. As a beginning, young children can sort blocks into piles according to some shared feature—for example, color, size, shape. Older boys and girls can sort pictures, musical recordings, books, ideas, events, or poems, and be asked, "Do you see anything the same or similar in the two ideas? stories? poems?"

For the teacher who has had little experience in leading youngsters to compare and contrast, an easy beginning is through two tales that adhere to a rather similar pattern of development. Good for this purpose is the old and well-known story of the "Teeny Tiny Woman" and the Tennessee mountain version called "The Tailypo." Children who have listened to both versions and retold each to get the facts straight can identify happenings common to both: a person takes something that belongs to someone else; this someone comes to reclaim his or her property, making several visits and calling out when coming closer and closer. Then children identify differences: in one the object can be returned, in the other not so; in one dogs chase that someone or something away at first, in the other no dogs; in one the taker is probably safe at the end, in the other not so. As participants suggest different points, a scribe can record these on the board. Later, as a group or independently, children can write paragraphs that incorporate the points thought out together. In this way, thinking activity blends with writing activity.

As children become more adept at figuring out differences and similarities, they can contrast two or more retellings of the same tale. Many stories have been written by more than one adapter with each adaptation differing in some respects from others. Upper graders who have read or listened to two or three—such as *Beauty and the Beast* as retold by Marianna Mayer (Four Winds, 1978), by Madame de Beaumont (Bradbury Press, 1977), and by Philippa Pearce (Crowell, 1972)—can decide how they differ in size, pictures, words, story events, mood, and even in the personalities and motives of Beauty, her father, and the Beast. Other good comparisons can grow out of analysis of Tomie de Paola's *Strega Nona* (Prentice-Hall, 1975) and Paul Galdone's *The Magic Porridge Pot* (Seabury, 1976). In these instances, the first result of children's analytical thinking can be charts of comparisons and contrasts. Ideas listed become paragraphs created by writers working alone or in small composing teams.

Classifying.   Classifying requires the thinker to group similar items together and apply a label to the resulting category. Essentially, the words *red, orange, yellow* are labels applied to items sharing a common color. In the same way, labels such as *mammal, bird, reptile* are applied to items that share similar structures. When a person calls an animal that has wings, has feathers, is pecking on a tree in the backyard, and lives in a nest "woodpecker," he or she is classifying according to similarities and differences among organisms. But classifying is a more involved cognitive operation than comparing and contrasting. It is higher up the cognitive "ladder," so to speak.

Classificatory activity belongs in classrooms. Youngsters who have sorted piles of blocks can be asked to attach a class label to the piles—to verbalize their activity. Moving from the very concrete, they can classify books as biographies, histories, and novels; music as jazz, disco, rock, or country; human activity as related to communication, transportation, or production.

To write a definition is also to classify. In defining, the thinker-writer first identifies the larger class to which an object, organism, or event belongs. A definition of a horse might simply begin: "A horse is an animal . . . ," identifying the larger group to which horses belong. Then the writer identifies the characteristics of the horse that distinguish it from other animals: "A horse is an animal that has x, y, and z."

That many children have trouble handling this type of thinking is indicated by the typical way in which they begin to define: "A horse is *when*. . . ." To help children avoid this usage, the teacher can supply definition starters in which a determiner is included as in: "An elephant is an . . ." or "King George III was the . . . ." In this way children come to know and use the linguistic pattern in which this type of thinking is most precisely expressed.

Analyzing Qualitatively. Two objects are big, but which is bigger? Two people are tall, but who is taller? Handling qualitative differences such as those just mentioned, the thinker begins to refine his or her ability to propose more sophisticated contrasts. Based on analyses that focus on the amount of a quality someone or something possesses, the thinker can place numerous items that share a particular property in a hierarchial scheme.

To develop this thinking skill, children can do the same in simplified contexts. In many different settings they can determine—

- which is greener
- which is darker
- which is colder
- which is more complicated
- which has more steps

- which is louder
- which is farther away
- which is more difficult
- which is simpler
- which is quicker

And they can decide which is most complicated, quickest, farthest away.

At first the teacher must raise the questions that lead children up the cognitive ladder, asking "Which is more . . . ? Which is the most . . . ?" As children find answers, they later raise the same questions for themselves. To encourage independence as thinkers, the teacher begins to ask: "What kinds of things can we look at as we analyze this example? What kinds of questions should we raise?"

Analyzing Sequentially. Some written pieces tell how something happened or how something is organized. To write such a piece, a thinker must be able to identify the subunits of which an event or a communication is composed and must be able to figure out the chronology of an event or the organization within a communication.

These rather sophisticated thinking skills are similar to those necessary to tell how. The concern in both instances is with breaking an event into subunits and relating the sequential ordering of those units. The purpose of an analytical piece, however, is not simply to tell how to do something but rather to indicate how a communication is organized or how an event occurred. Much more figuring out is involved in the latter in contrast to the former.

In elementary schools, children should have opportunity to analyze events and communications to figure out sequential relationships. After children have read a story or seen a film, a teacher can ask, "What happened first? next? How did the story or film end?" After a talk by a guest, she or he can query, "What was the first point Mr. Janick made? the second?" After a classroom accident, an excursion, or completion of an art, science, or crafts project, the teacher can ask, "What did we do first? next? finally?" Activities involving new content—reading, seeing a film, hearing a speaker, participating in a project—may have value in and of themselves. These can also serve as springboards to develop analytical thinking skills if the teacher raises appropriate questions that trigger children to discover relationships.

Explaining in Terms of Cause and Effect. To explain why something happened, a thinker-writer identifies another happening that caused the first, identifies elements that tie the two events together, and states the relationship between the two. To do this, one must be able to distinguish between something that simply takes place before or concurrent with another event and an occurrence that actually has a causal relationship with the event.

Young children have difficulty making these associations, for they are still operating within the confines of a rudimentary perceptual system. As Piaget's studies show, young children perceive that pouring a volume of liquid from a cylinder to another of a different shape changes the volume, that stretching or flattening a piece of clay also changes its volume; in actuality, no volume change has occurred.

As a first step in helping children handle cause-and-effect relationships, the teacher can begin with manipulative experiences in which children can perceive the effects that physical manipulation has on concrete materials. Play activity with water, clay, sand, or solids is background for thinking about causal relationships. With older, more perceptually mature children, a teacher can trigger causal thinking by asking the "why" question: "Why did the accident occur?" "Why did the snow melt so quickly?" "Why did the plants die?" These questions can be part of a thinking sequence in which youngsters first describe and, when they have the facts straight, move up to analyze.

Explaining in Terms of Supporting Principles. Another way of explaining why is by referring to known generalizations. For instance, fill a glass with water so that its surface is level with the rim of the glass. Is it full? Some will say yes. Add more water, drop by drop. What happens? The water does not cascade over the sides of the glass; it "stands up," taking on a lenslike shape. Why? Molecules of a material tend to cohere. In making this last statement, we are using a commonly known generalization to explain a particular happening.

Of course, children writing explanations of why the water does not overflow need not employ the sophisticated terminology used in the generalization given above. They should, however, be given opportunity to make similar associations. Fifth graders, for example, can study mercury bowing upward in a narrow glass tube and talk about how the particles or molecules of mercury stick together. The students can pour water on an oily surface and talk about how the water molecules also stick together. They can pour cooking oil on a surface and talk again about how the material sticks together. During this type of activity children begin to build a generalization about how matter acts. Faced with explaining why water, added drop by drop to a glass filled to the top, does not overflow, they may be able to apply their generalization: Molecules of a material tend to stick together. Later, writing about what they have done, children express this relationship as the big explanatory idea of a paragraph.

Explaining in Terms of Rational Intent. Another way of answering the why question is through an explanation based on human purposes, motives, or intentions. For example, the question "Why did the little boy climb upon the counter?" is answered by suggesting that he *wanted* a cookie that was there. The more sophisticated question "Why did the American colonies revolt against England?" again is partially answered by indicating what the country *wanted* to achieve.

Since children are basically egocentric, a good beginning for helping them handle rational explanations is to focus on their own actions and motives. The teacher can ask questions to which children respond, "I did it because . . . ." He or she can encourage discussion of reasons for performing certain classroom procedures by asking, "Why did we do that?" Children will answer, "We did it because . . ." or "We did it in order to . . .," falling easily into the sentence patterns used to express human purposes and motivations.

In upper grades, the same kind of relational thinking can be transferred to explanations of historical and social events. As part of social studies, the teacher can ask:

- Why is the United States establishing new kinds of relationships with China?
- Why are some industries making efforts to manufacture safer products?
- In some cultures in the past, why did women bind their feet? Why is this custom disappearing?
- Why did people leave England to settle in Australia, New Zealand, Canada, and the United States?

At the intermediate level, children spend more time studying social studies and science than they do in the primary grades. This does not mean, however, that they should spend less time involved in language experiences. Teachers who are interested in helping children develop thinking-writing skills can structure work in the content areas so that skill development is an integral part of study. Children not only think about who, what, when, where, how but about why. And thinking leads naturally into writing.

Projecting Hypotheses, Theories, and Designs

Not only do writers reflect aspects of their world and identify relationships existing within it, but they also jump beyond observations to propose hypotheses, theories, designs, and plans. In proposing new ways of looking at and organizing the world, writer-thinkers are fundamentally involved in putting together elements to form a whole. They reorder parts, combine them in unique patterns, eliminate some elements, add others, ending with a product that goes beyond the original data. In brief, they concoct!

Much of what has been written on creativity applies to the process of projecting or proposing. Success in the endeavor requires an intellectual flexibility and a curiosity to play with ideas, to try different approaches, to attempt the outrageous, not to conform to established patterns but to construct new ones, to diverge from expected modes of performance and from traditional views. The results are really big ideas to be expressed—hypotheses, generalizations, theories, designs, and plans.

Hypothesizing.   A person can project a guess or a prediction based on certain basic data he or she has observed directly, heard, or read. The hypothesizer reasons, "If *a* is true, if *b* is true, then *c* must logically follow." An acceptable prediction is one that takes into account all data at hand.

One of the best reasoned hypotheses recorded in the annals of science is Mendel's belief that organisms carry two factors for each inherited characteristic. Although Mendel had not looked inside the cell to see or touch the two factors, he believed that all evidence pointed toward this explanation. He had crossed tall plants with short ones: the result was a generation of tall plants. But when he crossed these tall plants with other tall ones of the same kind, three fourths of the plants he obtained were tall and one fourth short. He reasoned that if shortness shows up in the third generation, then shortness must have been carried by the second-generation tall plants. If these plants carry a factor for shortness as well as one for tallness (since they were all tall), then—he reasoned— organisms must carry within a cell two factors for each characteristic. This hypothesis was the basis for his further research. It was also content for his writing.

We do not expect children to make such large-scale hypotheses as Mendel's, but we can give them opportunities to make intellectual leaps so that they will learn to hypothesize possibilities that are in keeping with known information. In *Applied Imagination* (Scribner's, 1957), Alexander Osborn suggests that one way to get thinkers to go beyond observable fact is to raise wild possibilities for which there are no factual answers:

- What would happen to an elephant if it had a longer trunk?
- What would happen if the elephant had an extra foot instead of a trunk?
- What would happen to object B if we made it heavier, longer? changed its shape, color, texture? What would happen if we added another block to our tower? took a block away?
- What would happen if the population of the world were to double in ten years?

Children can be asked to predict how stories will end, given only the beginning details. Working together and orally, youngsters can propose original endings, which they compare and contrast to those actually found at the ends of stories. Later, they can create endings for story beginnings they have read on their own. A wordless book that encourages creative predictions is Fernando Krahn's *The Mystery of the Giant Footsteps* (Dutton, 1977), the ending of which is mind-boggling.

In the same way, experiments can be set up so that children must predict the outcome before it becomes obvious. For example, after children have experienced the previously described observations of mercury, oil, and water beading, the teacher can ask, "What will happen if I add a little more water to this beaker, which is already filled to the top?" Children can make educated guesses based on their previous knowledge and then experiment to determine whether their hypotheses are valid. They can be asked to complete sentences with this pattern: "If we . . . , then . . . ."

Generalizing. To generalize is basically to think inductively: first, to select and group together related data; second, to study rather systematically the related data to attempt rearrangements and reorderings; third, to leap beyond the data to identify underlying general principles. Obviously, inductive thinking has shades of both analysis and synthesis. Attempting to perceive essential elements within phenomena, one is analyzing. Jumping the gap from fact to generalization, one is synthesizing—putting the individual pieces together into a unique whole.

To teach children to think inductively is often to teach inductively. Start with several related examples: for instance, ask them to analyze such words as *unit, cluster, harbor, cider, humor, target, erupt, glider, cactus, thermal, bonus*. Children can study these words to figure out how all are the same; in this case study can involve clapping to find out how many syllables are in each word. When children have generalized that all the words are comprised of two syllables, the teacher questions: "I am going to pick one word—*unit*—from the group. Some of the others share a feature with it; others do not. What word is like unit in some way? Who can pick another and place it over here with *unit*?" When a youngster has selected and placed a word, the teacher continues: "In this other pile, I am going to put the word *cactus*. Who can pick a word that structurally is like *cactus*?" Working at first by trial and error, children sort the words into two groups—those that resemble *unit*, those that resemble *cactus*. As more and more children find that they can add a word to one of the groups, the teacher asks youngsters to state the relationship. Youngsters familiar with vowels, consonants, and syllables may be able to verbalize the generalization on their own: in words of two syllables, divide between the consonants if there are two coming together and between the vowel and the consonant if there is just one consonant at the syllable juncture. In so doing, they are jumping the gap between specific and general to discover for themselves a generalization that can be used to explain these and related examples. They are thinking inductively.

Especially as they move into intermediate grades, it is important that children know how to generalize and conclude based on evidence they have compiled. This is especially so as youngsters conduct library investigations in which they collect data from references. All too often, papers written as a result of these investigations are nothing more than a collection of facts, for children have little idea of what should come next in the thinking-writing process—studying their findings to propose some general relationships or conclusions. For that reason, a pivotal question in the teacher's arsenal is "What can we conclude?" or "What can we generalize?" This question should be asked whenever young investigators have compiled any body of data. It can be embodied in an investigative guide in which a place is set aside for specific facts and another for conclusions that can be projected based on them. Figure 1.9 is an example of such a data-retrieval chart that could be used as part of a social studies investigation that leads into paragraph writing.

Designing. At some point children should be asked to stretch their minds to produce original plans, contraptions, and schemes. To help children develop skill in thinking of unique approaches, the teacher can apply brainstorming techniques by suggesting rather wild situations and asking children to propose plans of action. For example:

- What would you do if the water in your house were turned off for twenty-four hours?
- What would you do if the brakes on your bike gave way as you were coasting downhill?
- What would you do if you won the million-dollar lottery?
- What would you select if you had to leave your home to live somewhere else and could take only ten items with you?

In working with hypothetical problems, youngsters can be encouraged to propose all manner of possibilities, suggesting reasons to support their plans. Later, having listened and talked together, individuals can write their own plans: What I Would Do If. . . .

Designing may also involve inventing an original contraption or material—for example, a better mousetrap. To write this kind of content, one must describe the material to be made and tell the steps in its construction. But here, planning diverges from simple description, for the plan to be written is for something that does not exist, except in the mind of the inventor. To get children thinking in these mind-stretching terms, ask them to sketch a toothbrush, a skateboard, a can opener, a pen, a chair, a calendar, or whatever, which serves the same purpose as present models but has some unique feature. Sketches drawn become notes to use in writing about the invention.

Figure 1.9. A data chart for generalizing and writing

Culture Group (Name particular groups here)	Kind of Home in Which They Live (Describe)	Kind of Clothing They Wear (Describe)	Climate of the Region (Describe)
1.			
2.			
3.			
Generalize here: How does the climate of the region where people live affect the kinds of homes and clothing they use?			
Writing follow-up: Write four paragraphs. In one describe the way the first group of people lives—their homes, clothing, and climate. Do the same for each of the other two groups. Then write a concluding paragraph that tells the relationship between climate of a region and people's way of life.			

At other times, invention may begin with brainstorming: "Let's visualize how this would look if we cut it in half, changed its shape, made it longer, added a square block on top." In response, children can actually change existing objects and construct original versions to be described later in paragraph form.

Still another designing task is the projection of original classification schemes and taxonomies. To develop new ways of organizing materials, the thinker-writer must start by analyzing data and considering similarities and differences existing in them. Using these similarities and differences, he or she figures out ways to group items to highlight relationships. This cognitive task goes beyond simple comparing and contrasting, for the result is an overarching design replete with categories and subcategories to use in classifying.

Children who have had considerable preliminary work with classifying materials into given groups and in comparing and contrasting can be asked to devise a system for organizing groups of heterogeneous materials—a walnut, a plastic comb, an olive, a piece of paper, a ballpoint pen, a piece of chalk, a bobby pin, an onion. Possibilities are almost endless: use, size, reaction to light, hardness, color, whether manufactured, organic, or inorganic. Again, in a sense this is a brainstorming activity, so the more heterogeneous the materials the better, and the wilder the suggested categories, the more the imagination is stretched.

Personalizing

Written content, as we have seen, can reflect the world, suggest relationships existing in the world, and propose new relationships and designs. It can also express personal emotions and individual reactions. Differing more in the degree of logic upon which they are based than in any other characteristic, emotions and reactions are basically of four kinds: feelings, preferences, opinions, and judgments.

Expressing Feelings

LOVE IN THE WORLD
The world
needs love—
needs love
so much.
A kiss
will change—
will change
the world.
A kiss
brings peace—
brings peace
to all.

Erick, grade 4 (after listening to and
talking about "Flying" by the Beatles)

In "Love in the World," Erick expressed his feelings about the need for love and peace in lines of free verse. Poems often serve as vehicles for the expression of a writer's feelings. The poems of Langston Hughes flow with feelings of discrimination, poverty, and at times hope. In like manner feelings about the beauty of nature pour out of the poems of Robert Frost, feelings of love spill from those of Elizabeth Barrett Browning.

To write in this vein, one must be able to react with a full range of emotions and be open enough to share innermost feelings with others. This requires that one "know one's self"—know what is important to one's inner being, know what strikes one deeply. Only by being in touch with one's own feelings can a writer compose passages in which inner feelings are laid bare.

How do we prepare children to write about their feelings? If knowledge of self and an openness that allows sharing of those feelings are necessary ingredients in the writing of feeling-laden pieces, then it seems logical to propose that what's most essential is a classroom environment in which expressions of emotions are accepted uncritically by the teacher. The teacher must communicate to children that emotions are a quality of humanness, not something of which to be ashamed.

This can be done in many contexts. Having read to middle graders Judith Viorst's *Alexander and the Terrible, Horrible, No Good, Very Bad Day* (Atheneum, 1972), the teacher can help children explore similar feelings: "When have you felt the way Alexander did? What words could you use to express your feelings? What phrases would tell how you felt deep inside? Why did you feel this way?" The teacher can suggest: "Let's draw our feelings on a terrible, horrible, no good, very bad day. What colors can we use to express our horrible feelings?" As follow-up, the teacher can ask children to describe how they feel on very good, great, wonderful days and to express those feelings with an interplay of lines and color perhaps using finger paints or fluorescent crayons.

When children argue or even fight, the teacher can encourage them to talk about how they feel deep down inside. When they are taking pleasure in doing something, they can be encouraged to talk about their delight. And when children have actively enjoyed an experience together, such as building a snowperson, the teacher can suggest, "Let's draw our feelings into a picture and add words that show how we feel about our snowperson." (See fig. 1.10.)

Expressing Preferences.   A somewhat less emotional reaction is the expression of a preference. The thinker-writer states, "I prefer x to y." The x may be almost anything—a person, color, piece of clothing, type of food, a book, or a type of activity. It may be selected because it is really liked, because y is disliked, or even because it is the lesser of two evils.

In stating preferences, thinker-writers are involved to some extent in comparing; they must know about the things among which they are choosing. But thinkers must go a step further to inject personal views, jumping the gap from factual analysis to subjective determination. To do this, thinkers must be able to formulate a point of view and feel free to express it.

Figure 1.10.
"The Snowman"
—a concrete poem
by a fourth grader

To teach children to make defensible choices, a teacher must give children genuine opportunity for choice within the classroom. Which book would you prefer reading? Which seat do you choose? Which colored chalk do you want? Here are three ways we can carry out this task—which do you prefer? In selecting, children should be encouraged to examine the bases of their preferences by being asked why and being urged to reply, "I prefer this because . . . ." The statement of preferences does not require a lengthy rationale; a simple enumeration of reasons is all that is necessary—something within the range of possibility for elementary youngsters.

Expressing Opinions.   Another kind of idea expressed in writing is an opinion or belief about the rightness-wrongness, propriety-impropriety, or goodness-badness of a course of action, a happening, or even a person. In giving an opinion, however, the thinker-writer analyzes basic aspects of the situation he or she is critiquing before expressing a belief about it and supports that opinion with a simple statement of reason: "I believe we should do *x* because. . . ." Of course there are no physical connections existing between a situation and one's opinion of it; that a particular course of action is proper is a subjective determination. In stating an opinion, one goes beyond fact.

To state opinions, thinker-writers must know that to look at a situation and formulate an opinion about it is a valid mental activity. They must feel that their beliefs are worthy of expression, have the skill to analyze situations as a basis for their opinions, and must be able to identify reasons that logically support beliefs. Teachers can encourage the development of these skills, cognitions, and attitudes by giving children the opportunity to express their opinions about situations that concern them directly. What do you think about the new school dress code? What do you think about the new cafeteria rules? What do you think about the food in the cafeteria? What is your opinion on taking drugs, smoking, looting, shoplifting? The follow-up question is "Why?" Discussed in classroom groups, these questions can become beginnings for short position papers, which children later share in debatelike, round-table forum sessions.

Expressing Judgments.   As used here, a judgment is an evaluation in terms of carefully stated criteria. Obviously, a statement of judgment is a more highly reasoned kind of written communication than the outpouring of feeling embodied in a piece of free verse or the simple expression of a preference.

In judging, the initial step is the development of an external measuring stick. Since the intent of judging is to apply such designations as effective-ineffective, efficient-inefficient, consistent-inconsistent, wise-foolish, there is no way in which a quantitative measure can be made. The judge must apply criteria developed outside the context of a particular item being evaluated. These criteria are the standard of effectiveness, efficiency, or consistency against which each item to be judged is "measured."

The next step is to analyze the item under evaluation and compare its attributes, or qualities, to those identified in the criteria as effective, efficient, or consistent. If the item in question possesses the qualities previously deemed as effective or efficient, the judgment is positive; if not, it is negative. If some qualities exist but others are lacking, the judgment incorporates both positive and negative statements.

At first glance, judging appears to be a rather objective thinking operation. Not so! The proposing of criteria is a subjective process, based on a person's own value system. Try to get a group of people to agree on a set of criteria by which to evaluate. It quickly becomes obvious that complete agreement is an impossibility. Then, too, even if some agreement is achieved, individual judges apply the criteria in ways that lead to different evaluations. This is to be expected, for there is no tight connection among the criteria, the object being judged, and the final judgment. The human mind must bridge the gap between criteria and object, between object and judgment. Evaluating is a creative process in which elements are reorganized into a new whole—the judgment.

A teacher may want to attempt judgmental thinking and writing, especially with upper graders. Initially, teacher and children propose a list of criteria by which something is to be judged. A good beginning is the youngsters' own work. Faced with several samples of handwriting, children can suggest qualities that good handwriting exhibits. Then they can apply these criteria to the evaluation of their own work, coming up with a judgment as to which are their better productions, which their poorer ones. Children can do the same with samples of their own art, with the content of their compositions, and with oral presentations. In so doing, they are not only introduced to the process of formal judgment, but they are starting down the road of self-analysis, a process extremely important in writing, as we shall see in later chapters of this book.

Inventing

Some writing is pure invention. The thinker-writer develops characters who have never existed, though they may, of course, resemble in certain respects people encountered in real life. The writer goes on to paint pictures of scenes using words to develop colors, shades, shapes, and masses. He or she invents relationships among characters as they interact within this "painted" landscape. These relationships may resemble relationships in real life, but they do not exactly follow events as they have occurred at any particular time.

The products of invention are the characters, descriptions, events, interrelationships, and dialogue found in narrative poetry, plays, short stories, and novels. To compose this type of communication requires one to synthesize: to formulate the new, to re-view what has been perceived, and to let the imagination fly loose.

A teacher can encourage children to let their imaginations fly by allowing time for "let's pretend" activity. Very young children can role play Mother Goose characters; they can pretend to be Big Bird from

"Sesame Street," a muppet puppet, or a character from a favorite TV cartoon or storybook. Youngsters can be asked to speak as if they were animals or things. The teacher suggests, "let's pretend" you are—

- a fly sitting on the end of my nose.
- a poodle on a leash.
- a mosquito taking a bite of you.
- a banana being peeled.
- a turtle trying to cross a busy highway.
- a crocodile who lives in your bathtub.

The teacher then asks, "What would you be thinking?" "What would you say?" The teacher can record youngsters' animal-talk for them.

Similarly, art activity can carry very young children into inventive thinking. Instead of centering art experiences solely on real and observed events, the teacher can suggest that youngsters paint—

- an enchanted forest.
- a magical apple orchard.
- a wizard who lives in a cave.
- another planet where life exists.
- an elephant who can fly.

Song and story are other materials that stimulate inventive thinking. A little song about "Puff, the Magic Dragon" (Peter Pan Records) can encourage children to enter the world of "let's pretend." As children sing about the magic dragon who lives by the sea, they are toying with make-believe—something very meaningful to the fanciful young—and can be encouraged to talk about other things that the dragon might do and say. The same holds true with stories. Raymond Briggs's delightful wordless picture book *The Snowman* (Random, 1978) tickles children's imagination to think of other adventures the affable snowman might undertake—adventures young readers can express both in pictures and in spoken words. William Steig's *Tiffky Doofky* (Farrar, 1978) appeals to slightly older children, who can invent stories about other treasures that the friendly pooch can locate in the garbage trash and the adventures these treasures can lead to. Maurice Sendak's still popular *In the Night Kitchen* (Harper & Row, 1970) leads children to think about other things that could happen in the kitchen at night, or in the attic, or on the apartment house rooftops. In so doing, youngsters become involved in the kind of thinking and talking that results in inventive description, plot, character, and dialogue.

SOME SUMMARY THOUGHTS

In order to write, a person must be able to create ideas. This is the first assumption on which *Written Expression in the Language Arts: Ideas and Skills* is based. It means that to teach children to write is fundamentally to teach them to think—to reflect, relate, project, personalize, and invent. At times, therefore, "writing lessons" may not involve writing at all; rather, children may be actively involved in describing, retelling, summarizing, hypothesizing, generalizing, expressing preferences, judgments, and opinions, inventing characters and events as they talk together about the world of fact and the world of fancy. These oral-thinking activities pave the way for times when children express their ideas on paper.

A second assumption is that thinking is not a single-faceted cognitive operation. Thinking for writing is not only to create personalized feelings to express in poetry form; it is not just to invent or create original stories. It is also to describe what has been perceived, to summarize significant facts and develop conclusions, to propose similarities and differences, to figure out relationships and hypotheses. It is to come up with a personal preference or opinion and give reasons to support beliefs.

Because thinking has many dimensions, school writing programs must include varied experiences—experiences with poems, short stories, wordless stories, short descriptive paragraphs, summaries, explanations, opinion papers, systematic reports in which conclusions flow out of findings set forth, analyses, even sophisticated judgments in upper grades. To ask youngsters to write only stories and poems is to touch the tip of the iceberg.

A third assumption to which research evidence gives credence is that thinking operations differ in complexity and, therefore, difficulty. To propose relationships within a set of data is a more complex operation than to retell what one has heard or read. To develop a thoroughly reasoned judgment is more difficult than to state a simple opinion. For this reason, experiences with thinking cannot be centered solely in third grade, fifth grade, or junior high. We need to view teaching for thinking as a developmental process in which children at each level encounter cognitive activities that build on previous ones and that are somewhat more complex and demanding than those experienced at previous levels.

In sum, classroom writing activity must be conceived broadly, not narrowly. It must include oral play with ideas, encounters with a full range of thinking processes, and more demanding intellectual problems as children proceed through the elementary to the secondary grades. This is fundamental if they are to produce written pieces that communicate worthwhile ideas.

LET CHILDREN TALK ◄►
building a foundation
for writing

"The time has come," the Walrus said, "To talk
    of many things:
Of shoes—and ships—and sealing-wax—of cabbages
    and kings—."
                    Lewis Carroll, "The Walrus and the Carpenter"

On the façade of the Royal Oak Hotel in Keswick in the heart of the English Lake District, a plaque bears this inscription:

> This ancient hostelry, formerly the Oak Inn, has been from the days of Queen Elizabeth the centre of the commercial activities and social life of Keswick. The headquarters in the 18th century of a thriving packhorse trade, this inn became subsequently, no less renowned as a posting establishment and halting place for stage coaches. No less celebrated are the literary associations of this house, for it was frequented by Robert Southey, Samuel Taylor, Hartley Coleridge, the Wordsworths, Shelley, Thomas de Quincey, Christopher North, and other Lake Land poets and writers. Here Sir Walter Scott wrote part of his "Bridal of Triermain" and here too Lord Tennyson and Robert Louis Stevenson were frequent visitors, while the "Skiddaw Hermit" and John Peel of hunting fame were frequently to be seen within its walls.

The Coleridges, Wordsworths, and Shelleys of that day came to inns such as the Royal Oak because there they could talk about their experiences and feelings. After solitary walks amid the lakes and hills, a

writer could share ideas with others. Warmed by a crackling fire and encouraged by companionship, a writer could mentally play with impressions and express them orally. In this environment, embryonic ideas
gathered substance.

Children can gain even more from "talk" than did the Coleridges
and Wordsworths. For them oral sharing is an important first step in the
process of translating ideas into the verbal patterns of written expression.
This is especially so for young children. At a developmental stage when
youngsters are concerned more with actions than with words, they need
considerable opportunity to handle ideas verbally. Asking children to
consign thoughts to paper before talking about them is asking more of
them than they can deliver. For this reason, oral experiences are a vital
part of any writing program; talk lessons are essentially preliminary
writing lessons.

In the context of written expression, "talk" in elementary programs assumes a number of forms. These include such verbal interactions as conversations, informal discussions, brainstorming, group
writing, informal oral presentations, and dramatizations. They include
such nonverbal activities as pantomime and drawing. In this chapter, we
shall consider these ways of letting children "talk" as a prelude to
writing.

CONVERSATIONS

Conversation with children as a way to encourage expression need
not be a formal activity. Indeed just the opposite is true. The teacher
welcomes children with conversation as they come into the classroom in
the morning, chats with them in the playground, and talks informally
with them during individualized learning activity. Topics of conversation
are those highly meaningful at this stage. How is your new baby sister?
What did you like most about your trip to the beach? How did you feel
as you ran through the snow on the way to school this morning? How did
you feel when the lights blacked out last night? Is there still no heat in
your apartment? Did you like the Muppets on TV last night? Did you see
The Grinch Who Stole Christmas? What do you think about it?

Although the topics become broader and less focused on personal
affairs, conversation with the teacher is significant too for older elementary school children. The teacher may trigger talk with such openers as
these: Who do you think will win the Superbowl? What did you think of
the biography of Martin Luther King Jr. by Eve Merriam that you just
finished? What happened to you and your friends on the camping over-

night? Who do you think is going to win the election? Why?

Youngsters who do not have the advantage of conversation with adults at home have a special need for conversation in school. When parents do not have time to listen and do not realize the importance of talking with their children, youngsters may become idea-disadvantaged. They may have almost no ability to create ideas to communicate and may benefit considerably from informal talk with the teacher.

Conversation with fellow students can also aid in the exploration of ideas. Dividing students into conversation-pairs is one approach to encourage talk. Children select a conversation-mate, and time is set aside during the day for mates to talk about some feelings or thoughts they have had. At first, the teacher can suggest talk-topics with which to begin:

- One thing I didn't like in school today.
- What I'm going to do after school.
- An argument I had with someone and how it made me feel.
- What happened to me on the way to school.
- What my brother (sister, mother, father, dog, cat, canary) did.
- The coming election, ball game, or space exploit.
- A program I saw on TV.
- A book I read.

If children deviate from suggested topics, the teacher should not consider the talk-time unsuccessful. Children have identified areas in which they have genuine ideas to express, and that—after all—is the ultimate goal.

Conversation among children on a less formal basis can also trigger ideas. In one class, for example, children created Rorschach inkblots from yellow and blue paint blobs pressed against the folds of a piece of paper. Asked to study their blobs and write about their perceptions, children at adjacent tables began automatically to share ideas. This exchange encouraged some children to think more deeply and more creatively. To have required silence in the room at this stage of writing would have been counterproductive.

INFORMAL DISCUSSIONS

Informal discussions with the whole class can stimulate children to express their thoughts about a shared experience. For instance, upon returning from a nature walk through the park in the fall, one teacher encouraged talk with the following questions:

Auditory Sense

What sounds did we hear when we kicked the leaves?

What sounds did the leaves make as they fell to the ground?

What sounds did you hear when we picked up large piles of leaves and threw them high into the air?

How did these two sounds differ?

What kinds of sounds did we hear when we stood perfectly still?

Visual Sense

How did the trees look in the woods?

What colors were the leaves?

Did some kinds of leaves look different from others? How did they differ?

What other things did we see on our walk? What words can we use to describe them?

Sense of Touch

How did the leaves feel when we touched them? What words can we use to describe them?

How did they feel along the edges? the surface areas?

What other things did you touch in the woods? What words can we use to describe their feel?

Sense of Smell

What odors did you smell in the woods? What words can we use to describe them? Which odors were pleasant? unpleasant?

How did the odors of the leaves compare with the odors of the wild flowers? Which did you like better?

How do the odors of your kitchen compare with those in the woods?

When we snapped the twigs and smelled them, how did this make you feel?

General Reactions

What part of our trip did you especially like? Why?

What part of our trip did you not like? Why?

How did you feel deep inside as we started out? as we started back?

Would you want to go again? Why? Why not?

Through this questioning sequence, the teacher helped youngsters sharpen their perceptions and encouraged them to translate their impressions into words.

Another teacher used a discussion period as a prelude to written expression. She took her fifth graders for a "wind walk" to feel the wind that was blowing rather fiercely that day. When they returned, the children talked in detail about how the wind made them feel, what they saw the wind doing, and how the wind sounded in their ears. Then they paired off to write just one line that began "Wind blows . . . ." Later a composing team put the lines together to form a cooperative poem:

WIND BLOWS . . .
Wind blows big gusts against our faces.
Wind blows our skirts in whirls around our legs.
Wind blows into our jackets and turns them into balloons.
Wind blows so hard it lifts us off our feet and carries us running
    down the street.
Wind blows into the trees and turns the branches into dancing arms.
Wind blows around corners to make whistle sounds.
Wind blows big slaps of air all around.
Wind blows . . . .
Wind blows . . . .

Upper elementary students can talk about impressions in triads, "quads," and "quints." These small group prewriting experiences can be structured at first by the teacher, who can supply a guide for groups that have not operated independently before. After a city-street walk, for instance, the talk-guide might include the points shown in figure 2.1. Talk can lead into writing; after students have talked for five or ten minutes about noise pollution problems they have encountered first-hand, they can write a piece describing the kinds of noises that spoil the environment, what can be done to cut down on noise pollution, or their personal reactions to environmental noise.

Book-sharing sessions with small groups can be conducted in a similar way. Youngsters who have read the same book or seen the same movie or TV show can talk together about their general reactions before attempting individual writing. Again, for groups with little experience in independent discussion, a discussion guide such as the one in figure 2.2 can be helpful.

Informal discussion with individual children as they compose can also have positive results. Discussion may cause a child to go beyond superficial consideration to look for the more unusual impression. A fourth-grade boy made a creative drawing by dipping string in green ink and swirling it across the page. As he studied his artistic outcome in an attempt to produce a story based on it, the teacher walked by and asked, "What do you see?"

The boy responded, "Don't you see the frog sitting on the leaf?"

The teacher answered, "Could that frog be sitting on something

Figure 2.1. A guide for a prewriting talk-time

QUESTIONS FOR TALKING ABOUT

NAMES OF PARTICIPANTS IN THE TALK-TIME: _____

1. List all the noises you heard. Next to each noise, list three words or phrases you could use to describe the noise. Then note down whether each noise was pleasant or unpleasant.

The Noises   Descriptive Words   Pleasant/Unpleasant

   a.

   b.

   c.

   d.

2. Noise pollution means that the environment is being spoiled by too many extremely unpleasant noises. Decide in your group: What specific things can each of us do to cut down on noise pollution?

other than a leaf—something more far out that could carry the frog into adventure?'' The result was an imaginative story about a frog that landed by chance on a magical feather that carried it away to the Land of Green.

The same need for talking is evidenced in this composition by a sixth-grade girl:

MY SUMMER VACATION

This summer I went to Canton, Maine, with my mother, father, and sister. My uncle and his family went too.

When we got there, we played ping pong and went swimming.

Figure 2.2. A guide for independent small group discussion

TALKING ABOUT BOOKS AND SHOWS

NAMES OF PARTICIPANTS IN THE TALK-TIME: _____

_____

1. Begin talk-time by having each group member describe an incident in the book or show that he or she either liked or disliked a lot.

2. Decide: Were there more incidents that most members of the group liked or more incidents that they disliked? List the incidents using summary phrases on this chart:

Incidents Most of Us Liked   Incidents Most of Us Disliked

3. Decide cooperatively whether you would recommend to friends that they read the book or see the show you have been discussing. Finish this sentence: We would recommend that our friends (see / not see), (read / not read) _____ because

We stayed there for a week, and then we came home. My cousins came home with us.

One day I went to Little Squam for three days. We had a very nice time. When we came home, we had some company.

Dorothy, 6th grade

Clearly, although Dorothy's composition is grammatically acceptable, she had not really thought through her experiences. She needed to talk about specific happenings with a teacher who asked questions that probed for additional insights. With this child, talk could have included:

- Tell me about the place where you went swimming.
- How did you feel when you went into the water?
- What was the water like? cold? deep?
- Did anything happen while you were playing in the water? Tell me about it.
- Tell me about the people with whom you went swimming. What did they say? What did they do?

Any one of these questions might have stimulated a discussion that could have elicited ideas for writing and perhaps for oral sharing.

BRAINSTORMING IDEAS AND WORDS

In the two instances just recounted, brainstorming could also have stimulated children to go beyond superficial examination. Brainstorming is an anything-goes, free association strategy that asks participants to think of words, ideas, or feelings related in a direct or remote way to a given topic. Using brainstorming with a youngster writing about a frog, a teacher might have suggested: "Together let's list all the things that the frog might be sitting on. Let's be as wild as we can in our thinking." Going farther, the teacher might have encouraged, "Let's think of many words that describe this unique frog. Let's think of things that the frog might say if it could talk." Items brainstormed could be written along the perimeter and the outline of key body features to produce what has been called a "thingumajig." See figure 2.3 for an example.

Figure 2.3.
A kitty
thingumajig dictated
by kindergarteners

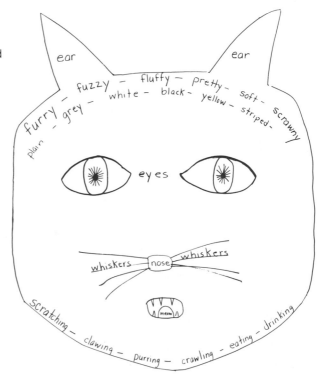

Ways of Using Brainstorming

Brainstorming is one of the most powerful strategies that teachers have in their instructional armories to get children thinking in an anything-is-acceptable situation. In lower grades, the teacher typically serves as leader and scribe, raising questions that ask youngsters to explore additional avenues and recording on board or chart each and every offering suggested by participants in the "idea-storm." Useful in stimulating thinking are such probes as:

- Think of words that describe how this looks.
- Think of words that describe how it moves.
- Think of what this object, animal, thing does.
- Think of other animals or things it resembles.
- Describe specific parts of it.
- Think of words that give your feelings about it.
- Think of things this object or animal might say if it could talk.

In upper grades, youngsters can raise additional directions for brainstorming and can take the teacher's place as scribe. Generally, more than one scribe is necessary to keep up with ideas as they are tossed out by many participants.

First experiences with brainstorming are generally most profitable if a number of youngsters join in to proffer wild ideas. Beginning brainstorming activity usually works best if youngsters handle a mind-stretching, imaginative topic that forces them to think of the unthinkable, to consider the impossible, to go beyond the confines of reality. Later, having thought wildly together, they can move into small groups to produce far-out words and ideas on a related but different topic. And even later in the sequence, youngsters can individually brainstorm words before writing on their own.

Take, for example, the way Dwight Frank used brainstorming with his sixth graders. Mr. Frank began by sharing Shel Silverstein's *The Giving Tree* (Harper & Row, 1964). Half the group listened for and thought about "tree/giving words," the other half for "people/taking words." Following the listening time, the sixth graders divided the board into two sections—one labeled *tree*, the other *person*—and began to brainstorm. They tossed out *apples, leaves, shade, trunk, branches,* and *stump* as tree words found in the story; they listed these on one section of the board. On the other they listed *gathering, swinging, climbing, playing, sailing, boating* as people words, again drawing directly from the word content of *The Giving Tree*.

But this was only a beginning. Children contributed more words and phrases to the board, triggered in their thinking by such questions as: "What words can we use to describe any tree? What words tell us how a tree moves in the breeze, in the wind, in a hurricane? What words describe this particular tree? What would this tree have done if it had the ability to get up and walk? What would it have wished if it had the ability to wish? What other things might it have said to the young boy? the older man? the very old man?" Having filled the board with more tree words, the children did the same with people words.

At that point, the youngsters zeroed in on feeling words, encouraged by questions that asked them to consider how the tree and the boy felt at the beginning of the story, in the middle, and at the end. They squeezed these words onto the already jam-packed board. Not until then did the youngsters begin to write—in this case, diamantes that contrasted tree with person. In composing, youngsters could "help themselves" to any of the words written higgledy-piggledy before them. Here are two in a longer series the class composed cooperatively based on their brainstormed listings.

TREE	TREE
Tall, stately	Cut, broken
Blowing, billowing, shading	Giving, loving, sharing
Branches, apples: friend, time	Stump, chair: wrinkles, cane
Gathering, swinging, climbing	Sitting, resting, waiting
Young, playful	Old, tired
BOY	MAN

Mr. Frank's use of brainstorming suggests just how this strategy can be integrated into a writing sequence. In his case, he began with an oral sharing of a story, which supplied some of the initial words and ideas for brainstorming; the story got the "storm" blowing. For the listening-time, he could well have substituted individual reading or researching or a direct experience followed by general talk. In any case, the introductory activity in the sequence would have provided youngsters with content to think about. This is essential, for, after all, inspiration favors the prepared mind.

Secondly, Mr. Frank's lesson demonstrates a fundamental characteristic of brainstorming sessions—recording words and ideas for future use. Mr. Frank chose to record on the chalkboard with participants later transferring words to cards that they taped up on the word wall. In this classroom, the entire space beneath the chalkboard areas was given over to words printed on cards that children had encountered in their studies; this area was called "The Working Word Wall," for youngsters were to try to make these words work for them as part of their speaking and writing activity. On other occasions, scribes recorded on charts, which continued to hang for several days so that children would have the words and ideas available for use.

In sum, Mr. Frank structured his writing sequence so that listening—or data collection—preceded brainstorming and so that recording accompanied the outpouring of ideas. Only then did children begin to write. Figure 2.4 shows the key steps in the sequence.

Figure 2.4. A writing sequence

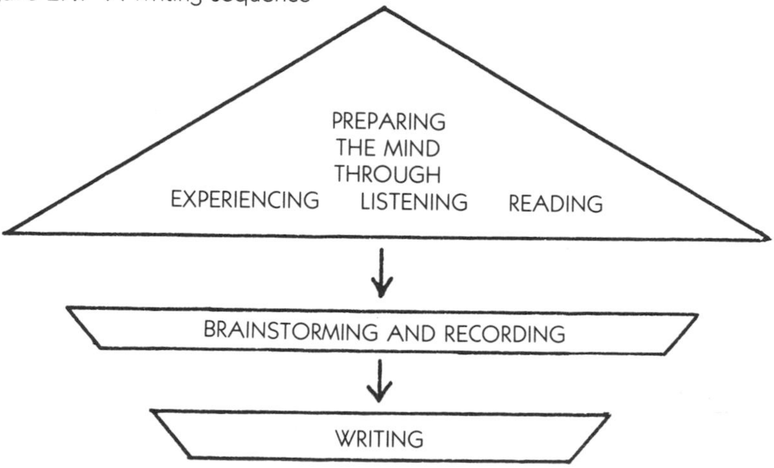

PREPARING
THE MIND
THROUGH

EXPERIENCING   LISTENING   READING

↓

BRAINSTORMING AND RECORDING

↓

WRITING

What Brainstorming Contributes

Mr. Frank's tree-person sequence also suggests what brainstorming contributes as part of writing activity. In the first place, it provides actual words and phrases that children can use in writing. If youngsters of widely differing abilities, interests, and backgrounds brainstorm together, the resulting list of thoughts will be far more comprehensive than if one youngster were to sit down independently to identify words related to the same topic. Then, too, some of the words that surface during the "storm" may be unfamiliar to a few participants; children who proffer these must explain them, telling how they are used and perhaps checking the dictionary for meaning and spelling before words are added to the board. In this respect, brainstorming is a strategy that contributes to children's functional vocabularies.

Spelling during writing becomes less a burden for those youngsters who normally encounter spelling problems as they write. Words to use—correctly spelled—are readily available as youngsters go on to write. All the young writer must do is look up at the word wall and find an appropriate word. To help slower youngsters, some experienced teachers ask participants to read in unison and aloud all the words recorded during the "storm." By doing this, the teacher helps poorer readers and spellers associate the visual image of a word with its oral equivalent.

Equally significant is the boost that brainstorming gives to thinking. Often a word suggested by one child triggers another child to identify a related word. In this way ideas mushroom as youngsters explore first one dimension of a topic, then another. Teachers who have brainstormed with their classes have been repeatedly amazed by the quality of the ideas to surface; they themselves never anticipated some of the words and expressions suggested during the anything-goes exploration.

GROUP WRITING

When Mr. Frank's sixth graders composed diamantes based on their listening-brainstorming experience, they did so cooperatively. Led by their teacher's probing questions, they talked about which adjectives of all those brainstormed best described the young tree. Children suggested pairs that communicated specific meanings in ways that "sounded nice together." They suggested groupings of -*ing* words to express young tree actions and noun words they associated with young trees and boys. They went on to put together clusters of -*ing* words and adjectives that described the young boy. The pattern for writing is shown in figure 2.5; developed by Iris Tiedt, it helps children who have trouble composing in more open formats to get started writing.

Figure 2.5. The structure of a diamante

Noun I

Two adjectives
describing Noun I

Three participles that go
with Noun I

Four nouns: the first 2 about Noun I,
the second 2 about Noun II

Three participles that go
with Noun II

Two adjectives
describing Noun II

Noun II (opposite of Noun I)

What Group Writing Contributes

Youngsters can gain confidence in their ability to produce ideas for writing by participating in group writing sessions. These sessions can be teacher-guided; a small group or even an entire class can decide together what words work well to introduce a written piece, to develop the idea, and to wrap it up at the end. Of course, individuals within the group contribute specific lines to the developing piece, which is recorded on a chart or a board for all to see. But as lines are suggested, children talk out the component ideas, expand them, change them, restructure them until most of them are satisfied with what they have written.

In *teacher-guided group writing*, the teacher's role is to raise questions that help youngsters play orally with ideas that are developing. In the process of thinking together, youngsters may stumble on really creative ways of expressing ideas and powerful words that communicate meanings precisely. This is particularly important in the creation of poetry. In poetry sounds are fundamental; and as youngsters contribute lines for possible inclusion in a cooperative piece, they "try them out on their tongues" to hear the arrangement of sounds.

The teacher's role is also to help participants decide which suggested lines to include in the cooperative piece. Here the teacher may query, "Which of these lines paints the clearer picture? Which has a better ring to it?" Finally, the teacher may have to suggest, "Let's vote. Which way do we want it?"

In this respect, the teacher's activity during initial group writing sessions in which many youngsters participate sets the stage for independent small group cooperative writing. Children who have participated in writing together when guided by the teacher are ready to raise the same questions when they work in small groups on their own. They know too that some compromise is necessary so that the final piece produced by a writing team includes ideas of each member.

When they have involved youngsters first in teacher-guided group writing and then in independent team writing, teachers report that the amount of writing children later produce when they write individually increases. The talking-together that takes place as part of group writing "loosens up" thinking for writing—a "loosening up" that appears to carry over when children take up their pencils to write alone. Perhaps the reason for this is that through group writing children learn to explore ideas. They see their ideas incorporated in a cooperative piece and are reassured that their ideas are worthy of being written down. Another reason is that group writing can be exciting, especially if youngsters are encouraged to search for a humorous twist or an unexpected ending. In talking and writing together pupils get carried away and suddenly discover that writing can be fun.

Structuring Group Writing Sessions

A very useful sequence for getting children writing cooperatively is to combine group writing activity with informal discussion and brainstorming. For example, one third-grade class was studying the ways people live together in communities and was faced with the question, "How do people in our state travel?" To start the ball rolling, Myra Morse, their teacher, displayed a large map of the state that showed major cities, roads, rail lines, and airports. Children came forward to point out parkways, turnpikes, and interstates they knew from firsthand experience. They told how they had traveled along these roads, for what purposes they had used each, and the vehicles using each kind of road. Similarly, they located major rail links and airports and talked about the kinds of trips they would take by plane or by train. As children talked, they added key vocabulary—*train, railroad, airport, airplane, motorcycle, bus, car, turnpike*—to the ABC listings of social studies words mounted around the room. These listings were actually twenty-six elongated dictionary-like pages, one for each letter of the alphabet. To the *A a* chart, for example, youngsters added *airport, airplane,* and *automobile*; to the *T t* chart they added *train, turnpike, travel,* and *transportation* after checking the dictionary for correct spelling. In listing words, youngsters made no attempt to alphabetize entries on a chart; they listed words in the order in which they surfaced during the brainstorming and general talk-time.

Having gathered both ideas and words for writing, the third graders formed into three-person writing teams. The cooperative task of each triad was to compose a paragraph telling how people in their state get around, or travel. One youngster on each team served as scribe and recorded sentences as team members suggested them. A second served as dictionary vice-president to double check spelling by referring to the bulletin board ABC charts or to a handy dictionary. The third orally read each sentence after it was recorded to see if it said what the team meant. Once team members had completed their paragraph, they studied it together to find a title that summed up what it was all about. This they recorded on the top line of a second draft that one member had copied onto charting paper. Later the youngsters illustrated their transportation charts and hung them in the hall so that other classes could read them when passing by.

During the week that followed—as part of a combined social

studies/language arts experience—Ms. Morse's third graders continued to talk about different forms of transportation and the advantages and disadvantages of each. Some of these discussions occurred in the context of teacher-guided class groups, some in small talk-teams. On some days, youngsters as a total class created charts that summarized the ideas they had discussed; on other days they worked again in triads to produce a paragraph based on ideas brainstormed and discussed. Finally, after one rather involved talk-time in which youngsters had to tell about their favorite form of transportation and explain why they felt the way they did, each youngster was asked to write a paragraph alone—a paragraph in which he or she expressed a personal preference and gave a reason or two. In this way, youngsters had to demonstrate whether they could apply learnings developed through group writing and talking.

In this teaching-learning sequence, talking blends directly with writing. Writing together, children must voice their ideas sentence by sentence before writing them down. As a result, thinking becomes a key aspect of writing since in talking children are thinking out loud. In this context, grading children's expression as A, B . . . F has little place. There is no need to assign a grade to a child's idea contributed in a teacher-guided composing session. Similarly, there is no need to assign a grade to a team's summary paragraph. On the other hand, during team writing there is need for the teacher to move from team to team and raise questions that force members to think more deeply, to consider a related point, or to expand a sentence to give more detail. By interacting directly with youngsters as they contribute to cooperative writing sessions, the teacher soon learns which youngsters can produce really in-depth ideas and which need more help in playing with their thoughts and feelings.

INFORMAL ORAL PRESENTATIONS

On any one day children come to school with information, thoughts, and feelings that focus on a wide range of topics. Mark comes into the classroom bubbling with excitement, telling his teacher, "We have a new baby at home," or "We're going to move," or "Did you see the eclipse on television last night?" or "I went fishing and caught a fish this long." Then the youngster elaborates, eager to share details that are meaningful to him. A teacher who perceives oral expression as important in its own right and as a stepping-stone to written expression can build classroom activity on this child's enthusiasm for talking about events that are significant to him.

"Come and tell us all about it," the teacher responds, gathering other youngsters into a group to hear Mark tell about his big event. The teacher raises questions as Mark's story winds down. Other children are encouraged to ask questions and recount similar kinds of events in their own lives. In this context oral discussion is a natural component of classroom living.

It can easily lead into writing, for once Mark has shared he is ready to tell the story on paper. This is the time for the teacher to encourage Mark to visit the Writing Center where paper, flo-pens, and pencils are laid out within a grouping of cubicles, each one of which provides the privacy for individual recording. Other youngsters can withdraw into other writing cubicles to write down similar stories that happened to them—perhaps "borrowing" some of the very words that Mark used in sharing his story.

Important characteristics of individual oral presentations that serve as stepping-stones into written expression are informality, naturalness, and child interest. Children with ideas to share should not be forced to stand up straight in front of the class; such a procedure is more likely to discourage rather than encourage the lively sharing of ideas. Instead, the teacher should select and organize classroom props to allow for informality.

With young children, the primary-grade teacher can establish a sharing corner in the room, a piece of rug on which children can sit while listening or talking to a Mark. Perhaps Mark can be supplied with a hassock or a piano stool on which to perch as he shares his story. With older children, the swivel armchair made famous on television talk shows can serve the same purpose. The child with an event to share can relax in the Talk Show Chair as he or she recounts the happening or feelings about it. At the junior high level, a tall stool makes an exciting perch for sharing.

As youngsters move up in the elementary grades, individual oral sharing may become slightly more sophisticated, though not necessarily more formal, because of the greater complexity of ideas to be expressed. Youngsters may want to think through ideas before expressing them. They may wish to think ahead about the way in which they want to present ideas to classmates. The clipboard technique is a possible aid in this situation. A sharer jots ideas on paper, clips them to the board, and refers to them while reporting from the swivel chair or tall stool. Notes used for this purpose need not be detailed—just a skeleton of the big ideas to be expressed. These notes, added to even during the oral presentation as peers raise questions and make suggestions, become a writing guide when later the reporter becomes a writer and withdraws to the writing center to compose a paragraph or two on the same topic.

As thoughts to be shared grow in complexity and children want to share their opinions on controversial topics, a group sharing of ideas becomes profitable. Having read rather extensively on a problem, children form a panel of experts on that topic. As a panel, one at a time they present their ideas—often conflicting—and respond to questions from classmates. This activity can also serve as a prelude to actual written expression of ideas. Reporters might compose a paragraph that expresses their opinion on the topic; listeners might compose by selecting one view expressed and explaining why it appears most plausible. Again the words and thoughts of the talk-time become the words and thoughts to grasp and twist in writing.

CREATIVE DRAMATIC EXPRESSION

Viewed as part of writing sequences, oral presentations need not be restricted to reporting activity. Indeed, creative dramatizations—especially of the spontaneous variety—can provide some of the most effective leaps into written expression. This is particularly so when dramatizations are combined with follow-up brainstorming or informal discussion.

Spontaneous Dramatizations

Dramatizations within writing programs serve the purpose of encouraging children to express themselves freely and to explore the varied dimensions of a situation. For this reason, children do not work from a prepared script nor do they necessarily begin by writing a script. Rather, participants improvise, working from their conceptions of the characters they are portraying and the manner in which these characters would behave under various conditions. The result can be an action-conversation skit based on some predefined problem situation that children may have encountered at some point in everyday living.

For example, working with inner-city children who tended to define misery in terms of discrimination, John O'Neill divided his class into subgroups of four. These subgroups met briefly to decide what characters they each would be in action-conversation skits about discrimination; one group identified the Boy, the Shopkeeper, the Cop, and the Passerby. Then they talked about what could happen to these characters, moving on to create a story not in written-down but in on-the-spot dramatic form. Only after each dramatic group had spontaneously performed its original story did youngsters in this fifth grade attempt to write; even then they did not work individually but rather in cooperative teams whose task was to write a conversation story in which the same characters interacted.

In the same way humorous action-conversation skits on topics of current interest may be improvised by upper elementary school children. For example, handling ideas related to preservation of the environment, students can create spontaneously the action-conversation—

- between the lungs of a man who is smoking a cigarette and the man himself.
- among three fish and a turtle that live in a polluted river.
- among a garbage can, a man who has just littered, and a metal soda can.
- between Smoky the Bear and two boys who are building a campfire.
- among three pelicans watching an oil slick come toward them.
- among three birds sitting on a roof as they smell the foul gasses from a nearby chimney.

Once dramatizations are performed, they can provide the content for writing as acting teams work together to record "for posterity" the story they developed for oral presentation.

In the same way, too, dramatizations related to social studies content can encourage free expression preparatory to writing. Students who have investigated such topics as life with the Indians, Eskimos, or Egyptians, life in the Middle Ages, life at Valley Forge with Washington, existence on a slave plantation, surviving in Plymouth, or the struggle on the western frontier can dramatize original versions of what happened. They can begin by associating life with the problems inherent in survival within communities; problems of—

- securing food, water, shelter.
- determining governmental structure.
- achieving freedom.
- replacing war with peace.
- overcoming threats from outside the community.
- providing transportation.
- maintaining good health.

Within the context of a specific situation dramatized, such concepts as freedom, peace, and law have a concrete base. As a result, children can handle the concepts in a more meaningful way and express ideas that they may not have been able to perceive if they had begun with definitions and abstractions. The result can also be words, thoughts, and feelings to be expressed through writing.

Especially in the lower grades, stories are effective for involving children dramatically. Familiar and repetitive stories such as *The Three*

Little Pigs, *The Three Billy Goats Gruff*, and *Little Red Riding Hood* make good beginnings for this type of expression. The teacher introduces the story by sharing it creatively, using both body and voice to add drama to the telling. On further retellings the teacher pauses at points where a character speaks and asks, "What do you think the first little pig said then? How did he say it? Let's all be the little pig and speak and act his line together." Having gone through the entire story interpreting lines and actions in this way, specific youngsters volunteer to play the major roles—one becoming the pig who built a house of straw, a second becoming the pig who built of twigs, a third becoming the pig who built of brick, and a fourth becoming the wolf who huffed and puffed to blow the houses down. On other days other youngsters—perhaps aided by props they have created—can assume these roles to retell the story in their own unique way.

This type of dramatization leads naturally into reflective writing. Children retell the story on paper, selecting the part to recount that they enjoyed the best. To help slower youngsters and those just beginning to record on their own, the teacher can print key story words on cards affixed to the word wall; children who have reading and writing problems can read these aloud before writing.

Puppet Plays

A device commonly used to encourage children to express themselves freely in dramatic situations is puppetry. Those who normally have few ideas to share or who typically function as tongue-tied performers may lose their inhibitions when they are hidden behind a box, screen, or mask; it is the puppet who is talking, not the performer, so the verbal and nonverbal expression takes on new dimensions of creativity. Using puppets, youngsters interacting in dramatic-production teams can spontaneously put together an original tale—perhaps one modeled after a tale previously shared by the teacher and interpreted line by line by class members. Later dramatic-production teams can become writing teams to record their playlets "for posterity."

Generally speaking, puppets need not be complicated to be effective. Sometimes the most effective puppet is the one made rather quickly to supplement ideas that emerge in spontaneous story-making and need to be expressed in that immediate context. Styrofoam balls about three or four centimeters in diameter can serve as basic material from which to construct simple finger puppets. With colored felt pens children can add ears, nose, eyes, mouth, and facial expressions. A bow tie of string, a ribbon, yarn pigtails, shaggy ears, a mustache, and a paper hat can all be affixed with straight pins. On a finger, the puppet can become anything or anyone a performer imagines. Manipulated from behind a desk, one or more puppets can be used to tell a story that youngsters are creating together on the spot.

Stick puppets are similarly adaptable. Children can cut faces, animals, people, objects, and background scenery from heavy construction paper and color them with crayon or felt pen. They can also cut pictures from magazines and mount these on construction paper. They staple the resulting pieces to sticks to form the characters and scenery they need to tell their story. Again, children can manipulate their puppets from below the level of a desk or can construct a simple puppet stage from a shoe box by cutting a slit along one side of the box and moving their puppets along the slit. (See fig. 2.6.)

Figure 2.6. Shoe box puppet stage

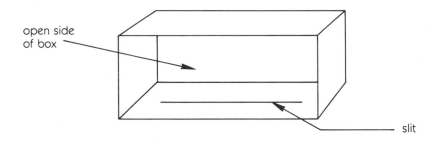

open side
of box

slit

Very much like stick puppets are head puppets. Children make masks and hold them over their faces during the dramatization to give themselves the feeling of being the characters in a story. Youngsters begin by cutting a circle from lightweight cardboard or locating some paper plates. With scissors they cut out ears, eyes, nose, and mouth; and with felt pen they add a little color. Even though not much time is required for construction, youngsters rather rapidly have puppets through which they can more freely express portions of a story taking form as part of a teacher-led or small team oral story-making activity.

Slightly more time-consuming to construct are body puppets. Each child stretches out on a very large piece of construction paper while a second child sketches the outline of the body on the paper, leaving approximately five centimeters of paper beyond the perimeters of the body. Children then color in features and clothing required for the characters to be portrayed and staple strips of heavy-grade cardboard to the back of arms, legs, and head for support. Performers hold their body puppets by central supports, using them to mask the entire body. Another way to achieve a similar result is to use large cartons. A hole can be cut in the top, through which the performer sticks his or her head. Holes are cut on both sides so that hands and arms can be extended. There is no bottom in the box so that the entire structure can be slipped easily onto the body. Again children color their puppets to meet the needs of the dramatization.

One of the simplest kinds of puppets is the type made from a small-sized paper bag. Students can affix pieces of construction paper to the flaps of bags to simulate hair and to the sides to simulate ears. They can draw features using crayon or felt pen. Performers then slip their puppets onto their hands and are ready to create a story as part of an oral story-making time.

Some teachers have discovered that for oral story-making with puppets to be productive, children require some preparatory teacher-guided work. To begin this work, the teacher introduces a puppet character that he or she has available. Particularly good for introductory activity are the commercially available hand puppets that are very colorful. The teacher begins, "Today I should like to introduce you to Oscar the Downcast Dragon. Let's talk about why Oscar is so downcast. What could be troubling him?" Children think in brainstorming style of all the possible problems that could have beset Oscar to make him so doleful. Possibilities are recorded on the board. Studying some of these problems, children follow up by suggesting way-out ways that Oscar could solve them. They decide which is the "best" problem—the one that would make the most imaginative story. Together they decide on other characters necessary for the development of Oscar's story and make some quick paper-bag puppets for these characters.

Having decided together on the overall dimensions of the story, teacher and children begin the story line. The teacher begins again, "Once there was a downcast dragon named Oscar." Children who hold puppet heads in hand must add a next possible line and then more and more. Cooperatively, they concoct good dialogue for each of the characters to say, and they think through a good way for the story to end. By working in this way, they are learning how to develop a story orally and creatively. They are acquiring thinking skills important when they create other stories independently.

Particularly with young children such cooperative story concoction through puppet play is often more meaningful than writing out a story from the very start. Youngsters are involved with actions as well as with words. They almost "crawl physically" into the story and identify with characters they are portraying. In addition, through oral activity, they are gaining the vocabulary and the sentence patterns to use when they write on their own.

TALKING THROUGH ACTIONS

In *Comparative Psychology of Mental Development* (Science Editions, 1948), Heinz Werner suggests that the younger the children are, the more likely they are to organize their world in terms of *activity* and in terms of the *self*. Within a total situation, younger children perceive action rather than specific elements; they create and fashion their world through a blending of motor-emotional activity and objects. Also, young children's organization of time and space is active and egocentric. Time to them is based on the great events in their own lives: wake-up time, breakfast, snack, nap, father's coming home. Their concept of space is similarly organized around themselves. Children use their own bodies to determine relationships in space; they physically interact with a situation to gain understanding of it. This is seen in the action of young children who enter an unfamiliar house: they run from room to room, physically sensing the size and exploring the shape of their new environment. Piaget calls this period of intellectual development the "pre-operational stage"—a stage when children establish "relationships between experience and action" by manipulating the world directly (*The Psychology of Intelligence*, Routledge & Kegan Paul, 1964).

As youngsters enter school in their fifth or sixth year, they are very likely moving into the successive stage, the "concrete operational," in which they learn to manipulate symbols and represent the external world symbolically. At this stage, children depend on a concrete referent to gain symbolic understanding; they are still very much tied to their perceptions. Only as young people move into junior high at approximately twelve years of age are they able to handle abstract relationships without reference to the concrete.

L. S. Vygotsky, too, considers the manipulation of things in the environment important for young children. Youngsters do a lot of talking aloud to the self. This is called *egocentric speech* and is accompanied by manipulation of concrete objects and materials found in the immediate situation (*Thought and Language*, M.I.T. Press, 1962). This type of oral activity, combined with active manipulation, paves the way for inner speech, or for the talking-to-the-self that takes place "within the head." Adults talk to themselves in this way, a way that is very important to the writer working independently with words and ideas. As James Moffett explains:

> If we concentrate our forces on fostering the highest development
> of inner speech, we shall automatically not only teach excellence in
> writing but lift other subjects along with it. . . . [To foster the

development of inner speech we use] "any means that will exercise thought itself . . . games, practical problems to solve, imagining, and dialectic with others; much experience in small-group process where all sorts of good conversing can be practiced—task talk, topic talk, improvisation . . . ; copious and wide-ranging reading . . . ; rich physical and social experience with the things of this world so that inner speech has much to reflect from the outside. (Moffett, "Integrity in the Teaching of Writing," *Phi Delta Kappan*, 61:276-79, December 1979)

These ideas suggest to the teacher working with young children that a broader conception of writing that includes a variety of activities is imperative. One form this activity can take is pantomime—a form of expression requiring children to translate their impressions of the world into physical activity and perhaps encouraging youngsters to use inner speech to think about what they are doing.

Pantomime Actions in Primary Grades

Children can interpret musical selections through their physical motions. Youngsters who enjoy "let's pretend" activity can become rabbits, involving their whole bodies in rabbit actions. They can be elephants, camels, lions, fish, or any other animals that intrigue them at this developmental stage. The preschool or primary teacher who is skilled at the piano, with the guitar, or even with an instrument like the cello has an advantage here. The musically talented teacher can quickly produce a tune, change to another, and then change to still another as children react physically with a nonverbal, interpretive impression of an animal. The teacher who is unskilled in music should not give up, for recordings can be used in similar fashion. Rather than making the bass notes on a piano growl like a bear or the treble notes sing like a bird, the teacher can use such recordings as Prokofiev's *Peter and the Wolf*, in which a flute trills like the Bird, an oboe clacks like the Duck, a clarinet slinks like the Cat, the horns play the Wolf, the strings sing Peter's sound, a bassoon is Grandfather, and the full orchestra plays the role of the Hunters. Children can be cast in each of these roles, and as they recognize their themes, they can do their own impressions.

Other pantomiming activities useful with younger children include "let's pretend" we are—

- jumping jacks.
- floating bubbles in the air.
- riding on a subway.

- driving a motorcycle.
- bobbing up and down on the waves.
- riding a horse.
- walking in the mud, splashing in puddles, slipping and falling—all on a rainy day.

Again, musical accompaniment may provide the stimulus that will trigger freedom of expression and creative individual interpretation. Or, instead, children may supply related noises—the screeches, the squeals, the whinnies, the roars, the splashes, the crashes, the plops—that accompany the action. Noises can merge into words as children spontaneously add verbal sound effects to their pantomimes, sometimes contributing feeling words, sometimes describing words, sometimes action words. Even as children spontaneously call out words that come to mind as they get involved in the pantomime, the teacher can stand at the board to record words for later use in writing.

Shadow Play.   Still another device for translating impressions into actions is shadow play. Using a slide projector as a light source, the teacher can project a beam onto a screen. Primary graders are fascinated with the process of casting their shadows on the screen and will move creatively to produce original effects. They will dance, slink, hop, bob, gesture, and gyrate with little or no inhibition as they watch their shadows perform the same activities.

Interpreting Stories.   Reading and listening to stories can also lead into creative nonverbal expression. Having heard Gerald McDermott's *The Stonecutter* (Viking, 1975), children can become the humble stonecutter, the magnificent prince, musicians and servants, the mighty sun, the powerful cloud, the mighty mountain, and finally at the end the stonecutter again. They can retell the story using only their bodies to communicate actions and feelings. These are other picture storybooks with strong action sequences that are particularly adaptable for nonverbal telling:

> Verna Aardema, *Why Mosquitoes Buzz in People's Ears* (Dial, 1975).
> Janina Domanska, *The Turnip* (Macmillan, 1969).
> La Fontaine, *The Miller, the Boy, and the Donkey* (Franklin Watts, 1969).
> La Fontaine, *The North Wind and the Sun* (Franklin Watts, 1964).
> Maurice Sendak, *Where the Wild Things Are* (Harper & Row, 1963).
> William Steig, *The Amazing Bone* (Farrar, Straus, 1976).

Such familiar tales as *The Three Billy Goats Gruff, Jack and the Bean Stalk*, and *The Three Bears* are also easy to interpret nonverbally. Having nonverbally interpreted one of these stories, youngsters can suggest words to describe each character—words that tell how the character walked, acted, felt. In this way nonverbal activity leads into brainstorming, which in turn leads into writing.

Since nursery rhymes very often embody actions, they too can be interpreted physically and used as part of a sequence similar to that just described. As children chorus a rhyme such as "Ride a Cockhorse to Banbury Cross," they can move their bodies to emulate the motion of the horse. With "Jack be nimble, Jack be quick," they can jump over the candlestick at the appropriate moment. Very young children can pretend to be Humpty Dumpty falling off the wall, Little Miss Muffet sitting on her tuffet, or Little Jack Horner putting his thumb into the pie. Later, they can translate their nonverbal experiencing into words, supplying words to describe their actions.

Pantomime Actions in Intermediate Grades

Upper elementary students can participate in more sophisticated pantomiming experiences to encourage them to be more perceptive of events, people, and things. These experiences, which may be a prelude to talk activity and to writing of descriptive paragraphs, are oftentimes most effective if they occur as part of total class expression and interpretation. For example, all members of a class can participate in an exaggerated "train chain." In this, pantomimists become wheels, doors, passengers, bell ringers, and so forth, using a lineup of about seven or eight chairs strung out down an open area of classroom or gymnasium to simulate a train. "Passenger players" sit upon the chairs, pretending to sleep, read newspapers, watch the passing scenery, and/or gyrate their bodies to the rhythm of the moving train. Next to the chairs seven or eight young people line up as "door players." They each extend one arm and pivot about ninety degrees to open and close. Next to the "door players," seven or eight players kneel to become "wheels." They produce wheel motion by rotating one arm in a clockwise direction. At the front of the line several "engineer players" stand who ring the bell. Before putting all the action together, each group of pantomimists practices synchronizing its act so that wheels move and bells ring in harmony, doors open simultaneously, and passengers disembark and embark as a group.

Then the full pantomime begins. The teacher starts the action initially by standing at the front of the "train" and calling verbal directions: "Bells ring. Wheels spin. Bells ring. Wheels stop. Doors open. Passengers climb on. Doors close." After a few run-throughs with oral directions, the group can shift to nonverbal directions; the teacher or a student "conductor" simply points or nods to groups to initiate or halt action. As children gain skill, children can exchange places so that wheels have a chance to be passengers, passengers a chance to be engineers. A natural follow-up is to list words that describe actions performed by passengers—words that are used later in writing descriptions.

Not only can a total class become parts of a train, but it can also become an orchestra or band with different groups pantomiming the activity of violinists, trombonists, drummers. In like manner, experienced pantomimists functioning in small groups can put together a pantomimed circus, parade, rodeo, printing press production, truck, with each participant contributing a component action.

Having functioned as a member of a group pantomime, some may volunteer to "go it alone." For instance, a perceptive upper grader may mimic the actions of—

- a banana peeling itself.
- a person fighting off a mosquito in the night.
- a person trying to locate a key and unlock a door when both hands are loaded with packages.
- a boy or girl who overslept and must rush to get to school on time.
- a person walking on a sheet of ice.
- a person washing a window.
- a person foolishly crossing the street in the middle of the block.

In acting any of these situations, children must think in concrete rather than abstract terms. In so doing, they may identify elements to express that they might not have noticed if they had begun by taking pen in hand or even talking about the situation.

In *The Composite Art of Acting* (Macmillan, 1966), Jerry Blunt describes the intricacies of pantomime so that the teacher who has not included pantomime within the language arts may feel more secure about using it. According to Blunt, skilled pantomimists can perceive in a situation all the contingencies that could occur because they have studied that situation thoroughly and have actually become part of it themselves. For instance, the pantomimist who mimics the actions of a girl in a short, short skirt may include these acts: pulling down the skirt, easing into a chair, pulling the skirt down again, looking around with a satisfied air, glancing surreptiously downward, seeing an "unmentionable" showing, looking around to see who else notices, pulling the skirt down, pulling it down even more, looking around, noticing that she has dropped a handkerchief, bending down with a stiff body motion to retrieve it, sitting up quickly as the skirt rides up, holding the skirt down with one hand while reaching with a determined, deliberate motion to pick up the handkerchief.

Not all children are equally successful in pantomiming. In this area, as well as in others, individual differences are to be expected. Yet children who become masters of the art of nonverbal expression can supply a lifelike picture for other children. In so doing, they help the others see the complexities of situations that appear deceptively simple on the surface. They help others pick up points to include in describing, whether that describing takes place through oral sharing or independent writing.

PICTORIALIZING: TALKING THROUGH DRAWING, PAINTING, AND SCULPTING

Commenting in *Language Arts*, 54:739-40, October 1977, Janet Emig concludes: "Children move necessarily, and probably developmentally, among modes of representation—more specifically, for children, drawing and other forms of pictorializing seem to serve essential conceptualizing needs during the writing process." Left to their own devices youngsters shuttle between drawing and writing, first adding new details to their pictures, then to their writings. This conclusion is based on studies such as that by Donald Graves in which children's activity in writing was observed directly.

As Emig goes on to suggest, "The implication, of course, is that children and adolescents be encouraged to roam among the representational modes (can't be prevented from roaming?) and that, just as verbal versions will be vitalized by alternate representations, so the quality of drawings, paintings, sculpture may well be vitalized by dealing with the same experience verbally." The visual arts and the language arts blend for children; teachers should encourage this blending in classrooms.

Pictorializing in Primary Grades

The major way in which young children record their impressions of their world on paper is through pictorializing. This way is especially meaningful to young children, for at this point in their development they are oriented more toward the concrete than toward symbolic abstractions. Recording of words on paper produces only a symbolic record, whereas a picture, a clay sculpture, a schematic, or a shoe box diorama provides a more concrete representation of the world.

Firsthand experiences can provide the "stuff" of pictorializing.

Children can take their crayons, drawing papers, and drawing boards outside as they experience the world. Sitting on a grassy site, they can pictorially describe clouds, trees, birds, and the movement of the wind. Standing in a playground and watching a busy street, they can pictorially describe cars, pollution, police officers, shops, buildings, and people. Clustered by a cage at the zoo, they can sketch their impressions of lions, zebras, antelopes, monkeys, and bears. Back in the classroom, they can draw descriptions of the hamster, the canary, the turtle, and the rabbit kept as class pets. Later, children can tell about their drawings, translating their nonverbal descriptions into word pictures.

It is rather exciting to see how seriously young children can become involved in pictorializing about the real world. On a visit to the Mikimoto Pearl Island in eastern Japan, one of the authors chanced upon an entire school on an expedition to record ideas as pictures. The children began by walking around the entire display area; then each child selected a site from which to record the scene. The little ones clustered around the place where the diving girls jumped into the water to search for oysters; they were intrigued by the action. The older ones settled before the statue of Mikimoto; they were intrigued by its detail. Shortly, most of the children were actively producing a visual record of their trip.

Stories and reports can also be told visually. When children come to school bubbling over with excitement about an event they want to share, they not only can relate their stories to teacher and fellow students, but they can also tell them through pictures that can be shown to others. When children travel into the realm of fantasy and relate ideas about Halloween witches, fairies, and make-believe animals, again they can record ideas as pictures to use in sharing their stories with others. When an incident crops up in the classroom, children can recount it visually, selecting colors and lines that communicate their feelings as well as the facts.

Children quickly realize that ideas can be told through pictures when the teacher shares books that have pictures but no words at all. For instance, in *The Snowman* (Random, 1978) Raymond Briggs tells the story of a boy who creates a snowman. In a dream the snowman comes alive to encounter electric lights, hot stoves, and TVs, to dress in father's clothes, and to go dancing out over the city and country with its creator. Reading the book, youngsters can follow the plot to find out what is happening to the story characters. Both Mercer Mayer and Martha Alexander have illustrated a number of wordless books that can be used to introduce children to this form of expression.

Such early "reading" activity can motivate children to "write" their own wordless books, depicting everyday occurrences or fanciful tales. To start, every child can contribute a picture to a class-events book, or an individual child may compile his or her own book—*Me*. In *Me* the "writer" colors or paints events that have personal meaning: the arrival of a new brother, an argument with Mama, a fight with Josie, a trip, the acquisition of a family pet, moving, getting a new pair of jeans, a favorite toy. Whenever inspiration strikes, the child creates another page to add to *Me*.

Through a related technique, children can increase their ability to work with story sequences. If all the children have participated in a class trip, follow-up talk can center on things that happened. While telling about an incident, a child stands at the side of the room. The next child to relate an incident stands beside the first, either in front or behind, depending on the sequence in which the events occurred. As other children tell happenings, they stand in relative positions in the line until all have a place. Those children who cannot think of a different incident stand beside a child who has already told about a well-liked part of the excursion.

Having talked out their impressions, children return to their seats, and every child colors or draws the part of the trip about which he or she spoke. Later, children tape their papers end-to-end in the order of events being recounted. The teacher can tape the long strip of papers to rollers and run it through a viewing box or across the stage of an opaque projector as children tell about their pictures, each taking a turn so that events are told in sequence.

This story-line activity can be carried on even more readily with small groups. A storytelling group clusters around the teacher; together the children build a story orally. Then each child selects an incident in the story just created to pictorialize. Later the pictures are organized in a sequence that tells the story and are taped in a strip so that they can be

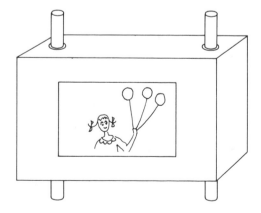

Figure 2.7.
A picture
story viewing box

shown in a viewing box. See figure 2.7 for an example.

As children move from kindergarten to first grade, pictorializing continues but with the added feature of written lines. Youngsters compose one or two sentences on lined paper stapled to their artwork. They tell their stories through two modes of expression, pictorial and verbal, perhaps working on both aspects simultaneously—adding a detail to their pictures and then expressing that idea in their compositions. Manuscript-drawing paper that has a large blank area at the top and several lines marked at the bottom is ideal for this purpose.

Pictorializing in Upper Grades

As Janet Emig explains, the need to draw as part of writing persists as children move into middle, junior high, and senior high schools. Their drawings do more than illustrate what they have written; illustrating serves as a mode of thinking that helps children elaborate on their impressions even as they write them down. By playing with an idea visually on paper, youngsters may be able to see new dimensions within a situation; and ideas may snowball.

Then, too, many children in the sixth grade are still functioning in the concrete-operational stage in which a concrete referent is essential if children are to handle abstractions with any degree of success. Pictorializing supplies a bridge between the concrete and more abstract symbolizations—words. Of course, there are some children who enjoy artistic expression more than written. If an experience blends both the artistic with the written, children who are uncertain of how to begin verbally may gain security by starting with what they can do well—artistic representation.

A student teacher, with whom one of the authors worked, tried an experience with upper graders that blended pictorializing with writing. The teacher began by brainstorming with young people. She asked:

> Wouldn't it be funny if we had dog arms on our bodies? How do you think we would live if we did?
> What if an elephant had a giraffe neck? How would it look? How would it have to live?
> What if a lion had a trunk like an elephant, wings like a duck, and stripes like a zebra? Can you imagine how it would look? How would it have to change the way it gets food? walks? sleeps?
> Can you put together a strange animal with characteristics like this?

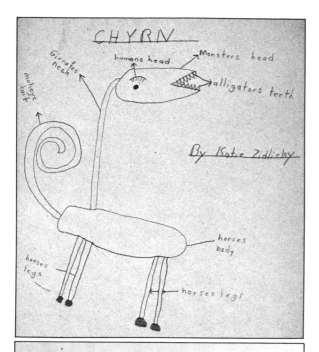

Figure 2.8.
The chyrn,
an animal invented
by Katie Zidlicky

CHYRN

This is a Chyrn, It lives in
the swamp in Africa. The trouble
is, that when it walk its neck
is so long that it breacks the
branches off the trees. It eats
leaves and small branches.
It also eats small animals.
It can run very very
fast. It loves the sun
when it is hot. When
winter comes it goes to
the oceon and goes and
buries at the bottom under
the sand. There he eats
the fish and sand until
it gets warm again.

The teacher next projected some drawings of "ziberiches," fantastic animals that combine parts from several different animals, and the children suggested crazy names for them. Then came their turns: every child pulled five letters of the alphabet from a hat to form a crazy name for an animal he or she was to invent. Each designed a "ziberich" on drawing paper and wrote a short paragraph of invented description about the animal created. Katie's invention was a "chyrn." Notice how she put her randomly chosen letters together to form a pronounceable name. Her drawing of a chyrn and her description are reproduced in figure 2.8.

There are many, many media to use in pictorializing: watercolor, felt pen, finger paint, clay, string dipped in paint, block prints, pastels, screen prints, charcoal, pen and ink, tempera. Children can cut construction paper into various two- or three-dimensional shapes, cut portions of pictures from magazines and paste them together to make collages, combine real materials in inventive patterns, wind colored yarns to form weblike designs, or use clay, papier-mache, or blocks to produce models. In so doing, their ideas become clearer and even more exciting to them.

When encouraging art activities, the teacher must exercise one caution—not to force on children a realistic, adult view of the world. Perceiving through creative eyes, children may represent snowflakes as green and blue upon a white background, rather than as white upon a green and blue background. They may represent sky as green, grass as blue. The initial reaction of the teacher may be to tell children to use a blue crayon for sky, a green one for grass. Yet if one does this, one is insisting on a realistic interpretation of the world, forgetting that even as written content may be a reflection of the world or an invention that goes beyond reality, so artistic representation can have elements of realism and impressionism.

SOME SUMMARY THOUGHTS

A basic premise of this chapter is that children need to be involved in talking out their thoughts as part of any program in written expression. In this context, however, talking takes on expanded meaning. It means expressing in conversations and informal discussions. It means brainstorming ideas and words, writing cooperatively in teacher-guided and independently operating groups, presenting ideas orally, and expressing through creative dramatizations. In addition, *talking* means expressing through actions, particularly through pantomime, and pictorializing—expressing via drawing, painting, and sculpting. (See fig.

2.9.) Through all of these means children are able to make their ideas blossom.

Seen in this context, a writing program has as its supporting framework activities that encourage children to express themselves in a variety of modes. Writing must be viewed as part of a larger whole, as part of the expressive arts.

Figure 2.9. The bases for written expression

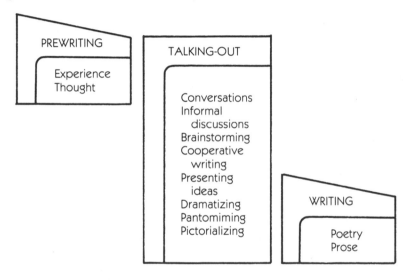

3

LET CHILDREN BEGIN ◄►
ways to introduce young
children to writing

In Creating, the only hard thing's to begin;
A grass-blade's no easier to make than an oak;
If you've once found the way, you've achieved
the grand stroke.
J. R. Lowell, A FABLE FOR CRITICS

Compare typical compositions written by first graders just learning to put words on paper with the talk of average first-grade children. As the compositions in figure 3.1 indicate, young children's written pieces show discontinuity of thought, rather simple structures, and words accidentally left out; in contrast the speech of first graders is more logically developed, employs more complex linguistic structures, and exhibits fewer accidental deletions. Such a comparison suggests that when young children verbally record their ideas on paper, they do so in less clear and complete fashion than in speaking. For them, written recording is hardly efficient.

Written recording is inefficient for young children because its production requires a visual, symbolic representation of ideas: children must physically construct letters and build those letters into words. Yet, at this stage youngsters are only being introduced to manuscript skills, and their knowledge of the written representations of words within their speaking vocabularies is extremely limited. Even when they have learned to control the pencil to produce all the letters in manuscript form, they are

Figure 3.1.
Compositions
by two first graders

browny was
a hoose.
he lived in farm
he littie the
Farm veary veary
much

The World is red i Like The Worldred
it is funny The Way it azk
The World is NAce GoUP At The World
                    i LiKe it
GiSS WantiDid   Elleh

handicapped by their slowness. Struggling to form words in manuscript, young writers focus on individual letters; in the process they may lose the thought they are trying to express. Of course, they also continue to work under the handicap of their limited spelling ability.

Because recording on paper is a slow process for the child, ways of recording that are less bound by children's skill in manipulating pencils and in spelling words must be employed preliminary to and parallel with independent written recording. In the previous chapter, a nonverbal way—pictorializing—was described. Drawing, sketching, painting, and sculpting are fine introductions to the idea that thoughts one carries in the head can be communicated to others in a visual form. In chapter 3, we will explore three other ways of recording: group dictation of ideas, individual dictation, and tape recording. In addition, we will describe ways of helping children make the transition from oral to independent written communication.

GROUP DICTATION, OR EXPERIENCE CHARTING

In *Understanding Language* (St. Martin's, 1977) Jean Malmstrom writes: "The language-experience method is a dynamic tool for drawing upon the students' oral skills in order to enhance learning to read." Clearly the method is a tool as well for teaching youngsters to write. Joining in a group led by the teacher and dictating ideas based on a shared experience, youngsters see as words written down the thoughts they have carried in their heads and have voiced. They see on paper and begin to read sentences they themselves have generated.

Ability to guide children's thinking as they dictate sentences is a fundamental skill teachers must acquire. For experience charting to be successful, the teacher must know how to structure preliminary activity so that children have thoughts to dictate as they interact together, ask questions that lead children to express their ideas, and keep children's attention as he or she records dictated sentences on paper. Let us consider how to do this.

Examples of Experience Charting in Primary Grades

Youngsters in the kindergarten at the West End School in North Plainfield, New Jersey, visited the Einstein-Moomjy salesroom to see the Oriental rugs and the many different kinds of carpets. Before they left, Mr. Moomjy gave each child a small sample of carpet to take back to school to use as a seat during group-sharing times. When the little ones returned to their classroom, they gathered around the recording easel to talk about how they could begin a thank you note to Mr. Moomjy and to suggest possible sentences to include in the letter. From the many suggested, the children chose two sentences for their teacher to write down in their letter:

Dear Mr. Moomjy,

Thank you for the rugs. We enjoy using them.

Your friends at West End

As an individual activity, every child drew a picture depicting what he or she would do with the carpet gift and signed his or her name to the drawing. All the drawings and the letter were stapled to a large piece of brown paper and were sent to Mr. Moomjy.

This type of group charting experience can be continued in the first grade and can, of course, result in forms of written expression other than thank you letters. Patrick brought his toy airplane to school to share during show-and-tell. After he had told his classmates how his airplane could fly and then demonstrated it, the children as a group suggested lines to write about it. The teacher recorded the children's words on charting paper in large manuscript letters:

THE AIRPLANE
Up and down!
See Patrick's airplane

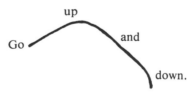

On another occasion the children in the same first-grade class talked about the fish in their class fish bowl. Afterward they dictated a report to the teacher; individual children suggested lines, and the total group decided which lines should be recorded:

THE FISH TANK
We have three fish in our fish tank. The fish are orange. We have two snails in the same bowl.

One day these first graders were talking about the possibility of a snowstorm. Using their tremendous excitement as a stimulus, the teacher gathered the youngsters around the recording easel and printed these lines as children suggested them:

SNOW

The air is cold.
The sky is gray.
The wind is blowing.
Will it snow today?

After an excursion that took them down to the railway station and for a short ride on the train, the children talked and then dictated:

OUR TRIP

We went for a walk to the train station. We saw an old furnace in the middle of the waiting room. The station man gave us little tickets. We had a good trip on the train.

Similarly, a second-grade teacher gave youngsters their first experience blowing bubbles and followed it up with group poetry writing and dictation. With the typical bubble-blowing equipment—bubble pipes and soap solution—the youngsters blew iridescent bubbles into the air on a morning when the sun was streaming into the room. As the bubbles danced upward, children called out their impressions, which the teacher recorded:

BIG BUBBLES

Bubbles are fun.
We like to blow
    big
    bubbles.

They burst on our shoes.
They pop on the ceiling.
They make rainbows in the air.

Bubbles are fun.
We like to eat
    big
    bubbles.

Guiding Children's Group Dictation Activity

To prepare children for the kind of composing activity described in these examples, experienced teachers begin by urging children to talk in general about what they have experienced or are experiencing. These teachers encourage: "Tell me about what we did. Tell me what we saw. Describe what happened there. Describe what happened next." They follow up with feeling probes: "How did this experience make you feel inside? What words describe your feelings? What was your favorite part? What part did you not like? Why did you dislike that part?'' After youngsters have shared their thoughts and feelings in a general way, teachers ask, ''Who can give me a good first thought to write down at the very beginning of our group chart? What would be a good thought to write down next?''

Experienced teachers also tend to involve children to some extent in the writing process. Responding to a child's suggested sentence, they answer, ''Yes, that would be a good beginning sentence. Should I start the sentence with a lower- or upper-case letter? Let's say the first word of Jill's sentence together and listen for its beginning sound. What letter do we use to record that sound?'' Since youngsters start to develop understanding of sound-symbol relationships in kindergarten and first grade, they can begin to apply their understanding as part of the dictation process. They can also apply their growing ability to record individual letters. If, for example, the first word of a sentence or line is *Bubbles* and children have been practicing writing upper-case *B*s, a teacher can continue: ''Who would like to come up and write the upper-case *B* into our chart to start our sentence?''

In a similar fashion, the teacher can help participants work with the sounds of a sentence recorded as punctuation. Having recorded a sentence suggested by the group, the scribe may pause and direct, ''Let's all read this sentence together and listen to what happens to our voices at the end.'' Children cooperatively decide whether the sentence is a stating, questioning, commanding, or exclaiming one. The decision made, a youngster adds the appropriate mark to the experience chart. In this way, the notion of sentences and different sentence endings becomes an integral part of the charting activity.

The next step in a typical experience charting sequence is reading what has been written. In some cases, the total group begins by chorusing the dictated lines together. This is especially helpful in the lower grades where youngsters' reading skills are relatively undeveloped. Or children can volunteer to read the lines of a story, poem, or report after the teacher has recorded them on large charting paper mounted on the easel. A number of youngsters read each line and then make a copy to include in an individual volume of the class-events book.

Modern technology has the potential to speed up the teacher's recording of dictated lines. Instead of recording on a chart, the teacher can type children's words into a microcomputer. Sentences appear on a television-like screen so that youngsters quickly see their ideas in written form. If the microcomputer is attached to a printer, a press of a key on the microcomputer triggers that printer to produce a typed copy, which comes rolling out of the machine in a matter of seconds. The coming years may well see microcomputers revolutionize the way we teach writing.

Advantages of Experience Charting in the Early Years

Group dictation activities contribute much to a young child's understanding of the writing process. Linguists tell us that language is essentially that which we speak; they look upon written words as simply oral language written down. From this point of view a learning strategy that begins with sentences spoken out and guides children to see how these sentences can be recorded on paper is a sound one; the movement in the sequence is from oral to written.

Second, there are always things going on in an activity-centered primary classroom that can supply the content for written expression. As children experience, they talk; a natural outgrowth of experiencing and talking is recording ideas on paper. If the teacher can perceive the writing potential inherent in most classroom situations, writing becomes an integral element of the developing curriculum. Writing is not a contrived activity; rather, children begin to see that written expression is a normal facet of living and that recording ideas on paper is a valuable means of communication.

Third, group charting is not at all a time-consuming activity in primary grades. Most of the pieces presented in this section were composed in less than ten minutes, making possible the inclusion of more informal writing experiences within a classroom day than would be possible if the teacher relied totally on individual approaches.

Fourth, as the examples given suggest, experience charting is not only a means of involving children in the idea-content of writing but also a means of teaching children how to record. Children can decide how to place words on the page, whether to use upper- or lower-case letters, and even what letter to use in beginning words to be recorded. Additionally, they contribute to the recording by actually getting up and printing beginning letters, punctuation marks, and eventually short words on the class chart.

Fifth, group dictation brings with it the added advantage of written products that serve as highly meaningful material to be read. Children enjoy reading and rereading sentences they have dictated. As they do, they add sight words to their reading vocabulary—sight words that are significant to them personally for these are within their listening and speaking vocabularies.

As part of the reading program, charts can be used in a variety of ways. Some teachers make individual word cards including words from the charts, and ask youngsters to match the word cards with the same words on the charts. On other occasions, primary teachers cut the charts into component sentences and ask children to put the sentences of the story "puzzle" back together again so that it tells the story in correct sequence. On still other occasions, they ask each youngster to make a copy of the chart and illustrate it. Later youngsters pair off, each to read and reread their personal versions to a listening mate. Using the products of group dictation in these ways, teachers are approaching reading from a language arts perspective, integrating it with writing, speaking, and listening.

A sixth advantage of group dictation is that it encourages cooperation among children. Youngsters deciding on which sentences to include in their piece are involved in a common enterprise. If their written record is to be used for some formal purpose—to send to the station agent, to include in a class-events book, to post in the hall, to be shared with youngsters in other classes—they tend to pull together to achieve that purpose. In this respect, social as well as language skills are outcomes of experience charting in the primary grades.

Using Experience Charting in Intermediate Grades

Group dictation is not an activity restricted to the lower grades. At the intermediate level, it has been used successfully to trigger ideas and to help youngsters see the fun to be had in playing with words on paper. For example, Joan Soroka's inner-city fourth grade reacted to a rainy day and, prodded by their teacher's questions, dictated the following piece of free verse:

RAIN
Rain means it is wet outside.
Puddles form on the ground.
People sink in the mud.
Umbrellas must be opened.
Thunder can be heard.
AND I HIDE IN THE HOUSE!

Similarly a fifth-grade teacher in a semirural area of New Hampshire helped youngsters record their impressions of an ice storm that had covered that part of the world with a blanket of glaze:

ICE DAY
Icy branches
Sparkle in the sun.
Trees
Bend down to touch the snow.
Roads
Are slippery with ice.

A rather different approach was employed by Philip Chensky, a sixth-grade teacher. He encouraged his youngsters to keep a running record of the growth patterns of tomato and radish seedlings, which the students were growing on a table near the window. To determine the effect of competition between different species on the development of each species, the youngsters planted a box of radish seeds, a box of tomato seeds, and a box of radish and tomato seeds. In each case, the same number of seeds was planted. The seeds were planted the same number of centimeters apart, and each box was given an identical growing environment—the same amount of water, the same temperature, and the same exposure to sunlight. Whenever groups of children worked on the project, they dictated what they were doing and what they observed to a student recorder, who entered the data in the "Experimental Log":

LOG—EFFECT OF COMPETITION ON PLANT GROWTH

April 2: We planted the radish seeds in Box A. We planted thirty seeds in all. We placed each seed three centimeters away from the next one. We poured on half a liter of water.

We planted thirty tomato seeds in Box B. We placed each seed three centimeters away from the next one. We poured on half a liter of water.

We planted fifteen tomato seeds and fifteen radish seeds in Box C. Each seed was planted three centimeters away from the next one. We poured on half a liter of water. This is the way we did it. (See fig. 3.2.)

April 4: We added a quarter of a liter of water to each box. We turned each box so that the opposite end was toward the window.

April 6: We added a quarter of a liter of water to each box. No seeds have begun to grow.

Figure 3.2. Pattern for planting   **Figure 3.3.** Recording data

R	T	R	T	R	T
T	R	T	R	T	R
R	T	R	T	R	T
T	R	T	R	T	R
R	T	R	T	R	T

R = radish
T = tomato

Box A	11 seedlings germinated
Box B	8 seedlings germinated
Box C	9 seedlings germinated

etc.

April 9: We added a quarter of a liter of water to each box. Some seeds have germinated. (See fig. 3.3.)

The log was kept during the total period of the experiment, which was most of April.

Advantages of Group Dictation in Intermediate Grades

Although group dictation has a lesser role to play in intermediate grades, it still is a valuable strategy. First, upper graders learn creative ways of recording on paper by making decisions together about how to record dictated thoughts. Youngsters in Joan Soroka's inner-city fourth grade decided cooperatively that it would be effective to write down all the words in the last line of their *Rain* piece in upper-case letters. Fifth-graders who created the *Ice Day* piece decided to break each sentence between subject and predicate in recording it as part of their poem. Ideas such as these blossom as children create together.

Second, because creation starts orally, youngsters are more aware of the sounds of what they write. They try out different word orderings as they search for an arrangement that not only communicates a clear thought but also sounds "nice on the ear." Punctuating also becomes an automatic aspect of writing as youngsters record changes in intonation and pause patterns as punctuation marks. In the case of the fourth graders who wrote *Rain*, they discovered the need for an exclamation mark only after chorusing their cooperatively created piece together. Saying that last line AND I HIDE IN THE HOUSE! very loudly, they knew that a period did not communicate their feelings with enough emphasis. And so they added the exclamation point!

Still another advantage of group dictation strategies in upper grades is the ease in which they can be integrated into study within the content areas. In the case of the plant experiments just described, group dictation occurred as part of science investigations and with a student serving as scribe—an approach that has almost endless possibilities in grades five and six when young people undertake small group study projects. In other cases, youngsters who have completed a reading assignment related to science or social studies may dictate a summary paragraph either to the teacher, who helps them organize their ideas, or to a fellow student, who serves as group recorder. Here the emphasis in the dictation period may be more on skill development than on creation of ideas. For this reason in-depth consideration of how to handle the activity will be reserved until Part II.

INDIVIDUAL DICTATION

Experienced teachers of young children typically set aside short periods to work individually with them on written expression. During the personalized dictation session, they chat informally with a child about emerging ideas, encourage him or her to think further about those ideas, and culminate the session by taking dictation—recording word by word, sentence by sentence, what the child dictates. In short, teachers become stenographers, inscribing the letters, words, and sentences that represent what the child is saying.

Children take pleasure in seeing their own words neatly written on a page. Even though they themselves may not have printed those letters, they identify the story with themselves and feel a sense of both possession and pride. They perceive too that their own words have value when recorded on the printed page: the words may be reread at a later time and shared with classmates. They begin to comprehend that the spoken word has its counterpart on the written page. Through individual dictation, children see writing as a valid form of communication.

Organizing Individual Dictation Activity

Individual dictation should parallel group dictation activity, especially in the early primary grades, and should occur on a daily basis. When one of the authors was teaching first grade, she found that children looked forward to the time when they could sit with the teacher and dictate. After several dictating experiences, they obviously anticipated their turn and had almost prepared for it by thinking ahead about the content of their dictations. They had selected the topic on which they wanted to write before they came up to the teacher, and they began with relatively little encouragement on her part.

The topics of "free" compositions selected by the children related generally to animals, nature, and "let's pretend"—as shown by the following samples taken from "Our Class Storybook," a first-grade publication:

A LITTLE INDIAN

Indian Two Feet wanted a horse, but he could not find one. He walked a long way. He went to the Chief. The Chief said, "If you keep on walking, you will find a horse."

Bonnie

A RAINBOW

One day we went for a ride, and it rained. Then we went home. After that we saw a beautiful rainbow in the sky.

Nancy

SPRING

In spring
The buds start coming out on trees.
In spring
The flowers begin to bloom.
In spring
The grass gets green.
In spring
The snow melts away.

Sara

FALL FRIGHT

As I was walking down the street,
I was scared right off my feet,
For I saw a witch
Who made me twitch.

Scott

JACK FROST

When I got into bed, I heard noises coming from outside. I got up
to look out of the window, but I didn't see anything. I went back
to bed.

Since the noises continued, I tiptoed to the window again. As I
looked out, I saw little people painting leaves red, orange, yellow,
and brown. Jack Frost and all his helpers were making the trees
colorful.

Patrick

A BIRD

Once there was a bird who lived in the woods. He decided that he
didn't want to live in the forest any longer because he didn't have any
friends. So he flew to China.

On his journey he passed over a bridge. As he flew, he saw a castle.
The Chinese people captured him and took him to the King. The
King decided that the bird was valuable and made him his friend.

Bobbie

Oftentimes in early primary grades, children dictate reactions to
experiences they have enjoyed as part of ongoing class work. These experiences may be firsthand involvements, or they may be vicarious ones
through listening or reading. In either case, the topic is supplied by the
experience rather than chosen freely by the dictator. The pictures in
figure 3.4 are examples of children's dictation of this type; following a
listening time in which the teacher orally shared the familiar story of
Goldilocks and the Three Bears, youngsters were asked to tell what
Goldilocks would do if she came to their house. Their telling was first by
pictorializing and then by dictating to their teacher, who kept on the

Figure 3.4. Two youngsters' pictorial answer to the question, "What would
Goldilocks do if she came to your house?" The words were written
by the teacher, Donna Russo, according to the children's dictation.

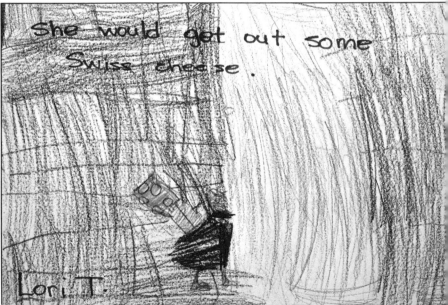

move and recorded children's statements directly on the top of their drawings.

Some teachers may question the amount of teacher or scribe-time that individual dictation requires. Although the time spent with each child is rather short, the total time necessary to record for all the children in a class can be considerable. Yet this time need not be blocked into one continuous period; it can be spread across several days or sandwiched between other activities. The teacher may work with one child as the rest put on their coats. Or he or she may fit three students in during an art session, four others in while the class is cleaning out desk areas. After all, every teacher should include some one-to-one verbal interaction within the daily program, and what better way to structure that interaction than to focus on primary language development in speaking, writing, and reading.

The authors know of one teacher who overcomes the time problem by training linguistically competent sixth graders to take dictation from her kindergarten children. She believes that both groups of children gain from the experience. First, the little children gain because they have many more opportunities to dictate: the sixth graders come for a half-hour each week, and with five sixth graders participating, every little child has an opportunity to dictate at least every third day. Second, the sixth graders must exercise their recording skills—punctuation, spelling, capitalization, and handwriting—and at times must even refer to the dictionary. In producing a written record for someone else, the sixth graders have even more reason to produce accurate copy than if they were writing personally.

In other schools, parent volunteers or paid aides assist in taking dictation. In some places, too, the volunteers or aides go a step farther: they type up what children have dictated to them, returning on another day to help the youngsters read and reread what they have "written." Where microcomputers are available, aides can type children's work into the computer and store it for future use. Later unaided, children can "tell" the computer to flash their stories on the television-like screen and can reread their stories to one another.

The Purposes Served by Individual Dictation

One advantage of individual dictation as an introduction to written expression is that children do not associate failure or drudgery with their initial writing activity. Encouraged by the teacher's personal attention and interest, and stimulated by the teacher's questions, children often produce much more than they themselves think at first that they can.

Then, too, the writing experience is not a laborious struggle. Children produce stories in short order without having to labor over the formation of each letter and without having to figure out which letters to record. At a time when children's attention spans are short, this is a definite advantage.

Needless to say, if individual dictation is to be a pleasurable introduction to the process of writing down ideas, it should take place within an environment completely free of pressure to produce. When children cannot think of ideas to dictate, they can chat informally with the teacher about happenings in the classroom or at home, about books they have been reading, or about things they would like to do or have. When a teacher perceives that children are not in the mood, or perhaps not ready to dictate, he or she can adapt the situation to meet children's unique needs. One child is channeled to express through a concrete, visual medium to which the teacher adds a dictated line or two. Another is channeled toward an overt acting out of feelings. Still another is asked to supply a list of words on the given topic. In work with beginning writers, the teacher's first objectives are to have the youngsters relax, enjoy the verbal interaction, and begin to express themselves in ways that may culminate in written expression.

A second advantage of individual dictation is that some of the most relevant content that children can read is material they themselves have written. It has more personal significance than the stories found in the best basal readers. The words are most assuredly within children's speaking vocabulary, so understanding of the conceptual content is not a problem. Therefore, after Bobbie dictates his story, the teacher reads it aloud to him and has Bobbie in turn read it back. The boy is encouraged to share his story of birds, Kings, and China with his friends, reading it from the page printed by the teacher. He can put his page into a folder and later read it again to another group of classmates. Dictated writing inherently has this additional value: the product can be used as content for personal reading.

Dictation is not only of value in the beginning school years. Some youngsters in the upper elementary grades gain from dictation. First, a youngster with a learning disability involving eye-hand coordination may have trouble simply forming letters. An eighth-grade boy with whom one of the authors worked recorded only indecipherable scratches on his paper; he did this so other youngsters would think that he too could write. Dictation became his major way of completing written assignments in the content areas. Second, children with extremely short attention spans may gain from dictation. If left at their seats to work alone, these youngsters probably cannot concentrate for the length of time required to produce most forms of written communication. Oral dictation to the teacher focuses their attention on the task at hand, while the accompanying conversation with the teacher may help them project an idea to be recorded. Third, some youngsters may have trouble projecting ideas to record. Perhaps because of unpleasant experiences with writing that occurred in earlier years, they have a mental block associated with writing; their minds freeze when they take pen in hand. In some cases, dictation circumvents the block.

TAPE RECORDING

Audiotape and videotape recorders aid teachers in structuring writing-recording experiences for children. These are effective devices for individuals and small groups to record ideas starting in kindergarten and extending throughout the elementary grades.

Audiotape Recording

Very young children enjoy recording their thoughts on audiotape. After a youngster has explored an idea individually with the teacher, he or she may propose: "Let's tell your idea on tape so that later we can share it with our class." With youngsters of this age, lightweight cassette recorders are most efficient. Having recorded, children themselves can operate the machine to review what they have created. The cassette recorder brings an added advantage; as children gain in ability to create ideas, they need not rely so heavily on the teacher to record for them. They can use the machine as a teacher-substitute, turning it on when they get an idea, recording, and then listening to what they have produced.

Older students can also use the tape recorder as a self-instructional recording device. On their own, they can orally try out ideas with which they are toying, then listen, consider, reorder their thoughts, and perhaps try again. After projecting a sequence of ideas in a way that they themselves approve of, the dictators transcribe on paper the thoughts they have recorded on tape. Some youngsters actually find this a more productive way of writing than the more typical way of recording ideas directly on paper. The pens of these children cannot keep up with the speed of their thoughts, so ideas get jumbled as they wait in line to get written down, and points are forgotten. When spoken into the tape recorder, children's ideas can spill out and be recorded as fast as tongues can move. Likewise, children handicapped by lack of spelling, punctuation, and capitalization skills are not affected by their handicap at a point in composition when idea-generation is most significant. How to spell a word, where to place a comma, and which letters to capitalize are not concerns to the composer working with a tape recorder. The major concern is with thinking through and developing ideas to be expressed.

There are limitations as well as advantages in using tape recorders for getting down ideas that eventually will be transcribed into written form. Children with speech problems may prefer to play with ideas on paper rather than on tape. Their awareness of their speech problem may hinder the development of ideas if those thoughts must first be expressed orally. Children with short attention spans who need the questioning presence of the teacher to keep their minds centered on idea-generation may similarly be less successful when using the machine. The insecure, too, may not be able to project ideas with only a mechanical teacher-substitute to record ideas for them. They may need the immediate personal reinforcement supplied by an empathetic human being. On the other hand, other shy students may have just the opposite reaction. They may fail when dictating ideas to a human being but succeed in expressing themselves when the recording device is an inanimate object totally within their control.

Videotape Recording

Videotape recording can play a parallel role in a writing program that is an integral part of a larger language arts program. Videotaping can be used to record children's ideas expressed through action and dramatization. Several youngsters may wish to have their improvised dramatization of a story recorded on tape to share later with other classes. Individual youngsters may want to have their pantomiming sequences recorded for later viewing on class TV. Children may want to be recorded on videotape as they express themselves with physical action in response to a musical selection, as they dramatize a poem, or as they tell an original story, complete with props that communicate—pictures, dioramas, flannel board figures, or puppets.

Generally, children are highly motivated when given the opportunity to express before TV cameras. With a total lack of inhibition, children will gesture wildly, dance expressively, contort both face and body, hop in rhythm, dress themselves in costumes that transport them into make-believe. Their anticipation can be so great that they can hardly wait to see themselves in playback. They can be as enthralled watching the unprofessional rendition of a story they have invented as they are watching Miss Piggy on TV.

To propose use of videotaping in public school classrooms is not to dream the impossible dream. Some urban and suburban school districts have already moved in this direction and have videotaping equipment functional in their classrooms. One reason the purchase of videotaping cameras has proved feasible is that they can be used for multiple purposes: teachers prepare short segments of instruction on videotape for later viewing by students; teachers tape short episodes of their own classroom instruction to analyze as a means of improving their teaching techniques; children are encouraged to tape group activity; and equipment can be taken on nature walks to record sights and sounds.

Technological devices such as audiotape and videotape recorders give the teacher an alternate way of recording children's impressions. For some youngsters, that way can be more productive than the traditional ways of thinking and producing ideas. One youngster in sixth grade may end up pounding a typewriter or microcomputer; another may produce his or her most original work by dictating to a tape recorder; a third child, even in the upper grades, may write best by dictating to a teacher; and still another child may be most productive sitting quietly alone in a corner with a felt pen in hand. Even in recording ideas for written expression, children have individual differences that teachers must respect.

TAKING PENCIL IN HAND—FROM IDEAS IN MIND TO WORDS ON PAPER

Not only do young children differ in the recording technique that is most productive for them; they differ also in their readiness to move from recording by dictation to recording by taking pencil in hand. Some youngsters are ready to encode their own ideas very early in first grade and a few even in kindergarten; they have both the requisite manuscript skills and the ability to project ideas on their own. Others are not ready to encode until later in their primary school experience. Instruction in written expression in early primary years must take into account these differences in readiness.

From Individual Dictation to Independent Writing

The beginnings of individual encoding of ideas can flow out of dictation sessions with the teacher. If a child gives the teacher a sentence to inscribe that contains a word that the child is able to write down, the teacher may ask, "Lillian, do you want to try to write that word into your story yourself? I will help you with the letters." Building on this type of situation, the teacher may suggest on another occasion: "Lillian, I bet you can write that sentence yourself." Again, as this youngster tries to encode her own words, the teacher may help by telling Lillian the letters to write. And, of course, from early on, youngsters who have learned to write down their own names can return from an individualized dictation session to print their names on their story papers. In this way, individual inscribing becomes a natural, sequential outgrowth of previous writing-recording activities. It also occurs in a setting that is more likely to result in success for a child than struggling alone at one's desk.

As children begin to build their manuscript skills, another way to involve them directly in the process of writing down meaningful ideas is to suggest that they take a husky crayon or flo-pen in hand and trace over or darken letters printed large and lightly by the teacher. Many experienced first-grade teachers use tracing as the first step leading to independent writing. Children start by tracing their own names, which the teacher has printed lightly on art papers. Later as youngsters become skilled at wielding pencil, crayon, and/or flo-pen, they trace a sentence that the teacher has printed at their dictation on the top of a picture they have drawn. Later still, children trace several sentences the teacher has recorded for them on lined paper and then go on to illustrate their thoughts pictorially.

Domenica Swenson, a first-grade teacher in Edison, New Jersey, finds that, after youngsters have had several opportunities to practice their manuscript by tracing, copying over is a natural next step in the instructional sequence leading to independent writing. When children dictate to her, she records their sentences by skipping every other line. Returning to their seats after individual dictation, the youngsters copy each sentence that Ms. Swenson has recorded for them in the space directly below it. In this way, youngsters' eyes do not have to move far as children produce their own copies. See figure 3.5 for a sample of a page dictated by a youngster in Domenica Swenson's class. On it the reader can see the words printed by the teacher and the copy produced by the student.

Ms. Swenson also finds that patterned writing helps youngsters make the transition from individual dictation to independent writing. One day, for example, she asks youngsters to dictate starting with the words *I am happy when.* At this point, they go on to write by copying lines beneath the ones she has printed for them. On another day she asks dictators to start with the words *I am excited when.* Again she records for them and they copy their lines. On still another day she asks them to begin with the words *I am unhappy when.* This time, however, she shifts to a different procedure. She writes the beginning words on the board for the youngsters; they copy those words onto their own story papers and

Figure 3.5. A story dictated and copied over by a first grader

independently try to finish the sentence themselves. In this way they build up a basic writing vocabulary, specifically in this case such words as *I*, *am*, and *when*.

To help youngsters as they try to record for themselves for the first time, Ms. Swenson keeps on the move. Carrying a flo-pen and a large stack of index cards in her hands, she responds to children's waving arms by recording on individual cards words they want to use but cannot write down. Youngsters use the individual word cards printed out by their teacher as models for recording these words into their compositions.

They keep their cards in their personal dictionary boxes and on later occasions reach for needed cards as they compose.

At times, rather than giving children personal word cards to keep, Ms. Swenson stands at the board. Children ask for words they want to use, and she prints these clearly on the chalkboard for all to see. When a child requests a word already recorded on the board, Domenica simply points it out again, sometimes moving her finger beneath it from left to right indicating each letter of the word in turn. An advantage of this technique is that words suggested by one youngster trigger other boys and girls to start thinking, with the words to express those thoughts on paper readily available on the board for writing.

From Group Dictation to Independent Writing

Group dictation can also lead to individual inscribing. The teacher begins by suggesting, "Today I am going to give you a group of words to start our writing. They are *In the summer, we like to*. I will write these words for you on our chart. Let's think of all the fun things we like to do in the summer. Who can suggest one?" As youngsters proffer ideas, the teacher records them—perhaps using a flo-pen of a color different from the one he or she used to record the introductory group of words. In this case, too, the teacher lists all the suggestions rather than writing them in paragraph fashion and puts a number before each. When children have brainstormed a lengthy list, the teacher remarks, "I am going to give you some sentence beginnings for you to complete by choosing some of the ideas we have listed on our chart." He or she then writes on a second chart a composing pattern similar to the one given in figure 3.6. Returning to their seats from their talking-cluster around the charts, the

Figure 3.6. The framework for a framed composition

Summer Fun

In the summer, we like
to _____ and
to _____. We
also like to _____
_____.

youngsters must copy the sentence beginnings and compose endings by selecting items from the brainstormed list. In short, they must complete the *framed* composition.

Framing is a powerful tool for getting children started in writing on their own. When combined with brainstormed lists, the technique supplies children with words to use as well as with basic sentence patterns with which to begin. It can be adapted easily for use in content-area writing; children who have talked about the work of a firefighter can, for example, list the many jobs of a firefighter—climbing ladders, pulling hoses, carrying people to safety, and so forth. Working from this list, they can compose a paragraph based on sentence beginnings provided by their teacher: At a fire, firefighters _____.
They _____. Firefighters also _____
_____.

Especially as children begin to use writing in this way to communicate ideas in science and social studies, word walls and ABC word charts become imperatives so that youngsters have words available for use in writing. Bulletin board ABC charts are particularly valuable if they are cumulative and include short function words such as *into, then, from, but.* Emily Davis, another experienced first-grade teacher, begins her charts on the very first day of school. As children talk together about their new class, she gathers them for group dictation. On the first day, she records only one or two sentences, for instance—*This is our class. We will learn here.* Having dictated, children read and reread their sentences. Then Ms. Davis points to the first letter of the first word. "What letter does the word *this* begin with?" Since youngsters in this community are introduced to letter forms in kindergarten, most children can identify the *t*. Posted around her room, Ms. Davis already has twenty-six elongated charts, each bearing one letter in both its lower- and upper-case forms. The charts are posted in alphabetical order. "Who can locate the letter *t* on one of these charts?" is Ms. Davis's next query. As children watch, she carefully prints the word *this* at the top of the *Tt* chart, placing a number *1* in front of it. Children read the word she has written. On successive days, youngsters help Ms. Davis record *the, then, to, two, take* on the *Tt* chart, numbering them in the order given but not attempting any alphabetizing of words on any one chart. Now as youngsters begin to record on their own and need a word to use, Ms. Davis responds to children's requests by pointing to the appropriate chart, "Look at the *Tt* chart, Kevin. The word *then* is number 3."

As youngsters gain confidence and skill in writing for themselves, they can move into more open forms of written expression and rely less on patterned and framed writing. For example, working with a group of youngsters who have shared a series of community dictation sessions and who have begun to inscribe for themselves, the teacher may read a story, stopping before the end and asking, "How do you think the story will end?" Instead of recording suggestions, the teacher-guide encourages participants to talk about their ideas and then suggests: "Let's each of us try to write down our own ending today. Before we start, let's think of some of the words we might need in writing." As youngsters suggest words, the teacher lists them on chart paper or on cards that he or she posts on the word wall. Then the teacher distributes lined picture-paper to the children and reminds them, "If you have trouble writing a word, check the ABC charts and our word wall. If you cannot find what you want, raise your hand, and I will give you a personal word card." Again, the teacher can move from youngster to youngster supplying necessary words that youngsters, who have learned to alphabetize, can later record on cards, illustrate to show meaning, and place in alphabetical order in their individual dictionary boxes.

Grouping for Writing

As the preceding paragraph hints, a teacher may find it necessary to group youngsters as they begin to encode for themselves. Small group instruction in writing, based on individual differences and needs, is organized in much the same manner as group instruction in reading. Given three groups, Group A begins by talking about an experience with the teacher. Then the youngsters in that group record verbally on paper with teacher help. This recording is on an independent basis—not a dictation. Follow-up activity for them may be a related art experience, the writing of a second draft of the stories they have just composed, or the illustration of their personal word cards.

Group B begins by making a visual record of their ideas through a drawing. This they do while the teacher is talking with Group A. When the teacher is ready for them, the youngsters in Group B then move to individual recording based on a brief talk-time with the teacher. As they record, the teacher stays close by to help with difficult words and chat individually with members having trouble translating their ideas into written words.

Group C may not be ready to inscribe; the task may still be too frustrating for them, because their manuscript skills are not well enough developed. For that reason, Group C may join Group A for talk about an experience, but instead of attempting to encode, they are channeled toward artistic expression of their ideas and given some practice sessions with making letters on paper. Later, these youngsters dictate individually to the teacher and then trace or copy dictated sentences.

Individual youngsters may function outside the groups. Some children may be perfectly capable of inscribing independently: they enjoy thinking and writing on their own. Others may find a private corner to think, write, or dictate into a tape recorder. Still others during this time may pursue individual reading and study activities.

This organizational scheme can be modified easily so that it is functional in the upper grades. Groups of youngsters can meet with their teacher to talk about their ideas while others work individually at their seats on second drafts of compositions already begun, on pictorializing, or on finishing a display copy of a poem. Other groups of youngsters, for whom recording is still a struggle, meet later with the teacher, who gives assistance with the encoding process. The upper-grade teacher can also work with the individual child while others are working on written drafts at their seats or at the tape recorder. Youngsters in upper grades differ considerably in their skill to handle encoding of ideas, so the need for individual and small group instruction is just as essential as in the lower grades.

SOME SUMMARY THOUGHTS

Teachers of first-grade youngsters know that the process of getting young children to begin to record for themselves requires continuing and focused attention. Simply to talk a bit with children and then ask them to write on the topic is not enough; young children need step-by-step instruction that progressively involves them in writing activity.

Group and individual dictation are beginning tools to start children writing, as this chapter has pointed out. They lay the foundation for the times when children take pencils in hand to translate ideas-in-mind into words on paper. Working toward independence as writers, children start by tracing words and sentences their teacher has recorded for them, copying sentences beneath those the teacher has printed during individual dictation, writing in response to framed and patterned beginnings, pulling words to use from those listed on charts, board, or word wall, and relying on personalized word cards compiled into individual, dictionary-like boxes. The process is a slow one, as experienced teachers testify, but the rewards are great. There is no pride to compare with the pride of accomplishment that children feel on seeing their own thoughts printed in their own handwriting on papers tacked up at home on refrigerator doors for all to see. Children have visual evidence that they are growing up and can say to themselves: "I CAN WRITE."

4 | LET CHILDREN LOOK FOR IDEAS ◄► activities to keep children writing

But words are things, and a small drop of ink
Falling like dew upon a thought, produces
That which makes thousands, perhaps millions, think.
Lord Byron, DON JUAN

Once children have begun to write, they should compose on a variety of subjects and in diverse situations. They should express themselves on paper as part of literary, artistic, dramatic, and musical experiences. They should write as part of the study of science, social studies, and current events. They should contribute to group writing projects and compose individual pieces. They should write prose and poetry, fiction and fact. Only by working with a wide range of topics will youngsters learn to think and write about all manner of ideas.

How does the teacher motivate children to keep writing? Without a doubt, the kinds of firsthand experiences described in chapter 1 and the kinds of talking and expressive activities described in chapter 2 are sparks that ignite ideas. In addition, the teacher can structure meaningful activities as part of ongoing classroom programs. Let us turn next to ways that teachers can organize motivating activities that encourage youngsters to write and write and write some more.

STRUCTURED ACTIVITIES

We can all recall an occasion when a specific suggestion offered by someone else inspired an idea. The suggestion triggered a train of thought that otherwise would not have occurred. As teachers, we can use many kinds of suggestions to help children formulate ideas for writing. We can structure idea-stimulating activities through use of pictures, music, literature, characters, objects, titles, words, trips, newsworthy events, world and school issues, and the content of the sciences and social sciences.

Pictures and Films

In the magazine section of a Sunday newspaper, a fourth-grade teacher found a page of pictures that presented close-up views of the eyes of different animals. One was easily identifiable as the eyes of a fish; the others could be perceived by children as the eyes of almost any animal. Teacher and students studied the picture series together, brainstorming ideas as to whom the eyes probably belonged and about how these animals viewed the world. Later, writing in small teams, the children described the world through the eyes of one of the animals. Some rather good written work was motivated in this way.

Two other teachers used pictures in a slightly different way. One located large reproductions of modern abstract art, the second—adept at photography—took some rather unusual 35-mm slides of pebbles, water trickling down a windowpane, puddles, railroad tracks, jet trails in the sky, froth on beer, footprints in the sand, and ripple marks on a beach and used these to test the power of suggestion. They found that the unusual picture is especially effective as a teacher-intervention in the idea-development process. Individuals can bring their unique backgrounds to the picture interpretation, producing different ideas.

Children's abstract art can be used in a similar way. Studying their own finger paintings, collages, ink blobs smeared on paper, or creative sculpture in metal or glass, young thinkers and writers can build descriptions, stories, and poems to attach to their artistic pieces.

Film, too, can stimulate writing. Weston Woods (Weston, Connecticut) has produced a whole series of films based on outstanding picture storybooks that are good for this purpose. An excellent example is Weston Woods's production of Doris Lund's *Attic of the Wind*. Using the fine illustrations by Ati Forberg, the film takes the viewer into the magical world up in the sky where all the things carried away on a windy day—"butterflies that flew too high," "kites that snapped their strings," "golden sparks from a summer fire," "snowflakes that didn't light"—can be found. Having experienced the aural and visual delights of the film, children can create expanded lines that begin "I went to the attic of the wind and I found. . . ." The result is a cooperative poem filled with adjectives that paint clear pictures in the mind's eye.

Some films lead into prose writing activity. A fine film for this purpose is the National Film Board of Canada's *The Loon's Necklace*,

Figure 4.1. "Zebra," a story by a second grader

which relates a folk explanation of how the loon acquired the beautiful spotted collar around its neck. A viewing of the film can be followed by a listening time in which youngsters listen to a few of Rudyard Kipling's *Just So Stories*. Children who have seen the film and listened to similar tales have gone on to volunteer creative explanations about how the red-headed woodpecker got its cap, how the crow got its caw, how the skunk got its stripe, how the turtle found its home, how the elephant earned its trunk, and how the toad learned to hop. Figure 4.1 provides a sample of an explanation written by a second grader. Here is an example of a third-grader's piece created in reaction to the Film Board of Canada's film:

HOW THE OCTOPUS GOT LONG ARMS
One day an octopus was looking around. He found a whirlpool and before he knew it, he was stuck in it. A boat was over him so he put his arms on the boat, and the boat pulled one way and the whirl-pool pulled the other way. The octopus's arms stretched so much he could never pull them in again. That is how the octopus got such long arms.

Michael

The sound filmstrips that Weston Woods and Miller Brody (342 Madison Ave., New York, New York 10017) have created based on Caldecott and Newbery Award winning and honor books can serve the same stimulative function in a writing program. The selection and possibilities for written content are extensive; for example:

- *The Stonecutter*, from Weston Woods—middle graders can decide who was really the most powerful and write opinion papers that set forth their opinions supported with reasons.
- *Why Mosquitoes Buzz in People's Ears*, from Weston Woods—middle graders can create their own "chain reaction" stories in which one event triggers a series of other happenings.
- *Rosie's Walk*, from Weston Woods—primary youngsters can create similar "walk" stories in which an animal visits a series of places in succession, leaving chaos behind him or her.
- *The Planet of Junior Brown*, from Miller Brody—upper graders can describe experiences and feelings of their own similar to Junior Brown's.
- *King of the Wind*, from Miller Brody—upper graders can create similar tales of adventure that include a friendship between a young person and an animal.
- *The King's Fifth*, from Miller Brody—upper graders can identify the effects of conquest on the conqueror and the conquered.

The titles available from Weston Woods as sound filmstrips are also available as films. Some of these are striking. See, for example, the filmed version of *The Stonecutter*, a visual masterpiece!

In addition, some filmstrips serve essentially as story starters. Open situations are projected to which children can bring their own backgrounds as they react with ideas. Viewers must create original endings based on the filmed beginnings.

Music and Literature

"Ebb Tide" makes the listener feel as if he or she is standing in the sand, watching the sea race in and out. George Gershwin's *An American in Paris* brings the sounds of taxi horns in Paris. In Tchaikovsky's *1812 Overture*, the listener hears the sounds of cannons reverberating in the ears. One eighth-grade class produced some of its best written work in reaction to Ferde Grofé's *Grand Canyon Suite*. The young people really felt as if they were standing in the desert, witnessing a rising storm and the quiet that follows. They enjoyed the musical suggestion so much that they told their friends in other sections about the experience, and these students asked their teacher if they too could "write from the Grand Canyon."

Less sophisticated musical selections also have the potential to stimulate ideas. Little songs like "The Dipsy Doodle Dragon" and "The Unicorn," recorded by Peter Pan Records, are effective with younger children. The song describes the dragon or the unicorn in such a way that the child is encouraged to invent an original tale about an imaginary animal. The words from such songs as "My Favorite Things" can similarly provide an idea-suggestion for some children. After singing about favorite things, a child can let his or her imagination fly free and write about unusual favorites.

A little poem like Eve Merriam's "The Motor-Boat Song" in *There Is No Rhyme for Silver* (Atheneum, 1962) can provide a suggestion for writing—in this case, a suggestion that sounds of a particular phenomenon or event can be the substance of a poem. Children who have listened to the "Putta put-put," the "Tutta tut-tut," and the "Rock a pock" of "The Motor-Boat Song" can create their own sound-filled pieces in the form of a "Rain Song," "Motorcycle Song," "Typewriter Song," or "Marching-Band Song." One group tried this:

STORM SONG

Pitter-patter
Patter-pitter

> Swish-swash
> Swash-swish
>
> Karum-karum-karum-bang
> Bang-bang-karum-karum
> Lightning, thunder, swirls of rain
> Pitter-patter, swish-swash, karum-bang!

Eve Merriam has written a number of poems that can serve as models for children creating cooperatively together. Beginning from the inspiration of Merriam's "The Cheerful Blues," youngsters can create their own "The Brave Yellow"; starting with her "Geography," they can develop their own associations to go along with other states' abbreviations even as Merriam did in her short poem. See *There Is No Rhyme for Silver* for these and other very useful writing "suggestions." Gifted youngsters, scanning the volume independently, may come up with an idea for writing.

In like manner, independent reading of stories can serve as writing inspirations. Many books can trigger children to express related feelings. Byrd Baylor's story *Hawk, I'm Your Brother*, with striking black and white line drawings by Peter Parnall, can inspire third, fourth, and fifth graders to write about the need to be free, the feelings of being trapped (Scribner's, 1976). The more humorous *The Terrible Thing That Happened at Our House*, written by Marge Blaine (Parents, 1975), can cause children to express their feelings about similarly "terrible" things that happened at their homes—the coming of a new baby, a forgetting of their birthday, a gift that was not what they wanted. Leo Lionni's *A Color All His Own* (Pantheon, 1976) can help children explore their feelings about having something that is uniquely their own.

Older readers find that books such as Norma Klein's *Confessions of an Only Child* (Pantheon, 1974) stimulate them to think about similar happenings in their own families and the feelings they have inside themselves about these events. The search for a special friend, as in Constance Greene's *A Girl Called Al* (Viking, 1969), the adjustments necessary because of divorce, as in Rose Blue's *A Month of Sundays* (Watts, 1972), or the development of self-concept, as in Betsy Byar's *After the Goat Man* (Viking, 1974) are themes set forth in books to which children can react by relating feelings of their own.

Children can also react to books by expressing opinions about the rightness/wrongness of story acts and by explaining their reactions to specific characters. To trigger this kind of reaction, teachers can ask elementary youngsters such questions as these: Was it right for Juan de Pareja in Elizabeth Borton de Trevino's *I, Juan de Pareja* (Bell Books,

1965) to be treated as he was? Was it right for Mouse in Betsy Byars' *The 18th Emergency* to fight Marv? Was it really the honorable thing to do? Do you like Andy in Joseph Krumgold's *Onion John* (Crowell, 1959)? Would you have acted as Andy did when he makes friends with the local

Figure 4.2.   A child's picture and composition motivated by reading "Pippi Longstocking"

"bum," Onion John? Why or why not? These types of questions may spark a reaction in a one-paragraph paper written individually or by small groups that have read the book.

Reacting to a book read, children can write idea-content that is essentially a reflection of what is; they can tell in their own words an incident in a story. As figure 4.2 suggests, books that are episodical, composed of separate stories about a main character, are useful here—such old-time favorites as Eleanor Estes's *The Middle Moffat* (Harcourt, Brace, 1942), Robert McCloskey's *Homer Price* (Viking, 1943), and Astrid Lindgren's *Pippi Longstocking* (Viking, 1950). Marguerite, a fifth grader, retold one chapter of *A Wrinkle in Time* by Madeleine L'Engle (Ariel, 1962) in this review:

> One day a boy named Calvin O'Keefe was delivering newspapers at the most unusual house. It was owned by Mrs. Wasit. Meg and Charles Wallace were approaching the house to discuss a matter. Suddenly and mysteriously they were propelled right into her house. Mrs. Wasit had two other friends with her, Mrs. Who and Mrs. Which. Right in front of their eyes, they changed like magic. Then they told Charles and Meg that they would help them find their father. For this they had to go into the 5th dimension of space called tesseract or a Wrinkle in Time.

Reviews of this type can be shared with other youngsters who may decide that they too would like to enter the fifth dimension.

Books can also trigger children to create stories that are similar in theme. For example, a number of books for upper graders are survival stories in which a hero must use his or her own skill and strength to survive in a wilderness alone:

> Daniel Defoe, *Robinson Crusoe* (the classic survival story found today in many editions).
> Jean George, *Julie of the Wolves* (Harper & Row, 1972).
> Jean George, *My Side of the Mountain* (Dutton, 1959).
> Scott O'Dell, *Island of the Blue Dolphins* (Houghton Mifflin, 1960).

Having read two or more of these, children can compare and contrast the manner in which the theme is developed, the qualities embodied in the characters, the location in which the hero must survive. Comparisons and contrasts can lead into several paragraph reports in which young writers record similarities and differences on paper. These can lead as well into creation of original survival stories that adhere to the classic pattern—a hero stranded in the wilderness must face a series of endurance hurdles, which eventually he or she overcomes to survive. This type of reading-writing experience is an enriching one that teachers may wish to explore with more gifted upper graders.

Another kind of enrichment activity that focuses attention more on a book's story and word patterns is creating stories that "borrow" a structural feature from a book read. Particularly good for this purpose are books that are short and have a pattern clearly apparent to children whether reading or listening. Examples are Diane Wolkstein's *The Visit* (Knopf, 1977) in which almost every page contains a variation of the sentence *She walked over a leaf, step by step*, Kazue Mizumura's *If I Were a Cricket* . . . (Crowell, 1973) in which every page begins with the words *If I were a* . . . , and Pat Hutchins's *Don't Forget the Bacon!* (Greenwillow, 1976) in which each page represents a play with the sounds found on the first page.

Having heard Diane Wolkstein's *The Visit*, listeners functioning as a class group can compose their own tale about a fish who left home. Sentences to add to the cooperative piece would be simple ones: *A little fish left home. He swam under the bridge, stroke by stroke. He swam through the rapids, stroke by stroke. He swam close to the dam, stroke by stroke.* And in the manner of the ant's trip in *The Visit*, cooperative writers would bring their fish home *stroke by stroke* just before dark. Later, working in groups, children can compose structurally similar tales about the exploits away from home of a bird, a turtle, a grasshopper, or a worm.

As this section has demonstrated, literature can lead to a variety of writing activities. The traditional notion of a "book report" in which youngsters summarize big story events or even analyze a leading character needs to be expanded to include creation of stories with similar themes, structures, or characters, reactions that include a personalized element, and comparisons and contrasts among related kinds of books.

Objects

Specific objects brought into or made in the classroom can suggest ideas for writing. Here are a few idea-triggers:

Hats. Make a collection of hats: a helmet from World War II, a football player's helmet, a beret, a bridal headpiece, a mountaineer's hat, a skier's cap, a black fedora, a wide-brimmed Mexican sunhat. In discussion with the class, encourage the children to talk about the possible stories that the World War II helmet could tell. Ideas can be expressed orally. The children individually may select one of the other hats as the object of writing.

Coins.   Borrow a collection of coins from exotic countries, such as Thailand, Turkey, India, or Austria. Give the children time to examine the coins. Then talk together about one—"The Indian Rupee's Tale." Each child may select one of the other coins as the object of writing. This is facilitated by gathering all the coins in the writing center where youngsters can go to consider and write.

Pollutants.   Assemble objects or representations of objects that pollute—a light bulb, a model car, a cigarette, a model airplane, a bottle of insecticide, a box of detergent. With the children, talk about how each of these adds pollution to the environment. Each student tries to think of one practical idea for conserving the environment and writes a paragraph about it. Children who individually have trouble thinking of an idea can be grouped into idea-pairs to write a paragraph cooperatively.

Bags.   Collect different kinds of bags: an orange bag, a beach bag, an airline bag, a hat bag, a garbage bag, a grocery bag, a bowler's bag, a bag bearing a foreign label. Children talk about what these bags have seen and where they have been. Ideas stimulated in discussion become the content of writing.

Miscellaneous Objects.   Place a heterogenous assortment in a grab bag in the writing center. Without looking at what they are selecting, children choose three or four items from the bag. They must invent a story around these items. This activity can be carried out individually or in groups; the writing can be preceded by improvised dramatics or talk.

Examples of objects to place in a grab bag include a piece of cellophane, a Ping-Pong ball, a carrot, a marble, a glove, a coin, a twig, a feather, a raisin, a bill for a pair of shoes, a grocery list, a calling card, a spoon, a used airline or bus ticket, an old ribbon, a torn handkerchief. To lead toward the activity and build interest, have the bag available for a period of several days; children can bring in objects to include.

A Collection of Commercials and Advertisements.   Tape a series of radio or TV commercials and play them to an upper elementary class. At the same time, compile a collection of magazine and newspaper advertisements for young people to analyze. Students talk about some of the techniques used by ad writers. They devise a list of products to be advertised: Oh Ho, a new breakfast food; Caterpillar, a low-slung sportscar; Zing, a new toothpaste; Cho-Chunk, a candy bar. Young people work in groups to write commercials that they intersperse in a radio or TV program they are producing. (For examples of magazine ads see fig. 4.3.)

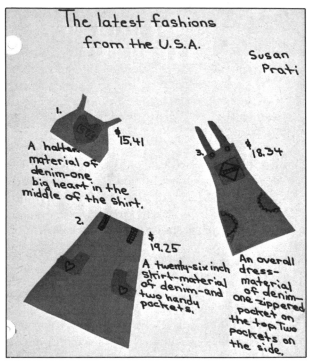

Figure 4.3. Advertisements from a magazine compiled by a group of fifth graders

Characters

The characters children have met as friends on television or in cartoons can spark ideas for writing. Children know how cartoon characters typically operate and they know what these characters tend to say. It is, therefore, rather easy to take their friends on further adventures. This is particularly true for young children who have spent many hours watching TV. The world of Snoopy, Charlie Brown, Tweetie, Bugs Bunny, Felix the Cat, and Popeye the Sailor Man is a real one to them.

Leslie, a kindergartener, dictated into a tape recorder her story about her friend, Bugs Bunny:

> BUGS BUNNY GOES SOUTH
>
> Bugs Bunny was walking, and a duck came up and said, "Hi, pal. Are you flying South for the winter?"
>
> "No, I am not," said Bugs Bunny. "Bunnies can't fly!"
>
> The duck said, "I will take you. Just hold on to my hand, and we will go." So they went to the South Pole for the winter.

Asked to tell about Oscar of "Sesame Street," Leslie dictated:

> OSCAR
>
> Oscar lives in the garbage can. He sings nutty songs sometimes. He pops up out of his garbage can when other people are talking.

About Charlie Brown and Snoopy, she recorded:

> SNOOPY
>
> Charlie Brown was walking one day. Snoopy came up and waved to Charlie Brown, but Charlie Brown said, "Get out of here, Snoopy," because Charlie Brown didn't want Snoopy that day.

Having worked with characters whom they know as television friends, children can be encouraged to invent stories about imaginary characters they have not encountered in film or book; for example:

Hippo, the River Horse   Herman, the Hermit Crab
Lester, the Lonely Lobster   Jennifer, the Jumping Green Grasshopper
Freddie, the Talking Parrot   Leopold, the Lion Who Curled His Hair
Aggie, the Acrobatic Spider   Prissie, the Friendly Porcupine

Names of animals can also be printed on slips of paper: the gorilla, the bear, the duck, the horse, the bee, the ant, the rhino, the egret, the porpoise, the skunk, the woodpecker, the caterpillar. Children select two slips of paper by reaching into a character grab bag located in the writing center. Around their two animals they must concoct a yarn. The results at times can be amusing as gorilla meets bee or duck encounters skunk.

Mix-and-match puppets lead to a similar writing activity. Youngsters in groups select four characters from a list they have been building all week: a hippie, a hold-up man, a grandmother, a witch, a human umbrella, a mixed-up horse, a police officer, a good fairy, a rabbi, a little girl, a laughing loon. Children in groups make paper-bag puppets, write a puppet show, rehearse it, and "do their thing" for the rest of the class.

Titles

Some children can take off into the realm of invention when given a push by a title that catches their imaginations or that relates to some aspect of a real-life experience. Not all titles will spark imagination in all children; titles relevant for one may "turn off" others. The list given below, therefore, is only suggestive of areas that may appeal to children. A teacher can use it as a basis for devising a list appropriate to a particular class:

Help! The World Is Cracking!	Foul Ball
The Night the Clocks Stopped	Run!
Caught in a Trap	Street Fight
Smoke in the Forest	Stranded on the Moon
The Ghost Who Lived over the Bedpost	Lion on the Loose
One Drop More	Overdose of Heroin
Panic or Pleasure	Pollution Does Us In
We Made Headlines!	"I'll Get Even"
Hurricane Alert	Run for Your Life!
Knocked Out in the Fourth Round	Champion in the Ring
All Alone	Lost in the Crowd
Who Am I?	Who Rang the Bell?
Stand Up and Be Counted	Excitement at the Airport
Friend or Enemy? I Didn't Know	My Gang—the Greatest
No School Today	Afraid to Move

One way to handle the title approach to written expression is to construct an eye-appealing bulletin board writing station that can be captioned "In the Mood to Invent?" A box of cards is attached to the board; each card bears a title. In independent study times, children may go through the cards and select one for writing. Finishing a story, writers pin it to the bulletin board if they feel it is worthy of publication. Every few days the teacher and a committee of students replenish the supply of cards in the box. Which cards "sell" give some indication of where student interest lies.

Word Bulletin Boards

Teachers who find that children react to bulletin board motivation can reorganize the activity just described to focus on words that can be combined and recombined in different idea-stimulating patterns. "Help Yourself to an Idea!" the bulletin board writing station caption read in one fifth grade. Over a large pink, bull-shaped pocket affixed to the board and filled with possible descriptive word-cards was the subcaption "Descriptive Word Bull Pen." Over a similar orange-colored pocket filled with object word-cards was the caption "Object Word Bull Pen." During independent work periods, children came to the station to reach into the pockets to draw out words they could combine to build a story.

Descriptive words: running, playful, frightened, brave, noisy, shy, mixed-up, shrewd, unhappy, oversized, lost, fantastic, soft, coughing, tired, wordy, hungry, forgetful, worn-out, sneezing, talking, naughty, foolish, strange, tiny, friendly, lazy

Object words: football, piano, spring, furnace, ant, whale, balloon, watermelon, radiator, elephant, fly, mosquito, nutcracker, nickel, dime, dollar bill, spoon, doorbell, river, baseball bat, apple tree, light bulb, banana, water faucet, elevator, rocket ship, violin, toad, horse

In writing at this station, children may select as many different words as they want. They may take one object word and one descriptive word, two descriptive words, and two object words, building word combinations that are rather far-out: the worn-out, sneezing whale; the tired water faucet and the coughing piano; the unhappy watermelon and the soft banana.

Another variation of this activity moves an "Action Word Bull Pen" onto the bulletin board in addition to the descriptive and object words or in place of one of these:

Action words: galloped, burst, chattered, tripped, flew, froze, acted, leaped, hatched, blossomed, laughed, smashed, prayed, ripped, yelled, whispered, careened, roared, slid, crept, cried, smiled, roared, crashed, fell

Again children build their own combinations by drawing word-cards from the pens.

Word phrases can be lettered on elongated cards and attached to a similar type of participatory bulletin board called "Pick a Pair." The words can be verb combinations as in *ripped* and *roared, slipped* and *slid, ranted* and *raved, tumbled* and *twisted, huffed* and *puffed, fretted* and *fussed*, *zipped* and *zoomed*. The pairs can be adjective combinations: *sleek* and *smooth*, *slow* and *steady*, *creepy* and *crafty*, *cold* and *clammy*, *tough* and *terrible*. The pairs can even be object words that can serve as major characters in a story: *the kangaroo* and *the ostrich*, *the water buffalo* and *the fish*, *the iron* and *the dish towel*, *the pelican* and *the eagle*, *the skate* and *the ski*, *the lawn mower* and *the horse*, *the bicycle* and *the baboon*, *the moose* and *the antelope*, *the lead pipe* and *the furnace*, *the organ grinder* and *the monkey*.

As children complete stories in reaction to phrases, they may, if they wish, mount their products on the board. If the display copy of all stories is written on the same size paper, one story can be placed on top of one previously displayed, turning the series into a book of short stories that children can read at their leisure and that can be sent to other classes to be shared there.

Occasions

Although adults enjoy holiday occasions, most children are enthralled by them. They count the days until Halloween, look forward to their birthdays, and build excitement in anticipation of a coming celebration. Thanksgiving, Valentine's Day, Christmas, Hanukkah, the Fourth of July, Rosh Hashanah, and the New Year are high points in their year. Teachers can build writing activities upon this natural excitement of childhood. Occasions can be used to trigger almost every kind of writing.

Reports. A birthday child is asked to write about one exciting, terrible, sad, or happy happening in his or her life and later on during the big day to share the report with other boys and girls. The birthday youngster can report the "where and when" of his or her birth and write "The Story of Me, Myself, and I." A Polaroid camera is a helpful addition to this type of writing activity. Another student in upper grades or the teacher in the lower grades can take a birthday picture of the child, which is projected with the opaque projector when the birthday youngster shares his or her report with the class. The picture is attached to the finished report that goes into the class book: "This Is Us!"

As a holiday occasion approaches, older children can find out how the holiday originated. Individually or in groups, children can write: "Where Did Halloween Come From?" "What Does Hanukkah Mean?" "Where Did Santa Claus Originate?" "Why Do People Put Up Fir Trees at Christmas?" "What Is the Meaning of Thanksgiving?"

Poetry. For Valentine's Day, children can make their own valentine cards to send to other children and to carry home as gifts. Working with red, white, and black construction paper, every youngster designs a card. Inside he or she tucks a humorous or serious verse that carries a holiday message. Little poems can be written as the message within birthday cards to be sent to relatives, teachers, and friends. A birthday card group can make cards to be given to each child in the class on his or her birthday. Likewise, children can design Hanukkah and Christmas cards to send to friends and family that carry holiday wishes in verse.

In Susan Haumacher's fifth grade during the December holidays, the children decided to have their own holiday fir tree that they would decorate with things they made themselves. Balls and other ornaments were cut from construction paper, were covered with glitter, and contained holiday verses they had written. Lisa made her tree decoration in the shape of a menorah and inscribed inside:

> Menorah—
> Jewish symbol
> proudly burning candles
> like seven fireflies.
> Hanukkah.
>
> *Lisa Roper*

Lisa also wrote inside an icicle-shaped ornament:

> Ice—
> frozen clear
> dripping from trees
> fun for ice skating:
> Slippery.

Another child designed a snowflake and wrote:

> Snow
> White Flakes
> Falling to Earth
> Beautiful Crystal Ice Stars
> Winter
>
> *Wendy Halsey*

Story and Play.   Children's interest in holidays can be channeled into writing realistic or inventive stories and plays. In many instances, children can devise their own make-believe or real topics for writing and then for sharing as the entertainment at a class holiday party. A group of children can perform a play they have written, or an individual can read his or her story. One fifth-grader, who invented her own title, wrote this story to share:

GETTING IT TOGETHER AS SANTA MOUSE

Scweek, Scweek, Scweek! I'm Santa Mouse! Did you ever hear of me? I live at the North Pole with Santa Claus. I dress up like him, except I have whiskers by my nose—you know like a dog does? On Christmas Santa yells out, "On Dasher, on Dancer, on Prancer and Vixen, on Comet, on Cupid, on Donner and Blitzen. Come on too, Santa Mouse!"

I'm Santa's little companion. I stick with him and the other reindeers, but most of all Rudolph. I look out that all the elves do their work correctly, not wrong. I'm busy most of the time. But I'm the one who wraps all the gifts! Not one or two, but all the gifts! I also put the goodies in your stocking!

Scweek, Scweek, Scweek! Merry Christmas!

June Neilson

For children who have trouble "getting it together," the teacher can offer holiday topics that may spark ideas for a play or story:

Thanksgiving
The Man Who Forgot to Be Thankful
No Turkey This Thanksgiving
A Pilgrim Came to Our Thanksgiving
What the Indian Said
Turkey, Cranberry, and Pumpkin Pie
I Was at the First Thanksgiving

Halloween
The Ghost Who Lost a Shoe
No Trick or Treat This Year
The Friendly Witch
The Orange Witch
The Crooked Broomstick
A Goblin Who Wouldn't Scare

St. Valentine's Day
The Valentine Card That Was Lost
A Broken Heart
A Valentine Card for Me
Nobody Loves Me
A Valentine Present for Paula
Cupid Got Lost

Christmas
The Woman Who Lost Christmas
Coal in My Stocking
He Didn't Want to Be a
   Christmas Tree
Santa—Lost in a Blizzard
The Flat Christmas Carol

Hanukkah
The Candles Wouldn't Burn
No Candles in the Window
The Fifth Candle
The Hanukkah Candles Talk

St. Patrick's Day
I Wished on a Four-leaf Clover
A Leprechaun Told Me
A Leprechaun Under the Bed
Leprechauns Are for Real

Birthdays of Lincoln, Washington, Columbus, King
He Did It!
That Was the Day
A Contribution to Remember

A Hero to Remember
One Hour in the Life of _____
This Is Your Life, _____

Trips

An actual visit to a locale may suggest a wide variety of writing activities: letters, papers recommending a course of action, descriptive paragraphs, editorials. The visit may also provide much of the information required for writing. Here are some suggestions.

Excursions to Industrial or Commercial Enterprises.   Take children to enterprises of unusual interest, such as a store displaying Oriental rugs, an inn dating from Revolutionary or Civil War days that retains some of the original flavor, an antique shop, an airport for small planes, or a tree nursery. Suggest that each child look for one item that strikes his or her fancy or that is particularly distasteful. Upon returning to the classroom, children can write—

- a thank you note to the manager.
- a letter to a student who did not make the trip, describing one aspect that was especially liked or disliked.
- a paper recommending how the trip could be improved another year.
- a paper describing a weakness or strength seen in the enterprise.
- a summary statement of the trip.

Excursions to Geological or Ecological Sites.   Take children to sites where erosion is fast eating away the land, where a forest fire has wreaked havoc, where a river shows signs of pollution, where strip mining is going on, where factories are polluting the air. Ask children: "What measures can we take to prevent continued destruction of the environment?" Have children write paragraphs suggesting solutions. If there is great enough interest, encourage them to write a letter to the editor of a local paper, describing what was observed.

Visits to Parks.   Take children to visit city parks or the school grounds to observe signs of vandalism and litter. On the walk, look for specific signs of littering, for flower beds and plots of grass ruined by people's walking through them, for broken statues, railings, and windows. Upon their return, children can write—

- a letter to a child who did not make the trip, describing what was seen.
- a position paper outlining a point of view about conditions seen.
- a letter to a park commissioner or a local paper, suggesting possible ways of correcting the situation.

• a script for a puppet show about what elementary school students can do to prevent destruction of school grounds and parks. (Perform the show for other classes.)

These assignments can be carried out individually in the upper-elementary grades and as a total class activity in lower and upper grades.

Newsworthy Events

The world in which we live is in constant change. Significant events occur almost daily. Today an oceanographer discovers a new form of life on the ocean's bottom; tomorrow an earthquake rocks Yugoslavia. One day there is a partial eclipse of the sun; the next a new mayor is elected locally. These and other events around the world are natural ways of stimulating children to report, to retell something read in the newspaper or heard on TV, and to summarize. A discussion of an exciting event and the children's reaction to it can lead to written expression almost without a teacher's suggesting it.

Events close to home are, of course, most meaningful for children. For example, a group of inner-city youngsters in an upper elementary grade came into school talking excitedly about the explosion in a nearby Standard Oil Refinery. The explosion had been strong enough to shake their homes. The children recounted what happened and what they felt at the time; then they expressed themselves in writing. One girl wrote:

THE EXPLOSION

When the explosion happened, it was about 12 o'clock at night. My aunt lives a few blocks away, and when it happened she fell on the floor. My cousin who lives with her was watching TV when all of a sudden he fell on the floor and he got up and said, "What happened?" My aunt said that a tank of gasoline exploded, so he immediately got in his car with my aunt and went to my house. There were a lot of people coming with children in their arms. My mother said that God surely looked after us.

Sports events may give youngsters in upper elementary grades ideas for writing. Many students follow the World Series, take interest in a heavyweight championship fight, or watch superbowl games on television. Then, too, as middle-class children are brought up learning to ski, sail, water-ski, skate, or bowl, they may follow related sports events on television. Depending on the geographical area in which they are teaching and the group with which they are working, teachers may find that a boy or girl with no interest in imaginative writing may enjoy writing sports reports. The topic may be a national event or a class or school game. The report may focus on one particular sport exclusive of all others. Such papers may be included in the school or class newspaper as part of the sports section.

World and School Issues

With children in upper elementary grades, a discussion of world, national, local, and school problems can spark an idea for realistic writing. Children today are becoming more aware of issues confronting the world, and they need to develop opinions that they can support in a rational way. Some widespread problems that have potential for stimulating both discussion and writing include war, dope, crime in the streets, poverty, environmental pollution (see fig. 4.4), juvenile delinquency, discrimination, unemployment, taxes, and inflation. Controversial issues within the local school scene that may be significant to children are school regulations, cafeteria food, school elections, homework, length of school day, and vacations.

Older elementary students can express their ideas on pertinent issues in a position paper outlining their reasons. A series of papers by different children on the same issue, which express different points of views, can be turned into a newsletter and distributed to other classes. Students can also write editorials in which they analyze some facet of a problem; these can be included on the editorial page of the school newspaper. Students can write letters to national and local leaders, communicating their ideas on an issue. A group of children can compose a

Figure 4.4. A fourth grader's position paper on pollution

petition, which they can sign and send to a person who may be able to effect change—a senator, a representative, a governor. A group can also write a script for a television or radio news special that outlines the dimensions of an issue. The program can be "released" to other classes. Still another kind of purposeful writing activity is the writing of a letter to the editor of a local paper on a current issue. Doreen wrote this letter to an area newspaper:

RECYCLING GLASS

Editor, *The Record*:

I am in the fifth grade and I go to Washington School. We are studying about pollution.

I read about the Coca Cola Company's collecting bottles to help pollution. I think they are doing the right thing. In our school we are recycling bottles to help pollution.

Doreen Kunz
Saddle Brook, New Jersey

Teachers whose children have developed ideas and written on relevant world issues generally agree that a preliminary discussion by the whole class is necessary. Children need experience in analyzing issues in order to understand the diverse ways of viewing an issue and to project ideas on their own. Recordings of radio and television newscasts and round table discussions and speeches on a topic can spark general discussion on an issue. So can a controversial editorial from a local newspaper, a controversial speaker, or a crisis in the school. The following two unedited papers, for example, were written in reaction to a picture showing a street scene in a poorer section of a large city. They were written after children had discussed their feelings about poverty.

WHAT I FEEL

I feel disgusted, we have food, money, a home, and they don't, they don't have a home, food, money, they don't have jobs. I would give all my money to them. I'm just lucky I have the things they don't.

Cameron Daggett

WHAT I FEEL

I feel sorry for them. They don't have any room. No houses. I feel bad. I would like to do something for them. They don't have anything. No cloths. No money to have things. They don't have good schools to go to. The fathers need jobs to support they're family's. They don't have enough experions. They haven't learned not much. They have no toys or jobs or even homes. They're going to get sick and thin. They won't have a life to live for.

Janine Sheppard

Sometimes children begin thinking about social issues by listing words that an issue brings to mind. City youngsters living in a high-crime area decided to write about crime in the streets. One seventh grader listed words that "crime in the street" brought to mind: *killing, fighting, mugging, shooting, cursing, kick, hit, rock, suicide, rapping, jump.* She went on to write:

P_____'S STREETS

There is a lot of killing on the streets of P_____, Governor and Main. You see of everything you didn't want to see. Every body there are bars on every corner. If you walk down on the street they say something to you. That's why people done like to walk on the streets.

Hanna

School issues can be the focus of writing assignments in the upper elementary grades as students increase their awareness of the intricacies of group interaction and show heightened interest in the decision-making process. Topics relevant to this age group may include "Smoking in School," "Marijuana in the Halls," or "Safety in the School."

Working in an inner-city junior high school, a student teacher began with a picture of a school hall scene in which an older man is confronting a younger one. The writer's task after a period of general discussion was to relate this picture to some issue in the school and suggest a story about what might have been taking place. The range of ideas, as well as what individual children read into the picture, was amazing. Each child identified an aspect of the picture with a major concern he or she had. Here are two unedited stories that resulted:

WHAT GOES ON IN SCHOOL TODAY

One day the principal was walking in the hall and he was going into the boys room when all of a sudden he opened the door and a boy about 6 feet tall was standing there looking straigh at him with a cigar in his mouth.

The principal said to him no smoking but the boy just ignored him so the principal kiked him out of school.

THE PUSHER

One day a boy came late to school. He was dizzy and walking like he was drunk. He had been smoking marawana. He's teacher quickly got him to the nurse, and got him to reality again. She asked him "Charlie where did you get that stuff? Is it being sold here on the play ground?" "Yes, Miss Smith, it is, a man out there told me I was his friend, he said if I took it I'd pass my exams today". Quickly Miss Smith ran down to the principal's office and told him what was going on! The principal, Mr. Caufman called the police. 15 minutes

later they had surrounded the play ground. The dope pusher was surrounded, it was no way out. The pusher ran into the school and hide
in the door frame of the boys room. The principal ran quickly to the
door. "Bang" the gun had shot off the wall and hit the pusher in the
leg. After that the police arrested him and took him away.

Teachers accustomed to having youngsters write about daffodils,
witches, and snow may be rather startled by the suggestion that young
people should be expressing themselves on such topics as these. Yet
smoking, dope, and even unwanted pregnancy are part of some elementary students' immediate environment; these are topics about which
students can write most meaningfully.

Science and Social Science Content

Children actively involved in science-related investigations find
written expression a natural outgrowth. For example, youngsters in middle elementary grades can set up a bird-feeding study. They can make
different kinds of food available to birds in several different ways:
crumbs, squash seeds, and cooked spaghetti can be scattered on the
ground; peanut butter, beef fat, and pork fat can be rubbed on the bark
of a growing tree; an actual feeding platform can be constructed and seed
placed on the platform. Children, of course, keep records of what they
do and what they observe. Their records include written statements, bird
sketches, and charts indicating the amount of food placed at each
feeding station. This can be organized as a group writing activity, with
one youngster serving as the recorder each day.

Children in Brenda Bryant's third grade produced the following
statements as they observed fish in an aquarium:

Our Experiment
1. Our fish were living in an aquarium.
2. We had four fish and three died.
3. In our aquarium we have only one fish left. It is a red
   fighter fish.

Later, hypothesizing about the cause of death, they wrote:

Our Explanation
1. Maybe somebody was breathing over the fish.
2. Maybe someone was feeding the fishes too much food.
3. The fish ate some of the grass in the aquarium.

In a similar manner, children involved in a study of weather can
make daily excursions out-of-doors to study such weather conditions as

cloud formations, temperature, humidity, and barometric pressure. They keep both graphic and written records of their observations, and they write their predictions on future weather.

Youngsters in the lower elementary grades are more than enthusiastic when they encounter this type of investigatory recording activity. Susan Renna, a student teacher working in a suburban area, helped her third graders study the behavior of solutions. Groups were given jelly jars, spoons, and possible solutes—sugar, salt, flour, pepper. The teacher poured measured amounts of cold and hot water into the jars for each group. The children then added a teaspoonful of a possible solute to a jar of cold water and a teaspoonful of solute to a jar of hot water. If the added solute dissolved, they added another teaspoonful of the solid matter. Each group worked with a different substance and was responsible for keeping records of what was done and what happened. After the investigatory session the groups met as a class and developed a large chart of results. Finally, they decided upon a conclusion, which they wrote together.

Working from scientific investigation, children have opportunities to produce varied content: descriptions, reports, comparisons, contrasts, explanations, hypotheses, conceptual schemes, designs. The written material incorporates charts, graphs, tables, and pictures that the children design to support and clarify ideas. Children just beginning to play with written expression in the lower grades can work cooperatively to produce written records. Older students can carry on individual investigations and keep their own records. Because of the number of options that exist, scientific study has much to offer an elementary school writing program.

The content of the social sciences can make a similar contribution to the formation of ideas. Having studied some period of history, children can gain retelling skills by recounting a significant event. A fifth grader who had studied the Pilgrims' journey wrote:

THE PILGRIMS

Some of the people of England wanted to worship in their own way. They decided to go to Holland where they had religious freedom. In Holland the young English children were learning everything the Dutch way. So they decided to go to the new world.

They planned the trip weeks before. They also asked the King if they could go, and he finally said, "Yes."

On the way over some died, but most were alive. They had many terrible storms, and many thought that they would never live through it. They finally landed. The people made friends with the Indians who taught them many things.

Writing about social science content is feasible at most grade levels. First graders studying about community helpers can describe in brief sentences what each community worker does. Studying about their school, children can begin by talking about what the principal does, what the nurse does, and so forth; their discussion can be stimulated by pictures from any of the good folios available commercially today. After talking, children can write sentences telling about workers in their school.

In the middle grades, as children study about people from other cultures, they can summarize their knowledge in written form. In upper elementary grades, they can begin to write explanations of events they have studied: Why do people in different areas live the way they do? Why do people in some regions change their way of life? Why is there more poverty in some areas of the world?

One activity related to social science that has high student appeal and tremendous potential to stimulate varied ideas for writing is the production of a newspaper that resembles a paper published during some historical period. To produce a "period newspaper," children must use their knowledge of the past to write headlines, editorials, news stories, weather reports, the social page, sports news, letters to the editor, political and social cartoons, comics, advertisements, and obituaries.

A particularly impressive job was done by Adelaid Lombardi, a sixth-grade teacher who had each child in the class select a part of the newspaper staff that he or she wanted to join. Even the layout of the final paper was the responsibility of one group. This group took the pieces written by the children, cut them up, and pasted them on a large, newspaper-sized, four-page mock-up of a real paper. (See fig. 4.5.) The headlines on the front page of the Revolutionary War *Daily Express* announced "Flatboats Collide." This was the lead story:

> On the Mississippi River yesterday, four flatboats collided. A witness to the accident said that the four flatboats were traveling down the Mississippi when the flatboat at the head of the line made a sudden stop. The three flatboats behind it collided into the first boat. Two of the boats sunk and the other two were broken up. Seven passengers were killed and twenty passengers were injured. The injured were taken to Fort Sink Hospital. Funeral services will be held at St. James Church. After hearing of the incident, Governor Sweeney made a law forbidding flatboats to travel close together.

Other front-page stories were "Chief Dies in War," "National Road Crosses Country," and "Grasshoppers Kill Crops." On the center spread were the classified ads, a political cartoon entitled "Stamp Out the Stamp Act," an announcement of an opening of a fair, an announcement of marriages and engagements, and the obituaries. There was also a version of "Dear Abby" called "Dear Alexandra."

Dear Alexandra,

My hands are lobster red. That comes from washing dishes. What can I do?

Reddy

Dear Reddy,

I know what it's like so mix some lard and blueberries together and that will solve your problem.

Alexandra

Dear Alexandra,

My mother makes me work when I want to play. I'd like to tell her without getting her mad. What can I say?

Work-hard

Dear Work-hard,

You know making a new country takes work, so bare it.

Alexandra

On the back page there were several news stories and a joke called "Revere Makes Mistake."

Yesterday Mrs. Snyder walked into the General Store and asked if they had any red coats. The salesman asked the manager if he had any red coats. Paul Revere was in the doorway. The sales manager said, "The Red Coats are coming." Mr. Revere rushed out the door, rode down hill on his horse, and yelled, "The Red Coats are coming; the Red Coats are coming."

A Point of View

When a teacher defines the dimensions of the writing program in terms of writing poetry, stories, plays, and perhaps letters, children have a restricted writing experience. Neglected is the writing of expository prose—reaction papers, reviews, laboratory reports, action reports, essays, petitions, research papers—which is a form of writing necessary for success in upper high school, college, and some phases of adult life. For that reason, a teacher must strive to balance activities that lead to creation of inventive content with those that lead to more information-centered content. Realistic writing stimulated by trips, newsworthy events, world and school problems, and the social and natural sciences has as significant a place in the writing program as does inventive writing.

Figure 4.5. A period newspaper by a sixth-grade class

2¢ ONLY 2¢ — WORTH ITS WEIGHT IN GOLD

Daily Express

PARTLY CLOUDY
CHANCE OF
RAIN STORM

FLATBOATS COLLIDE!

On the Mississippi River yesterday, four flatboats collided. A witness to the accident said that the four flatboats were traveling down the Mississippi River when the flatboat at the head of the line made a sudden stop. The three flatboats behind it collided into the first boat. Two of the boats collided sunk and the other two were broken up. Seven passengers were killed and twenty passengers were injured. The injured were taken to Fort Sink Hospital. Funeral services will be held at St. John's church. After hearing of the incident, Governor Sweeny made a law forbidding flatboats to travel close together.

By Maryanne DeLuca

I'm a farmer and I moved to the plains. When I grew crops grasshoppers came and ate my 500 acres of crops in two days. After that I decided to return East which I really hated to do .... After I reached the East I told everyone what happened. A man made made some sort of machine that scared the grasshoppers away and killed them.

by John Alexander

NATIONAL ROAD CROSSES COUNTRY

The National Road is being opened to the country. It travels into the Midwest from Baltimore to Vandalia first to Wheeling, then onto Columbus, Ohio, then to Indianapolis. This road ... ... The road is much ... ... than others because it is ... wider to prevent a wagon jam ... ... Indian attacks and hitting ... ... wagon or person ... ... the National road ha... ... ... stops to it ... a wagon breaks down there ... ... to help you. There are good ... ... the road is good ... ... the National road doe... ... ... and is a more direct ... ... roads. It is the best road going ... into the Midwest. I will be a good travel road for traders.

By Charles Gibson

CHIEF DIES IN WAR

Chief Screaming Eagle died in War. The arrow was sent by his own tribe.
Covered By Dave Stuttler

CHIEF DIES AT WAR!

By Bryce ...
Chief Screaming Eagle dies at war with white people at Fort April. Chief Screaming Eagle was killed by a flaming arrow sent by one of his own. By accident, his tribe is now moving west where they will kill each other. By stragg... ... ... them selves

Two Parents Die, Three Children Sprained

Thursday three children sprained their Ankles and Their parents died from an Indian attack. "Ma and Pa just put the baby to sleep and sat down. Luize and Lou were gettin ready for bed. Dad said he heard somthin outside. He went out. The next thing we knew Dad came in with an arrow in the

From left to right Connie, 14, Mr. And Mrs. J.H. Stevens, and baby J.H. Steven Jr., the twins Luize and Lou, 12

middle of his chest. Injuns started swarming in the house. Ma sceamed, "Get them children out of here Connie Go now!" I went up de stairs and Jumped out the winder with the children. We ran five miles to Aunt Lilys house." said Connie Stevens, 14 years old. The picture up in the right was taken last summer. The Parents were found dead (scalped) and full of arrows in the back yard. The children have sprained ankles from jumping. The children will be living with there Aunt + Uncle, Mr. and Mrs. Lou Paul Stevens, who have no children.

Written By: Beth Pivirotto

Indian Attack in Mississippi Valley, Indian Boy Lost on Tuesday, the wagon train going to California and Utah got attacked by the tribe of Natchez Indians. Many people were killed or captured. The Indians came with poisonous arrows and guns that they had taken. Some of the wagons got burned or they fell apart.

. Some people who survived say that a little Indian boy came with his father in his huge Knapsack. He first crawled out of the knapsack, then he crawled into a wagon. We believe that this boy survived the attack and went home with some of the survivers. He might be hiding away somewhere in town. If you know anything about this, please go to the sheriffs office or send a telegraph to Middletown.

By Lee Robb

British Get Out

Dear Editor,

I am writing to you to tell you about the British who are in my House. They make me cook they throw their clothes around they never pick up. I can't go to sleep because the General sleep upstairs in my room. I am not on their side I am for freedom in fact my son is one of the minute men. If they do not get out I will take one of my son's guns and shoot them all.

That General of theirs said this " We wouldn't fight" But he found out because we won the battle. He is going back to England because of it and another man is coming to take his place.

by
Robin Zuch

Revere Makes Mistake

BY BOB LOMBARDI

Yesterday Mrs. Snyder walked into the General store and asked if they had any red coats. The salesman asked if he had any red coats. Paul Revere was in the doorway, the sales manager said without hearing what the salesman said "The Red Coats are Coming". Mr. Revere rushed out the door, rode down hill on his horse and yelled "The Red Coats are Coming, The Red Coats are Coming.

It's A Joke

SEARCH IN REFERENCE MATERIALS

Sometimes we assume that ideas for writing will spring fully grown from our heads with little effort on our part, even as Minerva sprang fully formed from the head of Jupiter. Such an assumption is wishful thinking, especially when writing involves complex content. Search—the process through which a writer is saturated in source materials on a topic—is generally a necessity.

What is involved in the search for ideas? First, a searcher thumbs through material, scanning here, skipping there, reading in detail something that tickles an idea already beginning to germinate. Getting a spark of an idea, the writer-in-search-of-material jots it down. He or she marks a portion of an article for future reference or skims a second reference, reading only a line here or there. Then the searcher sits and thinks, juggling thoughts, putting facts together, searching for the thread that will give meaning to what is to be written.

A report that is nothing more than a sequencing of facts lifted verbatim from an encyclopedia results from an inability to use search as the base for writing. For some children, search erroneously degenerates into copying paragraphs of the reference encyclopedia into a notebook or onto index cards. The paragraphs copied get juggled around and actually become the report. To avoid such misunderstanding, we must teach children starting in third grade how to search for ideas.

Reading to Search

How can we teach children the techniques for saturating themselves in source materials? One answer is to have reading periods in which children thumb through magazines, looking here and there but not reading word by word. Good for this purpose are old copies of *National Geographic*, in which pictures play a major part and scanning can produce rapid understanding. Also, have children play at "reading" a magazine article. They should try to get the sense of it by reading only the first or last sentence of every paragraph. They can try the same technique with books: play at "reading" a book by reading only one sentence at the top of each page, one in the middle, and one at the end. Weekly newspapers such as *Our Weekly Reader* and *Junior Scholastic* can also be used to teach rapid skimming. Instead of reading in detail, suggest that the children first flip through the entire issue to discover what kinds of articles the week's issue contains and to determine which articles they would like to read in detail. On library trips, suggest that children skim through several books before selecting one to bring back to the class for thorough reading.

Another technique for teaching rapid skimming is first to collect newspaper articles on a topic. Distribute an article to each child. The child studies it for only three minutes; then he or she must pass it to the child behind, who gets it for three minutes before passing it on in turn. The process, which almost becomes a game, can be repeated five or six times, so that every child will have looked at five or six articles in fifteen or eighteen minutes. In the period immediately following the scanning, every child orally tells about something of interest gleaned from the reading. Then the teacher can follow up with the question: "If we were to write a paper on this topic to send to the other fifth-grade class, what would be the main message we would want to get across?" Ideas can be written on the board or fed into a tape recorder. If each of the articles has been numbered, children can also record the article or articles they consider particularly valuable sources.

To encourage children to read in varied sources to collect ideas for writing, teachers should use a variety of references directly in teaching. If the class is considering a problem of current social interest, the teacher can read a comment from a recent news magazine, illustrate a point with pictures from a newspaper story, or refer to editorials and articles in newspapers. If the class is studying a scientific topic, the teacher can refer to up-to-date material in *Scientific American.* As part of social science investigations, children can refer to the *Smithsonian, National Geographic, Consumer Reports,* or any of the oversized, illustrated volumes such as those in the Heritage Series. The teacher can share items from the *World Almanac, Guinness Book of World Records,* an assortment of atlases, encyclopedias, maps, and such specialized volumes as *Encyclopedia of American Biography, Who's Who,* and Van Nostrand's *Scientific Encyclopedia.* In addition, books other than texts should be made available for children to read a chapter or even a page. Instead of the teacher putting together a "reading table" of books on a unit, several children can go to the school library, check the card catalog, browse where the appropriate books are shelved, and return to the classroom with references for the "unit reading table."

Other Search Tools

Searching for ideas naturally takes one to written materials, but it is just as natural to consult other sources. Children can attempt systematic interviews, talking to people in the community with the assistance of interview guides planned by a group or the total class. Discussions with war veterans, writers of children's books, executives of electrical utility plants, or politicians can give children meaningful ideas for writing.

Children can systematically observe social phenomena. They can observe changing habits of dress and grooming, study at firsthand the characteristics of different neighborhoods, or observe the littering habits of people by recording behavior from the vantage point of a street corner. Again, both the procedures attempted and the results of the investigation can produce ideas for writing.

Search can take children to filmed materials. Encourage children to check the lists of films and filmstrips available on a subject chosen for writing. Suggest they study a film in depth, rerunning it several times to note down key points. Encourage children to find people with 35-mm slides or home movies that might give them greater insight into a topic. Help them to analyze what they are seeing to find meanings they can express in their own writing.

Search can involve listening to recordings. For example, children writing on Hawaiian life could search collections of island music done by such performers as Alfred Apaka, Mahi Beamer, and Haunani Kahalewai. From "Koni Au," "Hawaiian War Chant," "Papio," "Aloha Oe," and other songs, children can begin to know their subject and perhaps discover a theme for writing, whether that writing is prose or poetry.

Time—An Essential Requisite of Search Activity

As children grow older and become concerned with researching an idea, they must be encouraged to dig deeply into materials and ideas before beginning to compose on paper. While children are carrying on preliminary search activities, the teacher must serve as a sounding board, talking with them individually about facts uncovered, helping them identify the meaning of facts, and suggesting other directions the search can take. Talking about their findings sometimes enables students to put the pieces together. In upper grades, talking to other students about research data can serve the same function. Idea-pairs—two students who talk over ideas before writing—can be established at the start of a search-saturation period.

One of the major problems to be overcome is the inclination of some students to start writing or copying immediately; students begin to compose paragraphs based on information from only their very first reference. Sometimes, pretending to be detectives in search of evidence is a technique useful in getting children to prowl around in material. Conversely, some teachers have a built-in feeling that children are not being productive unless they are putting words on paper. One of the authors recalls a lesson in "creative writing" conducted by a student teacher. After less than five minutes had gone by, several fourth graders were still studying the picture that was to be their inspiration. The teacher prodded, "Come on! Get to work!" As teachers, we must remember that contemplating or pondering is work too!

And work takes time. When we ask children to search for ideas by saturating themselves in source materials, time should not be limited. All children should not be required to finish a paper in the identical time period. One child may take two hours to search for an idea; another may take two days. When we recall that Thomas Gray, the great English poet, lay for six months beneath a giant yew in an old country churchyard at Stoke Poges collecting impressions for "Elegy Written in a Country Churchyard," we should not get impatient with children who spend considerable time searching for ideas and contemplating them.

SOME SUMMARY THOUGHTS

This chapter has detailed a number of ways that children can be motivated to continue writing. How can such activities be integrated into the ongoing work of classrooms? Of course, the teacher can build a lesson or series of lessons around any one of the suggestions. But there is another, perhaps more functional, alternative. Writing can be included among the options from which students select during independent work sessions. For instance, a student may choose to write on a title displayed on the bulletin board, select a picture from the picture folio on the windowsill that correlates with a content unit in progress, listen to a story on a Weston Woods tape and react to it, or work with a group of other students on a "period newspaper" in progress. On another day, that same student may decide to check a plant growth experiment and record data, write a birthday report, or with two or three other youngsters write a cooperative play for later performing. Some of these activities can be structured so that youngsters can complete them in the privacy of their own desks, in a structured writing center, or in the group-interaction corner where students go to work together.

Through organizing such options into the independent study activity of the class, teachers can turn routine "seatwork" periods into meaningful learning-activity times and can involve children in written expression daily and continuously.

Part II | SKILLS FOR WRITING

The ablest writer is a gardener first,
and then a cook. His tasks are carefully to select and cultivate his
strongest and most nutritive thoughts,
and when they are ripe, to dress
them wholesomely, and so that they
may have relish.

J. C. Hare and A. W. Hare, GUESSES AT TRUTH

LET CHILDREN ORGANIZE THEIR THOUGHTS FOR WRITING ◄► creative and logical wholes

Manner is all in all, whate'er is writ.
William Cowper, TABLE TALK

   To write means to play with ideas. This is the essence of written communication, for unless one has an idea to express, taking pen in hand or sitting down at the typewriter to compose is meaningless. But the coin stamped "writing" has a second side. To write means also to capture ideas on paper through paragraph, sentence, line, and word patterns that communicate these ideas to others. Unless one can do this—and do it with style—ideas consigned to the written page lose their power.

   The way a writer organizes thoughts into logical and creative wholes—in other words, the way a writer designs paragraph and line patterns—is of prime importance in composing; it often determines the clarity of the communication. For this reason, school writing programs should be designed to teach children how to build thoughts into logical wholes. That such skill is sometimes lacking is evidenced by this unedited report composed by a bright eighth grader who was studying available vocational options before selecting courses to take in high school. Deciding that he might want to be a doctor, Steve located several references on the professional life of a doctor, studied them, and wrote:

DOCTOR

More people enjoy good health and live to an old age than ever before. This is because of modern medicine and the medical profession. I want to be a doctor. The main reason is because I like helping people.

Doctors diagnose deseases and treat people who are ill or in poor health. Doctors generally examine and treat patients in their own office and in hospitals, but they also visit patients at home when necessary. More than one third of the doctors are general practitioneers.

In offices through out the country, you will have to get a license to practice medicine. In every state it is required.

To qualify for a license, a candadate must graduate from an approved medical school and pass a licensing examination. Licensing examinations are given by State boards. Although doctors licensed in one state can usually obtain a license to practice in another without an examination, some states don't allow this.

Besides curing illness a doctor has to know how to prevent illness and also how to help prevent illness from spreading.

Among the qualifacations needed for success are a strong feeling that you want to be a doctor, above-average intelligence and an interest in science. A doctor must also have good judgment, he must be able to decide quickly in an emergency and remain calm.

He must also be healthy and strong. There are many hours in the hospital. He is also in contact with many deseases.

In order to be a doctor you have to have four years of college in premedical study. This includes courses in English, physics, biology, and chemistry in a good college. In your last year of college you take an examination called Medical College Admission Test. This helps you get admitted to a medical school. In the medical school you spend the first two years in labrotories and classrooms learning basic medical sciences and reserch. During the last two years, students spend most of the time in hospitals and clinics under the supervisim of experienced doctors. They learn to take case histories, perform examination and recognize deseases. . . .

Steven Rabin

That Steven has spent considerable time researching his topic and has compiled some significant data is obvious. But equally obvious is his problem in organizing ideas, which is much more serious than his random spelling errors—*labrotories, reserch, deseases, supervisim, qualafacations.* Clearly, Steve needs help in designing an overall structure for reporting his information, for he handles related ideas not as units but scattered throughout his paper. The result is discontinuity of thought. Similarly, he does not build ideas upon previously developed thoughts and does not use ideas to lead into successive ones. The result is lack of direction.

Paragraphs are also internally weak. Some ramble, not focusing on one big idea. The purpose of others is unclear, leaving the reader to question, "What is the purpose of this paragraph? What is it trying to say?" This problem is compounded by the fact that some paragraphs are very short—a single sentence in one case—suggesting that the writer has failed to think through details necessary to put "flesh" on his big ideas. Such short units make it difficult for any writer to develop ideas in depth.

In sum, Steve has a writing problem, one that is essentially a thinking problem. He has not mastered the basic thought processes or writing patterns needed for ideas to be communicated with precision. In this respect, he lacks fundamental organizational skills—skills that should be taught as part of school writing programs if we are to avoid generations of Stevens who have content to express but little control over how to express it.

This chapter, the first in a series of four on the skills of writing, describes what is involved in logical and creative organization and suggests ways of helping children organize their ideas for clear expression.

ORGANIZING THOUGHTS FOR WRITING

Organizing ideas for writing involves the ability to discriminate between what is significant within a particular context and what is insignificant. Basically, the writer must be able to answer two questions: What are the essential elements of my idea? What examples, details, and/or points do I need to support these essentials? Playing with these questions, a thinker-writer discards some points, while pinpointing others for inclusion. In this way, the writer climbs "inside" the idea and comes to understand its overall import. He or she identifies the big ideas to be expressed and the details that expand them.

A second subskill is the ability to perceive the psychological value of thoughts to be expressed through writing. In this context, the thinker-writer asks: What do I hope to achieve through my writing? Do I want to excite, calm, impress, cause to think, arouse to action, or transmit information? What will be the psychological impact of the ideas and feelings I am communicating? Playing with these questions, the thinker-writer decides what may be a psychologically sound way of introducing big ideas to the reader, organizing the argument, presenting facts, relaying emotion, and ending the written piece.

The thinker-writer must also be able to identify the logical relationships inherent in ideas to be expressed. First, he or she must be able to see which thoughts logically fit together, which facts relate most directly to main ideas chosen for inclusion, how one big idea relates to others, and how one idea can be used to build upon previous thoughts to form a sequential framework for writing. Second, feeling-laden ideas relate emotionally to one another; the writer must be able to perceive these emotional relationships within the material. He or she must sense that certain types of ideas communicate similar moods, with this similarity influencing the organization of a composition.

The preceding paragraphs do not imply that organizing thoughts for writing is only an analytical process involving the identification of big ideas, the psychological value of those ideas, and the relationships inherent within and between them. Organizing is a creative process as well, requiring the invention of a design for expressing. The mind must go beyond the material to reorder and assemble a new structure. In this respect, designing can be a creative activity—as creative as devising the ideas themselves. The designer mentally tries out different arrangements, plays with ideas by organizing them first this way and then that, places ideas in juxtaposition and then breaks them apart, turns them over, juggles them, and reorders again. The result is an original design or framework for communicating thoughts on paper.

How do we help children develop these thinking-writing skills? Clearly, to teach children to design frameworks for writing, we must begin by asking them to think in logical and creative ways. We must structure activities that ask them to group ideas into related clusters, visualize relationships within data, organize descriptive detail in terms of big unifying ideas, organize ideas gleaned from references, create unusual designs for writing, and compose titles and headings that reflect big ideas being expressed. In this section let us look at ways of doing this.

Grouping Ideas into Related Clusters

To design a structure for expressing ideas, the writer must be able to identify those that belong together because they share a common feature. He or she must build idea-pools—clusters of thoughts that fit together because of inherent emotional or logical relationships. These idea-pools develop into paragraphs and stanzas in which related ideas are organized into wholes.

A skill necessary in building idea-pools is the ability to perceive similarities and differences among ideas. This is a cognitive skill that can be developed rather systematically. Young children can begin to handle the grouping operation by sorting blocks of different colors, sizes, and shapes into groups that share a similar characteristic. Likewise, they can sort word cards into related piles. Words—*ax, bird, hammer, apple, banana, saw, giraffe, grapefruit, alligator, orange, baby, seal,* and *bee*—can be sorted into piles that share a similar first letter, or into piles labeled *tools, animals,* and *fruits.* Children should be encouraged to study words to discover other ways in which the word cards can be grouped—for example, the number of letters in the word, the number of letters repeated in it, or the number of vowels in it.

As children move through primary grades, they should perform grouping activities requiring finer discriminations. They can look at shells, leaves, or rocks, and make piles of similar specimens. Moving from the concrete to the more abstract, they can group related idea cards. For instance, given three major category headings (why I want to be a doctor, what doctors do, and what kinds of preparation doctors must have) children classify subideas under the major headings (I like people; doctors prevent illnesses from spreading; doctors must attend college; doctors must carry out an internship; I want to work with people; some doctors specialize in certain areas of medicine; doctors help people who are sick; I enjoy science). As children place their cards under a major heading-card, they explain why that card belongs in that location. Similar sets of cards for idea-grouping can be made by using main ideas and sentences from paragraphs in science and social studies books.

Children can also categorize according to emotional feelings and moods. "Let's group together happy occasions. Let's build another group of sad occasions," the first-grade teacher can suggest. "Let's categorize these events as quiet or noisy. Let's categorize these as boring or exciting," the third-grade teacher can urge. At the fifth-grade level the teacher can ask youngsters to propose word-pools on peace and war, honesty and dishonesty, fear and courage.

As the preceding paragraph hints, to develop skill in seeing relationships within and between ideas, youngsters need numerous opportunities at every level of schooling to classify according to similarities and differences. These opportunities should involve work with concrete materials, words, and ideas. They should involve encounters with both logical and emotional relationships. Through a developmental sequence of activities, children can acquire the ability to handle some of the thinking processes so fundamental to the design of compositions.

Visualizing Relationships

Even as youngsters search out relationships, they should attempt to organize ideas in a pictorial form that highlights which points belong together and what sequences are inherent in the material. Research by Donald Graves and others has begun to supply clues as to the importance of sketching and diagramming in the composing of young children. Experienced writers also know that, as they develop the design of a piece they are composing, at times they visualize that design by diagramming relationships on paper. They may plot out rough idea webs as in figure 5.1, which clarify what ideas are subsumed under bigger ideas and what the sequential relationships are.

One way to start children on the road to visualizing relationships among ideas is to have them create picture sequences that depict everyday events. Youngsters sketch what they did first, second, next, after

Figure 5.1. Idea webbing

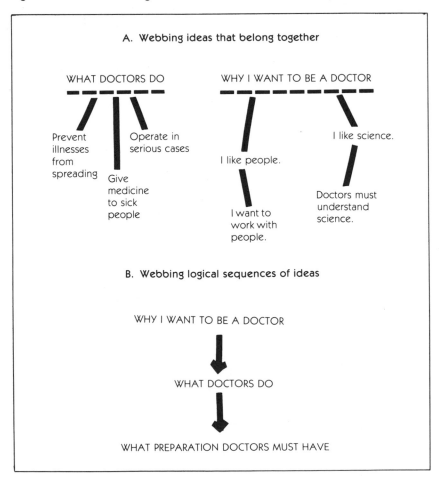

that, in a picture series that they later use to share the event with classmates. In the process, they begin to use the words *first, next, then, finally* that are so important in communicating sequential relationships both in oral and written expression. They draw arrows from one picture to the next in their series—arrows that show the direction of movement from one happening to the next. The result is an events flowchart.

In similar fashion children can create flowcharts to express sequential relationships found in science and social studies: steps in processes, sequences in historical events, directions from one place to another in geography. Youngsters simply sketch a series of pictures depicting steps or happenings and connect them with arrows. As students mature in the way they handle time relationships, they can plot such events on time lines, which help them visualize what happened first, next, and so on. With maturity, they can use maps for visualizing historical sequences, plotting the movement of migrating peoples on maps, again drawing arrows to show relationships.

In classrooms, perhaps the most useful material for helping children think in terms of relationships is the storybook. Having listened to a story told them, youngsters can select key points—or big events or idea-marks—in the story to crayon out on paper, again going back to connect events using arrows to indicate inherent sequences. This latter activity can be completed either individually or in groups with each participant contributing one drawing; drawings can be tied literally together by colorful yarn that links one event with those that preceded it.

Drawings too can be used to represent "belongingness." Having listened to a story, children can categorize events or characters and can place free-hand drawings under appropriate subheadings: characters who were wise—characters who were foolish; characters who were good—characters who were evil; characters who were important—characters who were less important; major events in the story—lesser events in the story. An example of this is shown in figure 5.2. Most of the traditional tales lend themselves to this kind of visualization, especially the fairy tales such as *Jack and the Beanstalk, Little Red Riding Hood, Hansel and Gretel, The Three Little Pigs.* The line between wise and foolish and good and evil is well delineated in all of them.

Relating Main Ideas and Significant Details

A major organizing idea of this chapter is that to write with clarity, a person must be able to grasp the logical relationships that exist within material; he or she must see which ideas "belong" together. The process of visualizing just described is one way that writers can lay out ideas to

Figure 5.2. Depicting story relationships

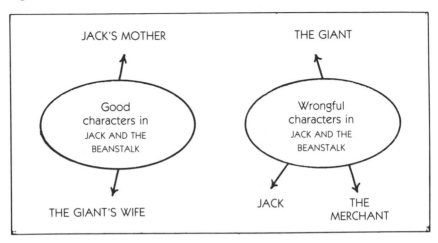

clarify relationships for themselves even as they begin to organize thoughts for writing. The process of systematically identifying the relevant who, what, when, where, how, and why detail is a second way—one that simultaneously allows the writer to put flesh on the idea itself.

Most teachers are familiar with the reportorial technique of describing an event or phenomenon in terms of the key who, what, when questions. Some writing programs are having children use these questions in a step-by-step manner to expand main ideas through the inclusion of related detail. For example, *Individualized Language Arts*, an ESEA Title IV-C Project carried out in Weehawken, New Jersey (Weehawken Board of Education, 1974), suggests that before youngsters begin to compose in paragraph style, they answer a few of these questions by listing several answers in brainstorming style for each:

- Who (or What) are we writing about
- What do they do (or What happens to them)
- What kind of (or Which)
- When
- Where
- How
- Why
- How many (much)

Using this approach with first or second graders as part of an integrated language arts-social studies experience, the teacher prepares motivational charts each captioned with a question: Who are the members of a family? What do families do together? Where do we find families? Why do people live together in families? Starting with a series of pictures that show families comprised of different numbers and kinds of members and families interacting in a variety of settings and ways, teacher and student add many possible answers to the captioned charts. The kinds of responses children typically give to the question *What do families do together?* are given in figure 5.3.

Later the teacher reads paragraphs about the family aloud to the brainstormers, asking children to listen sentence by sentence for more information to add to their already burgeoning charts. As each sentence is read, youngsters decide to which chart the new descriptive information belongs, because it relates to the main question printed there. Now a teacher guides simply by asking: "Does this information tell us who other family members are? Is it telling us why we have families?"

The Weehawken Plan suggests a similar strategy for thinking through relationships implicit in a narrative sequence such as a class trip. Here children first brainstorm in response to the big idea question *What*

Figure 5.3. An example of a main idea-question chart that can develop through group brainstorming of related detail

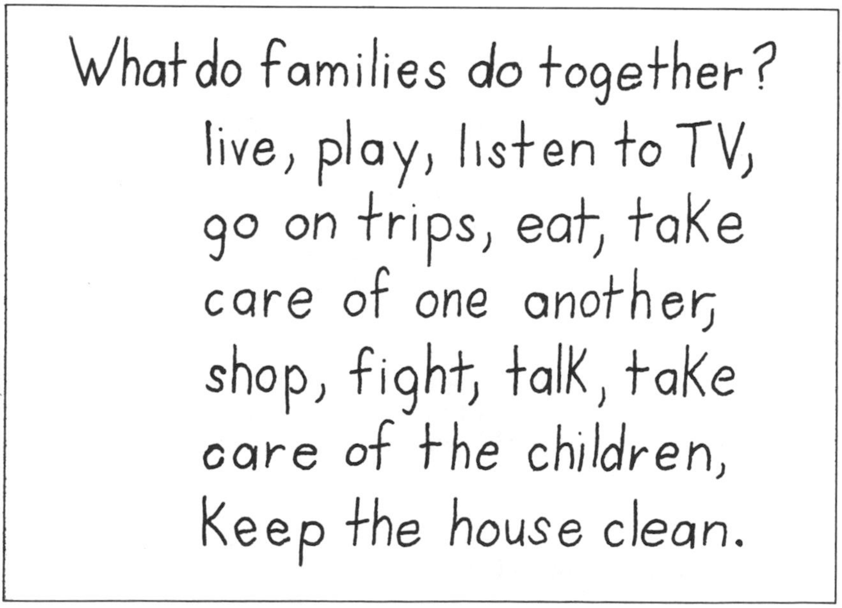

What do families do together?
live, play, listen to TV,
go on trips, eat, take
care of one another,
shop, fight, talk, take
care of the children,
keep the house clean.

happened on our trip? or *What did we do?* As children proffer items, the teacher lists on chart or chalkboard the points given in the order suggested and then asks:

- Which of these did we do first?
- Which did we do next (second)?
- Which did we do then (third)?
- What happened after that (fourth)?
- What happened last (finally)?

At this point teacher and students select from their first chart of random thoughts those items to list on a second chart in chronological order.

Even as children supply main ideas as to what they did first, second, third, and so forth, the teacher can ask them to put flesh on their ideas by supplying related details or descriptions. When children, for example, suggest that the first thing they did was to climb aboard the bus that took them to the museum, the teacher can ask, *What* time did we climb on? *Where* was the bus parked? *How many* of us went? *What kind of* a bus was it? *How* did we feel? *What happened* on the bus? The result is an expanded chart that provides both a sequence of main ideas and details relative to each big idea. The result also is some beginning understanding of the kinds of questions that thinkers use to expand upon and sequence their ideas in a logical way, especially in reportorial writing. Table 1 supplies a model that a group could produce in response to this series of teacher-projected questions.

If teachers attempt this step-by-step approach to help children think through descriptive detail and sequences, they should begin orally. The setting for initial question-asking, brainstorming of points, and charting is a teacher-guided group. In this setting, teachers can raise questions that guide children to uncover sequences and can prime the pump, so to speak, by asking "What kind of . . . ?" or "For what reason . . . ?" when children's minds go dry. Later, children working together in composing teams can use the charts as outlines for writing—a writing carried out not individually at first but cooperatively. Only after children have brainstormed orally in response to many teacher-raised questions and composed as part of a group should they be asked to use group charts as the basis for individual writing and to create similar charts independently.

Organizing Ideas Gleaned from References

Once young people have learned to raise key questions about events of which they have been a part and to chart out descriptive detail, they

Table 1
SEQUENCING AND EXPANDING MAIN IDEAS

OUR TRIP TO THE MUSEUM

Questions	Main Ideas	Details (Descriptions of Who, What, When, Where, Why, Which one, What kind of, How many)
What happened first?	Got on bus at school	Early morning. Bright, sunny June day. Front of Roosevelt School, 15 parents, 32 students, Miss Howard, happy, smiling, eager to see exhibits. Modern, red chartered bus, 20 minutes late because of heavy traffic, everyone impatient. Began singing camp songs on bus. (Etc.)
What happened second?	Bus took us to Main Gate, Museum	Arrived 8:45. Everyone excited, huge stone fountain, cool white sprays, gleaming steel sculptures of Zeus, Atlas, other Greek gods, 4-story red, black, and off-white building, cement and steel, no windows, high steps to bronze doors. (Etc.)
What happened third?	Saw more about stars, planets	9:15. Planetarium, high, dark hall, ceiling a black dome, little stars twinkling in it. Quiet, shadowy projector. Guide spoke in deep, level, calm voice. Whole universe springing from explosion (?). First stars streaking away from each other. Class, parents fascinated by one-hour program, craned necks to watch moving displays. (Etc.)
What happened last?	Arrived back at school	6:00. Front of school again. All tired but happy. Eager to see Museum again, because would need weeks to see all exhibits. Cleaned up bus before getting off. Said "Thank you!" to smiling bus driver for his cheerfulness, jokes. Learned a lot for science. (Etc.)

SOURCE: Data from "Individualized Language Arts" (Weehawken, N.J.: Weehawken Public Schools, 1974), p. 56. Reprinted with permission.

can apply these learnings to ideas they uncover in reference books. An easy introduction is through articles in classroom magazines and newsletters. Having read silently, children respond to teacher-raised questions: "About what or whom is this article? When did this happen? What happened? Where did it happen? What kind of people were involved? What were their feelings? Why did this happen? What is your reaction?" As children answer, a scribe records next to key *Who, What, When, Where, Why, How* words listed on the board. In this way, children come to know how important the question-asking words are as they gather information from reference materials.

Shortly these words become items on recording guides that students take along with them as they search references for information on a topic for writing. To start, guides for library search sessions should be devised cooperatively. If, for example, youngsters are each to locate data on a given bird, in preparation they need to chart out big questions to answer: What does this bird look like? Where does it live? What kind of food does it eat? What are its unique customs? Arriving in the library, young researchers pair off into two-person research teams to find answers to the questions they have previously brainstormed and list information on a chart in which main idea questions and related details are set down side by side. In completing their charts, teams must check out at least three different references on a topic and include information from each one. They need not note down information in complete sentences, for what they are compiling is a data-retrieval chart, not a paragraph.

Charts become outlines for later composing. Studying main ideas and related details, young people consider: "Which kind of information should we write about first? What material should come next? What material would be best at the end?" They number key questions on their charts in the order they think will serve best for talking about the topic on paper. (See fig. 5.4.) Still working in two-person teams, youngsters compose two or three paragraphs that relate information they have compiled on their charts.

This approach to writing based on research activity helps children overcome the weaknesses obvious in Steven's report cited earlier in the chapter. Student referencers often pick up one reference book and write a paragraph or two based on it. Then they move on to a second and again write several paragraphs based on it. In this way they move through their references and their report. As a result, as in Steve's case, ideas pop up more than once in a composition, and there is no overall design to it. Such students need a systematic strategy for compiling findings from several references. The use of key organizing questions can provide the system.

Figure 5.4. A research chart, including big idea questions and descriptive detail

OUR INVESTIGATION OF BIRDS	
Names of Researchers: _____	
Order for Writing	
1	What is the name of the bird?
4	Where is the bird found?
2	What does the bird look like?
5	What are its unique characteristics?
3	How big is it?

Creating the Unusual Design

The strategies for identifying big ideas and related descriptive detail and for handling sequences are essentially analytical and logical ones. In helping children gain skill in applying these strategies, however, teachers should not mislead children into believing that once an organization for expressing has been designed it is immutable. Anyone who has worked extensively with ideas on paper knows that the act of organizing changes the idea itself. The process of actually putting words on paper in sentence and paragraph patterns triggers related ideas; at the same time portions of the original idea no longer seem to "hold water." Similarly, other details begin to emerge, and different dimensions of the problem surface as more important.

An essential outgrowth of change in ideas is change in the original concept of how to organize those ideas for writing. Beginning to compose, writers hold a tentative design in mind. That design may be a rather vague notion: in the first part of this piece I will consider X, in the second part Y, and in the third part Z. The tentative design for other writers may be a listing of points to be included in the approximate order of presentation. But rarely does the final piece resemble in detail the organization of the original plan for writing.

Sometimes, too, writers must attempt several organizing patterns before settling on one within which they can function. They try this; they try that; they eliminate; they reorder; they put this first, then last; they combine; they divide; they jot notes on paper; they restudy the data. Then they reevaluate their options and begin again.

When teachers work with children in designing a framework for ideas, they may give the impression that designing is a relatively mechanical process. Children may be required to produce a precise outline complete with Roman numerals and upper- and lower-case letters before beginning to write. They may be required to follow it to the letter and even be graded on how closely the final product matches the original outline. No wonder children sometimes produce such unimaginative frameworks and dread writing, for the act of construction has been transformed into a boring academic exercise, stripped of excitement and elation. Also, structuring a complete, precise outline before beginning to write may prevent the fluid change in both ideas and organizational design so essential in composing.

It is the teacher's attitude that either discourages or encourages experimentation and change. Teachers must view the final dimensions of a written piece as an emerging product to be projected even as writing progresses. Teachers must accept differences in the way children approach construction, allowing this youngster to begin with only a mental design of what she intends, encouraging that one to jot down points that he wants to include, helping another with a highly systematic orientation to employ a traditional outline as a base for composing. Teachers can encourage children to modify projected designs even as they write and help them construct a first draft replete with cross-outs, write-overs, cut-outs, arrows, and stapled additions.

Selecting a Title and Headings That Reflect the Big Ideas

Selection of a title must be considered within the context of the overall design and purpose of a piece. Words selected for the title and subheadings are among the most important to be written. These words can provide a capsule view of the ideas, give some indication of the organization of what follows, or express the theme of the piece. They can indicate for whom the piece is intended, or they can be tricky, attention-getting devices.

In any case, writers do not necessarily begin composing by constructing a title. A title may emerge in the process of actual writing. As the words of composition or poem begin to take form on paper, the dimensions of the ideas to be expressed become clearer to the writer. Seeing where the piece is going, he or she constructs a title to communicate this direction. Accordingly, a writer may arrive at a title only after the paper is completed. Reading and rereading what has been consigned to paper, he or she identifies the one, two, ten, or twelve words that express the essence of the big idea. A title may also come from an association of words put together somewhere in the piece that in retrospect summarizes the piece perfectly.

With child writers, teachers often put the cart before the horse, asking them to start by neatly writing a title across the top of the page. Then we ask them to fit their ideas into that predetermined package, which is a rather impossible task. The product may be inconsistent with the title. Children may find that they cannot write on that title.

Instead, children should compile a list of possible titles as they write, leaving several blank lines at the top of the paper. When an inspiration strikes, youngsters jot it at the top. Completing the piece, children study the alternatives and perhaps add a few more. Youngsters can share their alternatives with classmates who decide which ones turn them on; based on such study, children create a big idea title—one that is more likely to capture the essence of the written piece than one constructed initially to fit the requirements of an assignment.

The place to begin creative titling is through teacher-guided group writing. Only after composing a piece cooperatively and editing to make the sentences flow smoothly do young people think in terms of a title that captures the mood and meaning of what they have composed. Then each participant thinks of one or more possible titles from which the group selects the most appropriate. One college-level group worked through this process, beginning a creative story by composing based on five words that they had to use in the sequence given: *monster, hole, centipede, slipped, hollered*. Here is their piece and their title—a title composed in retrospect:

FALLING FOR PUFFED RICE

Once upon a time in a dark, dreary hole at the bottom of a mountain lived a horrible, green monster named Sidney. He had a clumsy roommate named Harold, who was a centipede.

One wet, rainy day, Harold and Sydney went shopping for cornflakes. As they neared the raisin bran, Harold slipped on seventy-three of his hundred feet. Sydney slid after him! Picking themselves up, Harold and Sydney hollered, "To h— with cornflakes! Let's get some puffed rice!"

STRUCTURING PARAGRAPH PATTERNS

The test of a writer's ability to organize thoughts for expression is a series of paragraphs that flow logically into one another and each one of which communicates a major thought with supporting detail. A paragraph is considered by most authorities as a group of interrelated sentences that project a single idea. Often the idea of a paragraph is set forth in a sentence—the topic sentence—and it is this big thought that gives unity to the paragraph. All other sentences must in some way relate to the idea in the topic sentence.

There are a number of ways to construct unified paragraphs. Sometimes writers construct paragraphs that build inductively toward their major idea; they start with several sentences that relate details in a logical sequence and end with a topic sentence that ties up the whole. At other times, writers build deductively; they state their major point and then marshall the details to support it. At still other times, writers sandwich their topic sentence between two layers of related description, tucking the main idea somewhere in the middle of a paragraph. Sometimes, too, the topic sentence remains unwritten. Writers assume that their audience can perceive the interrelationships among the component sentences.

In some respects, composing is a technical endeavor; good writers know that paragraphs are generally constructed in certain ways and apply their knowledge in a rather systematic way. But composing paragraph patterns that flow smoothly from one idea to another is equally an artistic endeavor; good writers have an internal feel about the way ideas fit together. They sense when paragraphs do not develop smoothly and when a different arrangement of thoughts or a change in pace is necessary. As part of school writing programs, young people should acquire both technical skill and artistic sense.

Learning to Organize Paragraphs Around Main Ideas

To help children acquire skill and artistic sense in handling paragraph patterns, teachers must stress paragraphing from the very beginning and in a variety of contexts. Here are some ways of proceeding, starting with the first sentences that kindergarten teachers record for children on experience story charts.

Building Skills Through Charting. One of the most typical writing experiences in kindergarten and first grade is writing the "news of the day." Children contribute sentences about what has or will happen that day. The teacher prints the sentences on the board, and later, as seat-work, the children copy the news as a penmanship exercise.

In one second-grade class the news went something like this:

Peter got splashed by a car.
It was raining this morning.
Linda didn't come to school.
Janie fell in a puddle.
There was a large dark cloud.
Maxie was late because he found a big lake in the road.

As children dictated idea-sentences, the teacher recorded them in a list in the order given. Then the children proceeded to copy the "paragraph" in the same way.

In operating in that manner, the teacher was involved in what could well be called "mis-teaching." Sentences are not listed down in writing; they are grouped together in paragraphs. Third-grade teachers often complain that youngsters who have been "taught" by this method generally write their "paragraphs" in the same way—simply listing each sentence in random order, making no attempt to group related thoughts together.

In actuality such writing experiences as the news are golden oppor-tunities for teaching children logical paragraph development. Instead of asking children to copy the random list as if it were truly a composition, the teacher takes the obvious next step and continues: "We seem to have two kinds of sentences here. Which sentences tell us about things people did this morning? Which tell us about the weather this morning? Which kinds of sentences—about people or about the weather—should we rewrite first? Why? What sentence will be our beginning one? Let's put *1* in front of that sentence. What sentence will be our second one? Let's put 2 in front of that. What sentence will be our third sentence? Let's put a 3 in front of it." Having reordered all their sentences, children go on to identify the big idea of the entire paragraph and create a title that sum-marizes that idea. At that point, children can rewrite the sentences, following the order of the numbers and including the summarizing title:

IN THE RAIN

It was raining this morning. There was a large, dark cloud. Peter got splashed by a car. Janie fell in the puddle. Maxie was late to school because he found a big lake on the road. Linda didn't come to school.

What is being taught here is not only the projection of ideas for writing but the perception of relationships among ideas as well. For that reason, whenever children write prose together in teacher-guided groups, they should first be urged to share whatever ideas they have. After expressing those, children go back, as in the previous example, to organize ideas into cohesive wholes—paragraphs that start with the first word indented.

With very able first or second graders, a teacher might strive for an even tighter organization of ideas by asking, "What sentence does not tell us something that happened to us on our rainy day?" Children may identify the sentence about the black cloud as one that does not "fit" with the others. If they identify a sentence as "not belonging," youngsters can delete it from their paragraph.

Building Paragraphing Skills Through Group Writing. Most primary-grade teachers at some point use group experience charting as a strategy to involve children in writing. The process, however, has application at upper levels as a means of teaching specific writing skills. It is particularly useful when preceded by group brainstorming and categorization of responses and when followed by small group writing experiences, as is demonstrated in this lesson sequence designed for an upper elementary grade by Tina James, the teacher.

Ms. James's class had just completed a regional study of mountains as part of their unit sequence in the social studies. Concerned with having youngsters review major concepts about life in mountainous regions and at the same time cement their growing understanding of and skill in working with paragraph patterns, she wrote the following objectives in her lesson plan book:

Objectives
1. Having studied several mountainous regions of the world, students will be able to brainstorm a multitude of facts and ideas as a means of recalling and reviewing what they have encountered.
2. Students will see relationships between facts and ideas that "belong together," because these are on some common sub-topic of a larger topic.
3. Students will learn to write cohesive paragraphs containing points that are based on the same main idea.
4. Students will be able to work cooperatively together, learning to accept ideas of others working on the same task.
5. Students will be able to function as part of a large-class brainstorming group; they will recognize the needs of others, wait their turns, and confidently contribute ideas of their own.

In this instance, lesson objectives were drawn from both the language arts and the social studies. Since writing must have content, in school programs this content can validly come from any of the areas in the curriculum.

Next, Ms. James considered the materials she would need for the project. She listed:

Materials

1. Notebooks and references students have compiled.
2. Colored chalks and chalkboard space.
3. First draft paper, pens, and pencils.
4. Transparencies, transparency pens, and overhead projector.

Then she designed the sequence of activities that would lead children toward her specified objectives. She thought of the kinds of questions and structuring remarks she might use in introducing the sequence. These she wrote down in columnar fashion as follows:

Procedures

1. Place three student scribes at sections of the board; others refer to notebooks and texts they have been using during the unit.

2. Brainstorm facts and ideas about mountainous regions of the world. Students call out points in the order they come to mind and as fast as scribes can record on the board.

3. Students circle with yellow chalk points that focus on the same overarching topic (e.g., names of mountains, features of a geographic nature found in mountains, fun activities carried out in mountains, or economic activities); they circle with white points that focus on a different topic; they do this with different colors for the variety of main ideas represented by the points on the board.

4. Write a cooperative class paragraph based on the points listed

Questions & Structuring Remarks

2. Let's see what we remember about the mountainous regions of the world. Let's fill the board with facts and ideas galore. One at a time—but as fast as we can!

3. Which of these points relate to the same bigger idea? How are these points related? How do they differ? Which of these belong together? Why? What main idea label can we attach to these points?

4. If we were to write a paragraph about the points in this category

(*continued on next page*)

Procedures   *Questions & Structuring Remarks*

under one topic. A student scribe writes the sentences as dictated on the board. The class edits the paragraph.

(yellow), what would make a good first introductory sentence? What points would it be logical to state next? Why? Let's go back now to check our punctuation and spelling.

5. Divide next into three-person writing teams, each to compose a paragraph on one of the other main idea topics identified and circled in a color. Students write a first draft, edit it for errors, and print a copy on a transparency for projection.

6. Students project transparencies as viewers react to the logical organization of ideas and the grammaticalness of the written construction.

6. Is this a good first sentence? Why or why not? Does this point belong in this paragraph? Why? Are the points developed in good order? What might be a stronger order?

7. A group of compositors comprised of volunteers works on the paragraphs to see if they can put them together into a multiparagraphed sequence. Later they orally share their production with the class. Listeners decide if the transition words added to the paragraphs are adequate.

7. Let's listen to see if the flow of ideas from one paragraph to the next is smooth. What transition words did the compositors add? What other words may be necessary to make the transition between ideas clearer to follow?

Evaluation: Evaluation will be in terms of the scope of ideas brainstormed and the unity of the paragraphs written by teams.

Having planned out her objectives, materials, procedures, possible questions and structuring remarks, and the evaluation of the lesson, Tina James was ready to teach the sequence. Her focus was on mountains, but clearly the same sequence can be used within any topical area about which youngsters have acquired considerable information through previous study. But note that the sequence in terms of writing activity began with teacher-guided group writing. As children composed together, guided by their teacher's probing questions, they were actually learning paragraphing skills that they later applied during team writing. Only when they had participated in group writing experiences did they write paragraphs individually.

Teachers like Tina James have found teacher-guided group writing followed by team writing activity to be a powerful strategy for developing writing skills, especially those skills related to organization of thoughts into cohesive paragraphs. Writing together, children are thinking together and talking out relationships that exist within content to be expressed in paragraph form. Later, writing individually, children may use some of the same kinds of questions raised by teacher and teammates during group writing to organize ideas in their own compositions.

Building Paragraphing Skills Through Highly Structured Writing Assignments. There are a number of ways that writing assignments can be structured to build paragraphing skills. One way is to give young writers two topic sentences that are similar, but not identical, and have them write a paragraph about each, working first in small teams and then as individuals. Writing together, students must ask: "What kinds of thoughts belong in the first paragraph? What thoughts fit into the main idea of the second?" One of the authors has tried this even with college students who have trouble organizing paragraphs, asking participants to write two paragraphs, one beginning *The parking problem at the college has become a major concern of both students and faculty*, a second beginning *The spring season has made the parking situations at the college almost impossible.* In the first paragraph, students include details to prove student and faculty concern: letters to the editor of the school paper have appeared; students have spoken to their professors about being late to class as a result of the parking problem; professors have discussed the situation in faculty meetings; student sit-ins are being considered. In the second paragraph, students include details to show how the spring season has added to the problem: showers have turned parking lots into pools; grassy areas used for parking have become mud fields in which students can lose their cars; walking from the more distant lots is hazardous as students try to avoid water-filled potholes.

Examples of similar types of topic-sets for use in elementary classrooms, especially in the upper grades, are the following:

Example 1: People are becoming more concerned about pollution of the environment.
We are rapidly turning our rivers into cesspools of pollution.

Example 2: To play in the snow is fun.
          The snowstorm struck last night.
Example 3: Dogs should not be allowed to run loose.
          A person who has a dog should be willing to take care
          of it.
          A dog can be a good friend.

This writing assignment more closely replicates the actual task of writing
unified paragraphs than the traditional exercise of underlining topic
sentences in paragraphs from a language book. No relation exists between being able to underline topic sentences and being able to write
cohesive paragraphs. If children are to be asked to underline topic
sentences, they should work with their own paragraphs and underline to
determine whether each paragraph they have constructed is built around
one big idea.

A second kind of structured activity for teaching paragraph unity is
reported by a third-grade teacher, Elaine Winters. Ms. Winters constructs paragraphs that contain one sentence that does not relate to the
others. Her students take turns donning a detective's cap to identify the
sentence that does not belong in the paragraph. She then has them focus
on paragraphs they have written to detect any intruders.

Still another approach is reported in *Individualized Language Arts*
(Board of Education, Weehawken, New Jersey, 1974). In this program,
youngsters are given a series of related words to build into a sentence. To
start, such a series might be *bear, weather, often, see, many*. Later, they
are given more sophisticated words that they must build into a cohesive
paragraph. Again, to make the activity work, words must relate to some
general topic and be ones that children know through content-area study;
for example, *rapid, cities, energetic, resourceful, mind, plan, labor,
natural resources*. The Weehawken plan also suggests expanding given
word lists to include items children are learning to spell; for example, a
list for paragraph construction might be comprised of *astronaut,
module, Mars, space, they're, their, there*.

A related approach is to provide youngsters not with topics to
research in the library but with a topic sentence. In the library, upper
graders collect only data that relate directly to the big idea embodied in
the given sentence. Possible sentences to use here are *Thomas Jefferson
was a believer in religious freedom for all. Thomas Jefferson contributed
to his country by writing the Constitution. Thomas Jefferson valued
education.* Returning from the library and using their social studies texts
as a source of additional information, in teams youngsters compose
paragraphs that begin with the paragraph starters. Later, as they share
their products with the class, classmates listen to see if all data included

relate to the big ideas of the paragraph. Through such an activity, young people are learning basic writing skills even as they acquire understanding of the content areas that take up a substantial portion of classroom time starting in intermediate grades.

Learning to Sequence Paragraphs

In constructing effective paragraphs, writers must sequence their ideas so that one point builds naturally toward the next. As early as first grade, children should work with sequential patterns. They can be asked to line up objects according to size. Later on, they can make time lines on which they order events chronologically. At the same time, as part of oral interaction, a teacher can help children recap recent events. Talking together, they can list events, starting with those that happened first. A teacher can encourage children to recount steps by asking, "What do we do first? next? then? after that?" A teacher can have children orally give directions by asking, "What is the best way to get to Interstate 95? Where do we go first? Then where? Finally?"

As children record ideas on paper, similar kinds of activities can be structured. In this section let us look at specific strategies for building sequencing skills as part of paragraph writing.

Building Sequencing Skills Through Group Writing. Not only can experience story charting be used to develop organizational skills, but the strategy can also help children sequence their ideas in a logical fashion. For example, Maryanne Forest, a second-grade teacher, took her class on a short walk to the neighborhood stores. Upon returning, the children dictated a report on their outing:

OUR WALK TO THE STORES
Our class went on a walk today. We visited some stores. First, we went to Priscilla's Candy Shop. The lady gave us chocolate candy. Then we went to the pet store. We saw dogs, monkeys, birds, and an alligator. After that we went to the florist shop. We watched a lady make a bouquet. We saw roses, orchids, and big ferns. Our class had fun on our walk to the stores. We want to go again.

That the teacher helped the children sequence their ideas by asking guiding questions is obvious in the tight organization of the paragraph. Ms. Forest probably began by asking, "What did we do today?" and followed up with "Where did we go first? What happened at the candy shop? Then where did we go? What did we see there? What did we do after that?" Hers was an introductory lesson in the craft of writing that stressed intuitive understanding. Each question she asked helped children structure a sentence response that included a carefully chosen transitional word and detail that logically followed what was already written. In this way, she was teaching writing skills not by giving and explaining definitions and rules but by having the children experience the process firsthand.

This strategy of using highly structured questions to help students develop a logical pattern of sentences within a paragraph as part of teacher-guided group writing can be used with a variety of content—content from the social studies and science as well as from firsthand experiences. Its usefulness extends into the upper grades.

Building Sequencing Skills Through Work with Framed Paragraphs. Many programs recommend that children also work within the confines of paragraph frameworks in which a topic sentence and other key sentence beginnings are supplied. Children must build a paragraph around these beginnings. For example,

Title _____
Last week I went to the _____. I saw _____
_____. When _____
_____. Then _____
_____. At last _____
_____. I thought _____
_____.

Writing within such a given paragraph framework, youngsters can vary it as they see fit, for the purpose is not to stifle thought but to provide a logical scheme for expressing it.

Of course, some group oral experiences with framed paragraphs should precede individual composition, but the transition from group to individual writing can be a quick one since youngsters find it relatively easy to generate sentences when given some beginning points. Here, for example, are some paragraphs composed within the above framework by youngsters in Madeline Bruhn's third grade. The reader should note how much more syntactically mature the sentences in the paragraphs are as compared to average compositions written by third graders.

VISITING MY DAD

Last week I went to Rumson to visit my Dad at work. My Mom took me in the car. When I got there, I saw my Dad working. He was cutting wood with a power saw. He had been in the hospital so I helped him. Then I helped him by carrying wood. At last the house was finished and we went home. I thought it was time to eat because I was hungry from carrying wood.

THE CIRCUS

Last week I went to the circus. I saw striped tigers and large leopards while we were eating popcorn. When we came, we looked at the fattest lady in the world. Then we explored all around the circus looking at all the animals, insects, and mammals. At last it was lunchtime and we ate at a picnic table at the circus grounds and had tunafish sandwiches. I thought it was very much fun because the circus is always an exciting place, because I like seeing animals, and because I really like visiting everywhere.

THE BIG PARK

Last week I went to the big park in New York City. I saw big monkey bars and a big fat soft tire swing. When Mom came, I got mad because we had to go home. Then we made ham and cheese sandwiches. I thought it was fun because I got to go on the big swings.

Framing can also be used to get youngsters started in story creation. Paragraph starters can be devised by lifting the content from actual story beginnings, leaving only the key introducing words, which youngsters use to start their own stories. Here are five examples of beginning paragraph frames based on familiar stories.

- A paragraph starter based on *The Funny Little Woman* by Arlene Mosel (Dutton, 1972):

> Title: The Funny _____
> Long ago in old _____, there lived a funny little _____ who liked to laugh, ''_____ _____'' and who liked to make _____ out of _____.
> One morning . . . .

- A paragraph starter based on *Why Mosquitoes Buzz in People's Ears* by Verna Aardema (Dial, 1975):

> Title: Why _____
> One morning a _____ saw a/an _____ who was _____. The _____ said to the _____, ''_____, you will never believe what I saw yesterday!''
> ''Try me,'' said the _____.
> The _____ said, '' . . . .

- A paragraph starter based on *Once a Mouse* by Marcia Brown (Scribner, 1961):

Title: Once a _____
One day a _____ sat thinking about _____
_____. Suddenly, he saw a/an _____
about to be _____.
The _____ hurried _____. . . .

- A paragraph starter based on *The Story About Ping* by Marjorie Flack (out of print):

Title: The Story About _____
Once upon a time there was a beautiful young _____
named _____. _____ lived with . . . .
Each morning . . . .

- A paragraph starter based on *Someday, Said Mitchell* by Barbara Williams (Dutton, 1976):

Title: "_____," said _____
"Someday, I will be _____," said
_____. "Then I will . . . ."

Building Sequencing Skills by Working with Transitional Words. Very important in sequencing ideas is the construction of smooth transitions placed in juxtaposition. As writers order their ideas, either consciously or intuitively, they build in transitions according to the nature of the relationships they perceive in the material. Making a point and then wishing to modify it in some way, writers may pen, "However . . . ," "Nevertheless . . . ," "On the other hand . . . ," or "Regardless of this . . . ,". Expressing an idea and then wishing to add a related thought, they write, "Also . . . ," "In like manner . . . ," "Then, too . . . ," "Likewise . . . ," or "Similarly . . . ." Stating a generalization and then following it with examples, they write, "For instance . . . ," "For example . . . ," "Specifically . . . ," "An instance of . . . ." Describing a sequence of events, they pen, "First . . . ," "Then . . . ," "Later . . . ," and "At last . . . ."

A strategy to help children with transitions is a form of framing that requires the deletion of transitional words from a paragraph.

WHAT THE PROBLEM WAS
John liked Susan. _____ he did not want to take her to the dance. He had very good reasons. _____ he did not have the money. _____ he did not have a suit. _____ he did not have even the slightest knowledge of how to dance.

Given such a paragraph, students fill in the deleted words, using as many different arrangements as possible. As they propose alternate possibilities, they record transitional words on a large chart to be kept clearly visible during writing.

Children in upper elementary grades can also be asked to combine sentences, forming different transitional patterns. Take the first two sentences in the John-and-Susan paragraph. How can they be combined to communicate his liking and his not wanting to go to the dance? Students will propose:

- Although John liked Susan, he did not want to take her to the dance.
- John did not want to take Susan to the dance even though he liked her.
- Despite his liking for Susan, John did not want to take her to the dance.

Such patterns as these employ subordination to make transitions, a topic considered in chapter 6.

Building Sequencing Skills by Modeling Paragraphs After Those in Other Stories. In *Language Experiences in Communication* (Houghton Mifflin, 1976, p. 445), Roach Van Allen recommends that "Children who read and write in a language experience approach environment use the work of published authors as models for their own writing." In *Children's Writing and Language Growth* (Merrill, 1978), Ronald Cramer echoes this recommendation.

Repetitive prose and poetry patterns provide some of the easiest models for children by giving them clues as to how to organize paragraphs and stanzas in writing. Composing within these patterns, young writers learn different ways of handling language on paper through actual use. An instance in point is the cumulative tale, such as "The Old Woman and Her Pig," "The Gingerbread Boy," and "The Bremen Town Musicians." In these tales, at each new happening previous lines are repeated, and at each repetition new lines are added. Thus in "The Old Woman and Her Pig," when the little piggy won't go over the stile, the old woman meets a dog and commands him, "Dog, dog, bite piggy! Piggy won't go over the stile; and I shan't get home tonight." When the dog won't bite piggy, the old woman meets in succession a stick, a fire, water, an ox, a butcher, a rope, and a rat, none of whom will do her bidding to help get piggy over the stile. At last the old woman meets a cat and commands, "Cat, cat, kill rat! Rat won't gnaw rope; rope won't hang butcher; butcher won't kill ox; ox won't drink water; water won't quench fire; fire won't burn stick; stick won't beat dog; dog won't bite piggy; piggy won't get over the stile; and I shan't get home tonight."

Cat responds, "If you will go to the cow and fetch me a saucer of milk, I will kill the rat."

The old woman goes to the cow to ask for milk. The cow answers, "If you will give me some hay, I will give you some milk." The woman brings the cow some hay. As soon as the cow has eaten it, she gives the woman some milk, who in turn gives it to the cat, who kills the rat, who gnaws the rope, which hangs the butcher, who kills the ox, who drinks the water that quenches the fire, that burns the stick, that beats the dog, who then bites piggy, who jumps over the stile; and so the old woman gets home that night.

Children who have listened to the repeating pattern of "The Old Woman and Her Pig," as well as the same pattern in *One Fine Day* by Nonny Hogrogian (Macmillan, 1971), can create their own paragraphs in which a series of events is connected in a similar fashion and lines are repeated and added to in a cumulative way. In so doing, youngsters will have to model their use of quotation marks, commas, and semicolons after that of the writer of the tale. Again, before young people in upper elementary grades attempt the task on their own, oral, teacher-guided group writing demonstrates just how to proceed.

Other stories that lend themselves to modeling are Barbara Emberley's *Drummer Hoff* (Prentice-Hall, 1967), Remy Charlip's *Fortunately* (Parent's Magazine Press, 1964), Leo Lionni's *Pezzettino* (Pantheon, 1975), Judith Viorst's *Alexander and the Terrible, Horrible, No Good, Very Bad Day* (Atheneum, 1972), Pat Hutchins's *Rosie's Walk* (Macmillan, 1968), George Mendoza's *The Gillygoofang* (Dial, undated), and Eric Carle's *The Rooster Who Set Out to See the World* (Franklin Watts, 1972). Using any one of these, child-writers can borrow sentence and paragraph patterns and interject their own content to produce original versions of the story. For instance, modeling after the Viorst book, children can compose *Marvin and the Wonderful, Great, Not Bad, Very Good Day*; modeling after the Hutchins's book, they can create *Jennie's Swim*—the story of an alligator who leaves destruction in her wake; or modeling after the Lionni, they can write about a huge piece who feels dissatisfied with itself.

Poems in storybook form also can be used as models, specifically Julian Scheer and Marvin Bileck's *Rain Makes Applesauce* (Holiday House, 1964), Doris Lund's *Attic of the Wind* (Parent's Magazine Press, 1966), and Christina Rossetti's *What Is Pink?* (ill. by Jose Aruego, Macmillan, 1971). Using any one of these, youngsters composing orally together can brainstorm possible lines based on the model.

In the case of *Rain Makes Applesauce*, Gloria Franzblau's third graders brainstormed other weather words to substitute for rain—their results, *Snow makes popsicles*; *Sleet makes jellybeans*; *Fog makes sauerkraut*; *Sun makes asparagus.* To substitute for "Oh, you're just talking silly talk," they wrote, "No! We're just wishing funny thoughts." Then they went on to create lines not about stars, shoes, houses, dolls, wind, monkeys, and tigers as in the original poem but about boots, buildings, buffalo, bread, back stairs, and batons. In so doing, they were learning how to play with word meanings and sounds in a creative way and how to use repetitive lines to carry thoughts from one stanza or line to the next.

Building Sequencing Skills Through Chaining.   Another exercise for developing skill in transitions is chaining. A chain story is one in which a child begins a story but writes only a first paragraph or in the lower grades a first line. That child passes the story to a second youngster, who adds to it. This continues until several youngsters have contributed.

Smooth transitions are especially important as youngsters add on to a theme started by someone else. To aid in the process the teacher can supply charts that list—

- words to consider if you want to change story direction: *on the other hand, nevertheless, however, whereas.*
- words to consider if you want to continue with the same story direction: *also, now, the next, in the same way, therefore, as a result.*

The teacher can also suggest that children identify a key word or words in the material written by a previous contributor and for continuity repeat these key words in the portion they are adding.

Experience seems to indicate that chain stories on which three children work are more effective than those to which many children contribute a section. Perhaps there is a psychological reason for this: children retain a sense of possession for a story and do not look at the activity merely as a game. There may be a structural reason as well: short stories typically have a beginning, a middle, and an end. Each contributor in a group of three can more readily perceive how his or her addition relates to the whole. Three language-disadvantaged children in one fourth grade wrote the following chain story after enjoying several previous experiences with the activity. Notice that although the three show problems in the area of sentencing, they are beginning rather effectively to handle the sequential development of an idea.

THE BOGEY MAN

One night as I was in bed I saw a shadow. . . . It was very big. Mommy! Mommy! I called, but no one came. And then I reliezed it was the Bogey Man! He crept closer and closer. A bogey a bogey I'd scream if I could.

Second contributor: I got out of bed. I jump out the winow. I got lost out there.

Third contributor: There I saw a man. He had a cape it was scarey he said I'm the boogy man. Then the cape fell off. I found out it was my father. I screamed oh daddy you scared me halve to death! He put me in bed and the next morning he explained.

The End

Serving as poet-in-residence and working with upper elementary students, New Jersey poet Sam Hamod has found that chaining is an effective teaching-learning strategy even as children create poetry. He has youngsters chain in groups of five, with each youngster contributing only one line to which others in the group must add in a way that carries the idea forward. To get children's cerebral juices flowing, he sometimes supplies—not a topic—but a first line such as *Swimming in a sea of meatballs*; *Trapped in a can of sardines*; *Adrift in a tube of toothpaste*. According to Dr. Hamod, such lines have potential, for they ask children to react with all their senses as they create lines about smell, taste, feel, sound, and sight.

Such beginning lines also teach youngsters that a thought need not be started and finished in one line; it can be carried over to following lines as a means of carrying the thought forward. The running on of a thought from one line or couplet to the next is known as *enjambment*. This process can be part of chaining experiences, with youngsters creating lines that spill over into next lines, as in the following piece that Dr. Hamod helped one group create together:

> Swimming in a sea of meatballs, all
> red and squishy, I smell
> the lovely smell of garlic; diving down with my mouth
> open through a sauce crowded with chunks of peppers and
> onions, I have to be hungry; I'll keep
> swimming until I find the spaghetti.

Contributors to this group poem went away feeling good about poetry and about themselves. They also went away with a better understanding of how to bind thoughts and lines together, especially in poetry creation.

SOME SUMMARY THOUGHTS

An integral part of developmental writing programs in elementary schools is work with the thought processes and paragraph patterns so fundamental if youngsters are to learn to write in a manner that communicates their thoughts with clarity and style. For this reason, teachers must design writing activities that relate directly to organizational and thinking problems children are having—activities that ask children to group related ideas together, to visualize relationships, to relate main ideas with significant details, to organize ideas gleaned from references, to create unusual designs, and to select titles and headings that reflect the big ideas they are expressing.

As this chapter points out, this work and play begin with oral encounters with thoughts written down. Children participate in teacher-guided, group-composing sessions in which questions asked by the teacher lead contributors to operate mentally on ideas they are offering. Writing together, youngsters organize ideas into pools and sequence them in ways that facilitate communication. Such teacher-guided writing activity leads naturally into small-group writing in which youngsters apply and refine skills. Team writing in turn leads into independent writing in which developing writers create on their own. It is through such individual and group writing experiences that children and youth begin to acquire skill in manipulating ideas for writing.

6 LET CHILDREN
BUILD SENTENCES ◀▶
acquiring sentence sense

True ease in writing comes from art, not chance.
As those move easiest who have learn'd to dance.
Alexander Pope, ESSAY ON CRITICISM

Joe, a youngster in fifth grade, described a brief friendship with a dog in this unedited story:

HOW MY FRIEND KING AND I MET

One summer day I was walking to the store with my sister and a little boy. Suddenly a great big dog had our attention, there he was standing on the other side of the street. All of a sudden he came over to us, we petted him for a while then he looked very hungary and thirsty. So my sister went in the house and got some water the little boy got him some dog food because he had a dog all ready had a dog. Then we decided to call him King because he was so big. We played with him a while, then he got tiered and layed down for a while in front of my house. After he feel asleep and woke up again. The little boy brought out a cracker, then we wanted to see if he could do tricks. So I saw if he would beg. So I took a cracker and threw it in the air and he jumped up and gulped the cracker up. The next day my father found an owner to the dog in the paper. When the owner came to pick him up. We saddly walk him to the car. Then said Good by King we will always remember you!

THE END

Joe's story has some good features. The sequence of events recounted is easy to follow, and his choice of words is appropriate in the context of the story. His use of conversational style strengthens the story, making the ending more striking. But it is obvious to the reader that Joe lacks sentence sense. He often writes two sentences as one: "All of a sudden he came over, we petted him for a while." He also writes incomplete sentences: "When the owner came to pick him up." Then, too, he composes sentences strung together with a series of "ands." These sentencing problems weaken the impact of his composition.

Joe is not alone in his inability to perceive sentence boundaries. Writing incomplete and run-on sentences is a rather common problem that extends even into the adult population. It is a problem that teachers of written expression must tackle head-on, for the ability to handle sentence patterns is one of the most basic skills writers must possess if they are to communicate their ideas with any degree of clarity.

GETTING A SENSE OF SENTENCE IN THE EARLY YEARS

Instruction in sentencing should begin in the early years as part of experience charting; as children compose cooperatively, they dictate sentences to the teacher and then return to read what they have dictated. They also listen to and generate sentence patterns as part of general oral activity. In this section, let us look at ways that charting and listening activities can be structured to help children build sentence sense.

Dictating and Reading Sentences Together

The words *sentence* and *period* should enter children's listening and speaking vocabularies early in their school experience. For example, one kindergarten teacher, Evelyn Winters, uses the word *sentence* as children dictate on the very first day of school. On this day, children talk about things they see in their kindergarten room. They name objects they like. Then Ms. Winters asks, "Who can give me one sentence that begins 'I see a . . .' that I will print for you up here on my charting paper?" Children volunteer such statements as "I see a sink." "I see a big doll." "I see a green rug." As three or four children proffer suggested sentences, Ms. Winters records them on the chart, starting with a capital I and ending with a period. Having recorded three or four sentences for the children, Ms. Winters queries, "What do you see at the end of each of your sentences?" An observant youngster tells about the big dot found at the end of each. Other youngsters hop up to take turns pointing out the big dot, which Ms. Winters has begun to call *a period*. At this point Ms. Winters asks for one more sentence to add to the chart. Recording it, she requests the youngster who has dictated the sentence to come forward and add the period at the end. From then on, the children—not the teacher—become period makers, contributing the periods at the ends of sentences the teacher has recorded for them.

Following any dictation, youngsters and teacher return to their sentences to read and reread them. Children not only read words together; they "read" the periods. Guiding children's eyes from left to right across the page with her hand, the teacher pauses at the period, halting children's reading momentarily at this point.

After a number of experiences generating fundamental kernel sentences in this way, Ms. Winters introduces the "asking sentence." She herself at the end of a dictation suggests the last sentence. For example, she may proffer the sentence "Do we like our school?" as the final one in this dictated sequence:

OUR SCHOOL

In school we play. In school we learn to read. In school we paint
some pictures. In school we talk in a circle. Do we like our school?

Children read and reread their composition aloud and together. They listen to the sound they make at each sentence end. Then Ms. Winters may ask, "What happens to our voices at the end of the last sentence? Let's listen as we read together." As children rechorus the last sentence, they follow Ms. Winters's hand as it moves across the sentence and moves upward at the end. Ms. Winters changes the period already inscribed on the chart to a question mark to show the upward movement at the end of this asking sentence. In so doing, she uses the phrase *asking sentence*. Children go back to reread the other sentences—ones they have begun to call *telling sentences*. Now, whenever they dictate, children decide whether each sentence recorded is a telling or an asking one; they decide whether they should write down a period or a question mark. In each case, they decide by reading aloud and listening for the sentence sound.

As youngsters move on to read in groups and independently, they should be encouraged to interpret the punctuation sounds. Many beginning readers read sentences not as thought units but word-by-word. The teacher should suggest, "Boys and girls, let's read that sentence together just as if we were speaking it." The teacher joins in the oral reading and children model their interpretation after the teacher's, reading in a more flowing manner that more clearly communicates the overall meaning and helps them perceive the relationship between written and spoken thoughts and between vocal intonations and punctuation marks.

As part of reading together, the first-grade teacher can continue the stress on interpreting punctuation by focusing attention on the sounds of exclamation points and commas. Meeting a sentence such as *"Help! Help!" cried Bruce*, the teacher suggests, "Let's all read that sentence just the way Bruce must have said it." Having read it with great excitement in their voices, children look to see how they know that the sentence should be read that way. Now as they encounter other exclaiming sentences, they show the exclamation point in their voices.

Some of the relationships between punctuation and meaningful pauses within sentences can be taught in much the same way. Meeting a sentence in context—"Joe, Lou, and Betty found the lost letter"—they practice reading it to show the comma stops. In this context, emphasis is on reading to communicate clearly to listeners; later as children record through dictation or through their own efforts wielding pencil or pen, they begin to apply their growing understanding of comma stops to writing down their own thoughts.

Listening to Sentence Sounds

One of the simplest and most effective techniques for helping children apply their growing sentence sense in their own writing is to have them listen to their own sentences. Youngsters can be asked to read their compositions to the teacher. When reading aloud, children who have had considerable work with interpreting punctuation orally as described above will almost naturally pause at the ends of sentences they have written. Questions for the teacher to ask at this point are "Why did you stop there?" and "What punctuation mark do we use for a long pause?" Children can add periods wherever they naturally pause for "large-sized stops." Reading, *Do you have a tadpole?* children's voices will go up at the end—an upward movement to be shown on paper by the question mark. Similarly, reading *When the owner came to pick him up . . . ,* children will make only a "small-sized stop"—a stop to be recorded with a comma, not a period.

Observing in a third-grade class, one of the authors saw a teacher employ this technique with a child who had written the sentence *Why was Peggy a stranger in the city?* with a period as end punctuation. During an individual conference, the teacher urged the child to read the sentence aloud and then asked, "Is that a telling or an asking sentence?" The child's response was that the sentence was a question, and without prompting he added the question mark.

In a similar way, oral exercises prepare children to hear sentences in their own writing. The teacher of young children can read the following sentences:

> The dogs are barking.
> The girls are singing.
> The elephants are running.

After that, the teacher can suggest, "I am going to read some groups of words to you. Some will be sentences like the ones I just gave. They have the sound of a sentence. We can use them in writing. Some will not be sentences; we cannot use them in our writing. Let's decide:

> Barking in the woods
> The horses are eating.
> Eating peanuts
> Running home
> The boys are fighting.

By second and third grades the same technique can be used with run-on sentences. Sentences can be read to children, who must determine where the first sentence ends and the second sentence begins by vocally interpreting the set:

> All of a sudden he came over to us we petted him for awhile.
> We gave King a cracker he jumped up and down.
> The dog did tricks for us he sat up and begged for a cracker.
> The dog fell asleep he woke up again.
> The little boy got some water he gave it to King.

This type of listening activity can be structured most effectively with the assistance of an overhead projector. After the teacher has read a run-on set and the children have heard the sentence boundaries, sentences can be projected, and youngsters can put in the periods, or pause markers.

Sometimes sentence sets can be taken directly from students' papers for group analysis as in the activity just described—a technique called *sentence lifting* in the integrated Open Court Reading Program. Children working orally together in teacher-guided groups read sentences composed by one member and decide where sentences begin and end and what punctuation is needed to interpret the sentence sounds.

A related technique is *sentence dictation*—another approach that is an integral component of Open Court. The teacher dictates three or four sentences to children, who must record them on paper, and, in so doing, must translate sentence sounds into punctuation marks. Children take turns writing what they have recorded on paper onto the chalkboard. To test the accuracy of their placement and choice of punctuation marks, children chorus the sentences to listen for sentence sounds.

Sentence Building

Children who exhibit lack of sentence sense may benefit from writing activities that focus directly on writing kernel sentences. The topic should be a limited one and require youngsters to repeat the same pattern. Youngsters in lower elementary grades may begin by writing just one sentence that starts with one of the following phrases:

- Happiness is . . . .
- I wish that . . . .
- A friend is . . . .
- Dogs are . . . .
- Thanksgiving is for . . . .

Later they can write a series of sentences, each one beginning with the same sentence starter, as in:

DOGS

Dogs are fun to play with. Dogs are nice to have with you. Dogs are noisy sometimes. Dogs are friends.

Sometimes, if each youngster is asked to write one sentence that begins with the same two or three words, they can later build one paragraph by including a sentence contributed by each participant.

' In the same way a teacher can ask students to generate sentences that adhere to the same sentence pattern but differ in the specific words contained therein. An easy beginning is with a simple noun phrase and verb phrase pattern comprised of only three words:

| *Noun Phrase* | *Verb Phrase* |
| The penguin | hopped. |

Working from that beginning, children can create sentence ladders:

NP	*VP*
The penguin	hopped.
The crow	cawed.
The truck	crashed.
The building	burned.
The water	boiled.

They can go on to expand the thought by adding to the verb phrase to tell how:

NP	VP
The penguin	hopped into the air.
The crow	cawed loudly.
The truck	crashed into the wall.
The building	burned all night.
The water	boiled violently.

Today linguists tend to define the sentence in terms of a noun phrase/verb phrase combination. In some language arts programs this concept is introduced as early as first grade. Rather than simply having youngsters pick out noun and verb phrases, however, teachers should encourage children to generate sentences in the basic kernel patterns and then to expand on them by adding words that supply greater detail.

Carl Lefevre has identified four basic English sentence patterns with which children can play in upper primary grades. They are as follows (*Linguistics, English, and the Language Arts*, Teachers College Press, 1973):

	Noun Phrase	*Verb Phrase*	
Pattern I:	*Noun*	*Verb*	*Adjective or Adverb*
Examples:			
N V	The penguin	hopped.	
N V Adv	The water	boiled	violently.
N V Adj	The package	arrived	intact.

	Noun	*Verb*	*Noun*
Pattern II:			
Examples:			
N V N	The dog	bit	the mail carrier.
N V N	He	patted	the dog.
N V N	Mother	forgot	her sister.

	Noun	*Verb*	*Noun*	*Noun or Adjective*
Pattern III:				
Examples:				
N V N N	I	gave	Mary	a bicycle.
N V N N	She	considered	me	an enemy.
N V N Adj	He	made	his wife	happy.

Pattern IV:	*Noun*	*Linking Verb*	*Noun or Adjective*
Examples:			
N LV N	My brother	was	the winner.
N LV N	The explorers	became	heroes.
N LV Adj	Some children	are	unhappy.

Youngsters should have plenty of oral work with the patterns as a basis for writing. The format for this oral work includes these steps:

- The teacher supplies sentence models that meet the specifications of a pattern: "She touched the stove." "She cleaned the floor." "He washed the dishes." "The boys lifted the rugs."
- Children suggest more sentences that meet the specifications.
- Children and teacher analyze together the structure of the pattern and discover the pattern of the samples given as examples.

Using the sentences they have generated orally as models, youngsters eventually concoct sentences on paper, perhaps functioning in cooperative writing teams that race each other to see which can produce the greatest number of sentences in a given time period.

Another technique through which students can generate sentences is building from a given group of words. In preparation, the teacher or a child-scribe prints word cards: *elephants, the, ran, slowly, steadily, and, every, big, gray.* Each active participant receives a card. Cooperatively, they build a sentence from their words, placing adjectives and adverbs in appropriate spots in the sentence. Printed on cards, word groups such as *into the woods, through the fields,* and *of long grass* can be added to the sentence as children work with more complex structures.

This type of sentence work helps children acquire a sense of the word orders employed in standard English. Children who grow up speaking a nonstandard dialect of English may order their words differently and may need extensive oral work if they are also to become proficient in standard English word order. The same is even more true of youngsters who are learning English as a second language. Whereas children who hear standard word orders at home use them almost automatically, those who speak a different dialect or language may need many more oral activities as a base for writing standard English patterns.

Children build an intuitive understanding of what a sentence is through oral activity with sentences. Instead of beginning with a meaningless definition of a sentence, they gradually acquire sentence sense as they continually manipulate different kinds of sentence patterns. Emphasis is on generating sentences, not on naming, identifying, or defining patterns.

PLAYING WITH SENTENCES

For youngsters moving through primary into intermediate grades, transformational linguists offer several approaches to the sentence that not only help young people understand the way their language works but also have the potential to help them as they write. These approaches include sentence transforming, sentence expanding, sentence dismantling, and sentence combining through joining and embedding.

Sentence Transforming

The sentence *The lemon pie is in the oven.* can be transformed in a number of ways. It can be changed into a question by changing word order as in *Is the lemon pie in the oven?* It can be made to show negation by adding the word *not*: *The lemon pie is not in the oven.* The sentence can also be changed to show a different time relationship: *The lemon pie was in the oven.* or *The lemon pie will be in the oven.* It can be changed to indicate a difference in number: *The lemon pies are in the oven.*

Children can play with some of these kinds of transformations as a means of getting a hold on the sentence, for when play is carried out orally, emphasis is on the sounds of sentence patterns. Starting even in primary grades, children can listen to a piece and then play orally with it—a piece such as "One, Two."

ONE, TWO
One, two,
Buckle your shoe.
Three, four,
Shut the door.
Five, six,
Pick up sticks.
Seven, eight,
Lay them straight.
Nine, ten,
A big, fat hen.

Oral play can begin by chorusing together while simultaneously making comma gestures with the right hand at appropriate short pauses and period gestures with the left at longer pauses. Studying the alternate lines they have chorused, youngsters can select the one that does not pattern like the others—*A big, fat hen*—and can transform it into a line that commands—*Chase a hen.*

Chorusing can lead as well into transforming alternate lines into telling sentences, into asking sentences, and then into exclaiming sentences, changing the punctuation to reflect the changes in meaning.

Later, working in composing teams, youngsters can create their own original versions of "One, Two," deciding together whether to adhere to a telling, commanding, questioning, or exclaiming pattern. They can revise what they have written to transform sentences into a negative pattern. Responding to this cooperative assignment, one older group composed:

ONE, TWO
One, two,
Is the sky blue?
Three, four,
Do you want more?
Five, six,
Will you play tricks?
Seven, eight,
Are you coming late?
Nine, ten,
Can you start again?

Notice that each question begins with a different question-marking word; this happened because the teacher had recorded on the board possible question beginnings from which youngsters could select in writing alternate lines.

A number of poems found in such anthologies as *Childcraft Encyclopedia*, volume 1, *Poetry* can be adapted for language play with transformations of kernel sentences. Another easy example is Evelyn Beyer's "Jump or Jiggle":*

JUMP OR JIGGLE
Frogs jump;
Caterpillars hump.
   Worms wiggle;
   Bugs jiggle.
Rabbits hop;
Horses clop.
   Snakes slide;
   Sea gulls glide.
Mice creep;
Deer leap.
   Puppies bounce;
   Kittens pounce.
Lions stalk—
But—
I walk!

---

*Evelyn Beyer, "Jump or Jiggle," in Lucy Sprague Mitchell, *Another Here and Now Story Book*. Reprinted by permission of E. P. Dutton. Copyright 1937 by E. P. Dutton and Co., Inc. Copyright renewal © 1965 by Lucy Sprague Mitchell.

The teacher begins: "I am going to change the first line of the poem we have just chorused together. Listen carefully to my change, 'A frog jumps.' Who can change the second line in the same way—the line about the caterpillars?" Children who proffer changed lines must remember them so that when all the nouns have been transformed from plural to singular and when the last line has been changed from "But I walk" to "But he walks," each child can repeat his or her line in sequence as part of a choral speaking. Later, children can create original versions of the piece, first using a plural noun phrase and then a singular one. A good beginning is simply, "Birds sing."

This latter kind of work is an oral way of handling agreement of subject and predicate words. For children to handle this usage on paper, essentially they must be able to hear the sounds and feel comfortable with them. In short, "A bird sings" and "Birds sing" must sound normal; "A bird sing" and "Birds sings" are not normal to their ears. Such activity is particularly important for children who are learning standard English as a second language or dialect.

Sentence Expanding

Just as youngsters handle oral transformations of sentences, so too they can play with sentence expansions. "Jump or Jiggle," for example, can be used as a stepping-stone into expanding kernel sentences through addition of adjectives and adverbs and as an introduction to the notion that placing words in different positions in a sentence changes meaning and sound. A teacher can ask students, "Who can add a word between *A* and *frog* in our version of "Jump or Jiggle"? (A frog jumps; A caterpillar humps.) "Who can add a word between *A* and *caterpillar*?" The result can be an expanded piece that begins:

JUMP OR JIGGLE
A friendly frog jumps;
A fat caterpillar humps.
A long worm wiggles;
A baby bug jiggles.

Youngsters can also expand the verb phrase to produce such lines as "A friendly frog jumps carefully;" and "A fat caterpillar humps slowly." Dissatisfied with the sounds of these lines, they can look around for another location in the sentence into which they can move *slowly* and *carefully*. The result can be an expanded piece that now begins:

JUMP OR JIGGLE
A friendly frog carefully jumps;
A fat caterpillar slowly humps.

A long worm always wiggles;
A baby bug never jiggles.

Based on their work with a poetry model, children can create original versions that pattern similarly but have different content. They begin in this case by composing together orally a "two-fer"—a piece that has only two words to a line, a noun and a verb.

One way to get the sentence building going is to ask "Let's brainstorm things that happen on the highway. Give me only two words that follow the pattern of my line, *Horns honk*. Who has a two-word line like mine?"

Children will proffer such lines as *Cars race, Motorcycles roar, Trucks speed, Lights blink, Buses move, Children cross, Police chase, Horns blare, Sirens scream, People talk, Dogs bark*. At that point, the teacher helps by asking, "Who can give me a two-word line that rhymes with *Cars race*?" A probable answer is *Police chase*. Doing the same with a line such as *People talk*, participants may suggest *Children walk*. Working with *Horns blare*, children may offer *Lights glare*. Putting the three sets together, creators have an original two-fer to which they can add a summing-up with three words as Evelyn Beyer did in "Jump or Jiggle."

RACE OR CHASE
Cars race;
Police chase.
  Horns blare;
  Lights glare.
People talk;
Children walk.
  Trucks load—
  Along the road.

And, of course, children can expand their two-fers to form three-fers with three words to the line or four-fers with four words to the line. For example, "Race or Chase" can be expanded to a three-fer by adding adjectives:

RACE OR CHASE
Big cars race;
Watchful police chase.
  Harsh horns blare;
  Bright lights glare.
Happy people talk;
Young children walk.
  Heavy trucks load—
  Along the crowded road.

Figure 6.1. A sentence-building pyramid

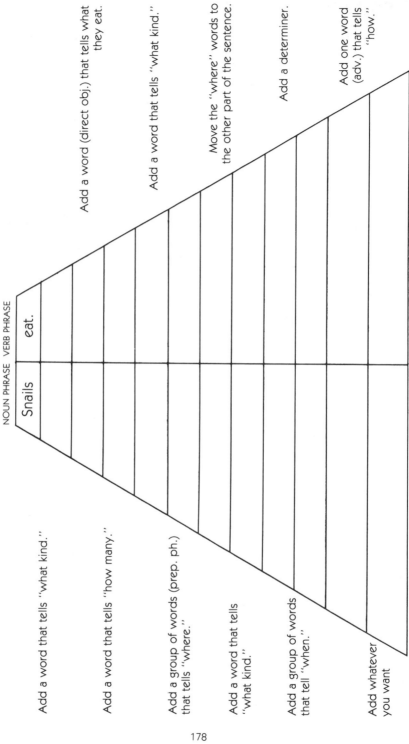

Add a word that tells "what kind."

Add a word that tells "how many."

Add a group of words (prep. ph.) that tells "where."

Add a word that tells "what kind."

Add a group of words that tell "when."

Add whatever you want

NOUN PHRASE   VERB PHRASE

Snails   eat.

Add a word (direct obj.) that tells what they eat.

Add a word that tells "what kind."

Move the "where" words to the other part of the sentence.

Add a determiner.

Add one word (adv.) that tells "how."

It can be converted to a four-fer by adding adverbs. A sample line would be "Happy people always talk," which adheres to the pattern Adjective-Noun-Adverb-Verb.

Another way to approach sentence expansion is through a sentence-building pyramid as shown in figure 6.1. The pyramid is divided into noun phrase and verb phrase sections, and a short kernel sentence is given at the top of the pyramid. To start, children expand the sentence by adding a word or phrase first to the noun phrase, then to the verb phrase, rewriting the sentence lower down in the pyramid each time they add to it. In upper grades when young people are on "speaking terms" with parts of speech, the teacher can give specific directions for each expansion: add an adjective to the noun phrase; add an adverb that tells how to the verb phrase; add an introductory prepositional phrase that tells when to the noun phrase; add a prepositional phrase to the verb phrase that tells where; add an adjective to the noun phrase; add an adjective within one of the prepositional phrases you have added; and so forth. The result will be a highly expanded sentence that tells not only who and what happened but also when, where, how, what kind, and how many. After children have handled the expanding operation in this way as part of oral activity, they can attempt it independently. In the latter case, directions for expansion are written on the sides of the sentence-building pyramid. In addition, upper graders can create sentence-building directions for their peers to follow by reading down the sides of a pyramid.

Sentence Dismantling

A natural corollary of sentence expansion is sentence dismantling. This is the process by which students strip words from a sentence—first one at a time, later two at a time, and still later three at a time—until they get down to the kernel structure, a simple noun phrase and verb phrase unit. The upside-down pyramid shape shown in figure 6.2 simplifies the activity for young people. On each line of the pyramid, children rewrite the sentence, each time stripping it of one more word. When they can no longer take out just one word and retain a sensible, typical English pattern, they can take out words two at a time. This latter step is necessary when handling prepositional phrases; both the preposition and its companion noun must come out at the same time.

Sentence dismantling can be carried out as an oral activity and probably should be done before youngsters attempt it independently. Some teachers have discovered that placing a very lengthy sentence across the top of the chalkboard and having each youngster in turn come forward to cross out one item and read the resulting product aloud is a

Figure 6.2. Sentence-dismantling pyramid

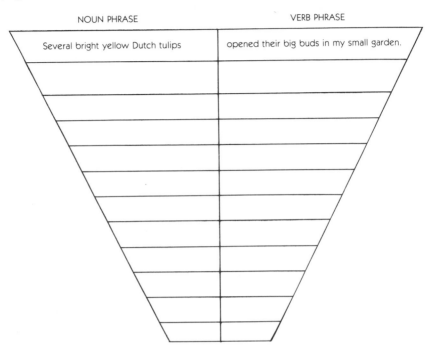

good way to stress the sentence sound. Listeners can decide whether what is left remains an acceptable English sentence. Upper graders enjoy doing the activity as a listening-memory one. Players must remember what words previous players have deleted, for deletions are not recorded on the board. Again, youngsters decide whether the end sentence is really a sentence. Does it have a noun phrase? Does it have a verb phrase?

One advantage of including sentence dismantling—or sentence reducing, as it is sometimes called—in elementary writing programs is that students must not get the erroneous idea that longer sentences that result from expansion are necessarily better. Wordiness is to be avoided, and children must learn to edit their own work by chopping out words that do not add power and that introduce awkwardness into the construction.

Sentence Combining

In 1965 Kellogg Hunt studied the progressive development of sentence complexity as children mature as writers. Describing his findings in *Grammatical Structures Written at Three Grade Levels* (National Council of Teachers of English, 1965), Hunt explained that as youngsters move from fourth, to eighth, and into twelfth grade, their sentence structures become systematically and progressively more complicated. His research indicated that young writers do not have the syntactic strength, or, in other words, the ability to use a variety of sentence-building strategies, as do more mature writers.

Hunt's findings were based on an original unit of sentence measurement—the minimum terminable unit, or what he called the T-unit. A T-unit is a main clause plus all subordinate clauses joined to it or embedded in it. In this context, a clause is defined as a grouping of words containing one subject or one set of coordinate subjects functioning with one verb phrase or one set of coordinate verb phrases. For example, *Steve drove the car* is one T-unit; it is comprised of one subject and one verb phrase. *Steve and Marcia climbed on the airplane and came home* is also one T-unit, because it contains one set of coordinate subjects with one set of coordinate verb phrases. Similarly, *When Marcia climbed on the airplane, Steve came home* is one T-unit, because it is made up of one main clause and one subordinate clause. In contrast, a sentence such as *Marcia climbed on the airplane, and Steve came home* is made up of two T-units, since there are two main clauses.

Using Hunt's technique to determine the sophistication of a piece of writing, a researcher counts the number of words in each T-unit and calculates an average number of words per T-unit in the total piece. That this proves a functional way of studying writing complexity is suggested by the fact that more mature writers do tend to use more adjective, adverb, and noun clauses. Syntactically mature writers are more likely to write a sentence such as *Long, long ago, at the bottom of the mountain lived an ugly, green monster, who was known far and wide for his bad temper.* A less mature writer might write instead: *Once upon a time there was a monster, and he was known everywhere for his bad temper, and he was very ugly, and he was green, and he lived at the bottom of the mountain.* The first sentence is one T-unit made up of twenty-four words. The second is five T-units with an average T-unit length of seven words.

Helping Children Build Syntactic Strength in Writing. Experienced teachers in the middle elementary grades know that youngsters have trouble joining their thoughts together. They rely overly on *ands* to link a series of thoughts or, once they have struck upon one alternate means of linking, they use it repeatedly as Brenda overused *and so* in this piece:

IF I WERE A GROUNDHOG

If I were a groundhog I would see my shadow so I could sleep more and so I would not have to go to work as sone as I wake up and so I would not have to go through all truble gist to find my shadow and so what if the people have six more weeks of winter it' good for the animals to sleep longer too and so my children would not have to go to school as sone as they get up and my wife woold not have to clean the house as sone as she got up and that should make her feel good.

THE END

As Jack Perron reminds us in *Language Arts* (September 1976), "Joining elements via *and* may be the easiest way to begin writing, but as children mature, its overuse limits the power of expression."

Researchers have used the T-unit to study whether it is possible through instruction to increase the average number of words per T-unit that children produce. In Perron's words, "The novice writer gains control over these [sentence combining] skills through a glacially slow process, currently without much direct help from teachers" (p. 652). He and others have investigated whether focused study of ways to delete excess verb parts, embed clauses in other clauses, and transform ideas into one sentence results in greater syntactic maturity in writing.

Perron's research carried out at the University of Indiana ("An Exploratory Approach to Extending the Syntactic Development of Fourth-Grade Students Through the Use of Sentence-Combining Methods," Doctoral diss., 1974) indicates that direct experiences with sentence combining (s-c for short) can help children gain more rapid control over ways of handling sentences on paper, a control that extends to their actual written expression. Dr. Perron's program included structured lessons with sentence combining tactics as well as games and activities of a concrete nature. Similar findings were reported earlier by John Mellon (1969) and Frank O'Hare (1973), both of whom worked with seventh graders, and by Hunt and O'Donnell (1970) and Miller and Ney (1968), who worked with fourth graders. These studies raise a fundamental question for the teacher: How do we encourage children to join sentences together and to embed one sentence in another? Let us look at some activities based on those employed in the studies by Perron, Mellon, O'Hare, and others.

Combining by Joining.   Through the use of the conjunction *and* in the sentence *Steve and Marcia climbed on the airplane and came home*, ideas from four separate sentences have been combined into one. Those four sentences are:

Steve climbed on the airplane.
Steve came home.
Marcia climbed on the airplane.
Marcia came home.

Joining is possible in this case because the same ideas are repeated in the verb phrases of the component sentences.

Perron suggests that as children work orally together, the teacher can ask them to combine repeated ideas into one sentence. For example, as youngsters dictate sentences that describe an object (perhaps a ball), they may proffer, "It is red." "It is big." "It is soft." "It is round." The teacher waits to record until many possible sentences have been proposed and then urges, "Let's see if we can create one sentence that describes the ball and includes all the ideas contained in our four sentences. Who wants to try?" The sentence *The ball is red, big, soft, and round.* is the one that gets recorded in the class chart.

The teacher may stretch the activity and suggest: "I can change our sentence another way: *The red ball is big, soft, and round.* Who can change it still another way?" Possibilities that children may offer orally are *The big, red ball is soft and round. The big, soft ball is red and round. The soft, round ball is big and red. The soft ball is big, round, and red.* By playing with a sentence and rewriting it in a variety of ways, youngsters begin to see that there is no best way to style a sentence. Goodness in styling is a matter of the sound and meaning the writer wants to achieve.

Perron describes another oral experience that lays the foundation for sentence combining in later writing—a game he calls "Double Up." Youngsters brainstorm words that can function as verbs as a scribe records these on the board. Each student "joins with a partner, and they produce two sentences together, using one of the words from the blackboard twice." Then they combine their two sentences into one by deleting the repeating verb. Perron runs this activity as a game, the winning pair being the team that composes the most double-upped sentences in a given time.

Youngsters who previously have had some oral work with sentence combining can work together to build combination sentences from sets of repeating ones provided by the teacher. In groups of two or three, upper graders can be asked to compose as many "combos" as they can out of each of the following and star the combo that sounds the best and communicates most clearly:

- The house is white. It is very large. It is vacant. It is run down.
- Martin's car is brand new. It is shiny red. It is small. It is expensive.
- Mrs. Cohen runs the insurance agency. Marie runs the insurance agency. Mrs. Cohen runs the bank. Marie runs the bank.
- Mike cleaned the stove. I cleaned the stove. Timothy cleaned the stove. Rod cleaned the windows.

- Kevin has a new skateboard. Ruth has a new skateboard. Kevin has a new bicycle. Ruth has a new bicycle.

The results of joinings may be compound subjects, predicates, objects, adjectives, prepositional phrases, and so forth, depending on the kinds of sentences with which children start.

Sentence Embedding. Of course, the process of combining by joining sentence parts through coordination only gets at the tip of the iceberg. Actually, more mature writers combine more often by tying ideas together through subordination. As Perron explains (*Language Arts*, September 1976), beginners may combine ideas to produce *There was a boy and he was tall and he lived down the street*, but mature writers tend to eliminate the extraneous *he* and the verb parts to produce *There was a tall boy who lived down the street*. The latter sentence contains an adjective clause embedded in it, *who lived down the street*. Other sentences contain noun clauses and/or adverb clauses.

Perron has devised another game, "Sentence Partners," to help children in an oral setting build sentences that include embedded clauses. In a group of eight, each youngster receives a card that is hung around his or her neck. The sign cards read:

- I know
- I wonder
- I hope
- I believe
- that this class will end.
- when we will get another vacation.
- you will be good to me.
- this period will be fun.

Each player carries a piece of paper on which he or she records as many sentences that can be formed by combining one partner with another. The results, of course, are sentences in which noun clauses are embedded.

The same can be done with embedded adjective and adverb clauses. Here are sentence parts that Perron provides his students:

- This is the day
- She is the girl
- They are the ones
- He is the boy
- that we get out early.
- who likes ice cream cones.
- who will never give up.

- I like to write
- I get up
- After we eat
- Unless we win
- because it's easy.
- when it is time to go to school.

- who rides bicycles
  backwards.

- we can play ball.
- we won't be the champs.

Upper graders can play "Sentence Partners" with twenty-four participants, each one wearing a card from the noun clause, adjective clause, or adverb clause game. Players write down as many sentences as they can by combining parts that other players wear.

Young people who have played a game such as "Sentence Partners" can create original sentence wheels based on embeddings they have already handled. Gertrude Lapare has her fifth graders create wheels for sentences containing adjective clauses by cutting three circles of differing colors and sizes from construction paper. On the large outer circle, students record around the edge possible noun phrases: *The clowns, The people, Those workers, The boys, The firefighters, The men and women, Some sad children, Five girls.* On the middle circle, they record around the edge possible adjective clauses that have the potential to combine with the noun phrases already recorded: *who were in the street, who were ready to go, who carried the flag, who won first prize, who came first, who sat in the front row, who had red hair,* and *who got on the truck.* On the small, central circle, students write down possible verb phrases: *were very good friends, were shouting at the top of their lungs, were afraid to do anything, were on the way home, were cheered, were soaking wet from the rain, must be the ones we know,* and *laughed.* When the three circles are superimposed one above the other and clipped together, students loan out their sentence wheels so that other youngsters can write numerous sentences by "spinning their wheels."

Punctuating Sentence Combinations.   Even as youngsters are involved directly in activities requiring them to join and embed sentences, they should begin to develop related punctuation skills. This is true not only as children combine sentences using noun, adjective, and adverb clauses but also as they play orally with such other sentence-combining tactics as indirect quotations, direct quotations, and appositives.

Attention to punctuation and capitalization patterns can begin as children compose in teacher-guided groups. If, for example, as youngsters create a story together, a child proposes a sentence such as *The dragon said that he was hungry,* the teacher can ask, "Is there another way we can say that same sentence? What were the actual words that the dragon spoke?" The result may be another more exciting, transformed sentence relying on a direct, rather than an indirect quotation: *The dragon said, "I am hungry."* Recording that sentence into the group story, the teacher may remark, "Watch how I am putting these quotation marks around the words that the dragon spoke. Look how I am putting the comma before the words that he spoke." Later in groups children can produce other sentences with direct quotations embedded in them, which are modeled after the ones written cooperatively during story-making. Used in this way, teacher-guided group writing provides an opportunity to build sentence-writing and related punctuation skills as well as an opportunity to talk out ideas and expand upon them.

In the same way, the teacher can help youngsters handle the punctuation conventions associated with appositives in writing. If youngsters dictate *Donald was a monster. He lived at the top of the mountain. He was unhappy. He was unhappy because he was all alone*, the teacher may suggest, "Let's see if we can put some of our sentences together." Children quickly see that they do not need the first *He was unhappy* and may delete it, going on to suggest a "combo" such as *Donald was a monster who lived at the top of the mountain. He was unhappy because he was all alone.* With guidance from the teacher, upper graders can make an additional move—inserting through use of an appositive: *Donald, a monster who lived at the top of the mountain, was unhappy because he was all alone.* Together teacher and students add the necessary punctuation. Later youngsters join in writing teams to create other sentences that pattern in the same way as the model included in the group composition. The instructional sequence here is (1) teacher-guided group composition, (2) teacher-guided group combining, and (3) team composing of sentences similar to the one combined.

One way to reinforce punctuation conventions associated with various sentence combining tactics is story reconstruction. After youngsters have listened to or read a story, they each receive a story strip on which is printed a part of a story sentence—usually either a noun phrase or a verb phrase part. Holding up their strips, participants decide cooperatively how to put the cut-up story back together again and lay out their pieces in the appropriate order using a large table or the floor as a reconstruction stage. With strips in logical sequence, youngsters proceed to add punctuation markers and capitalization indicators—little cards bearing punctuation marks and capital letters. If children disagree on how the marks and indicators should be placed, they check the written text to find out how it is done there. Then they generalize:

> Punctuation Generalization A: Put quotation marks around the words a character speaks.
> Punctuation Generalization B: Put the period at the end of a spoken statement inside the quotation marks.
> Punctuation Generalization C: Put the question mark at the end of a spoken question inside the quotation marks.

Punctuation Generalization D: Put the comma that introduces a direct quotation before the first quotation mark.

These generalizations that children have formulated for themselves can
be printed on charts and hung in the writing center where youngsters go
to compose. Compositions written after group composing sessions and
story reconstructions that focus on one kind of sentence combining tactic
should relate in some way to the syntactic pattern under consideration.
Having just worked orally and together on direct quotations, children
should try to write original conversation stories in which characters talk
directly to one another. Having just created a number of sentences by
embedding adverbial clauses, youngsters should try to include sentences
with *when, as, since, because, while, after,* and *if* clauses embedded in
them.

Teacher-guided group composition and story reconstruction are
two of the most pleasurable instructional settings for developing written-
language skills. The teacher introduces ways of handling ideas and ways
of punctuating sentences even as youngsters need them—in the very process of recording thoughts on paper. Then, too, the oral setting is a
helpful one, for often the pauses of speech patterns are the punctuation
marks of written patterns. Working orally together, students hear the
difference between *John, your brother, is here* and *John, your brother is
here*; between *We had chocolate, cake, and ice cream* and *We had
chocolate cake and ice cream.* In this way they understand the function
of punctuation in written communication.

BUILDING SENTENCE SENSE THROUGH READING

Written English differs from spoken English in a number of different ways. First, there is a tighter, more logical organization in
sentences written down to be read by someone else than there is in spoken
sentences. Similar ideas are grouped together and should flow logically
into one another. Second, more diverse and sophisticated syntactic or
sentence patterns are employed in written communications. Such patterns as direct quotations, appositives, and even parenthetical expressions are found less commonly in oral expression. Third, written pieces
are more terse with fewer extraneous words.

Because written expression does differ in these respects from oral
expression, contact with different kinds of written material can help a
youngster achieve an intuitive understanding of how English sentences
are recorded on the printed page. Working with college students, the
authors have found that those who can express themselves well on paper
are often young people who admit to having read widely as children and

teenagers. To teach writing, therefore, we must develop a parallel literature program that introduces children to the best literary styles so that they will be encouraged to read and read more. To teach the skills of reading is not enough; we must turn children on to books so that they search for more and more books to read.

This is not to imply that teachers should force children to analyze the sentence patterns in books and poems they are reading—not at all! That process is more effective as a means of turning children off to books. What is being suggested is a literature enjoyment program in which children listen to books written by some of the great writers for children of today and are encouraged to dip into these treasures on their own. Through these dips young readers come intuitively to know what to expect from Konigsburg, Dr. Seuss, Lionni, Sendak, McCloskey, and a host of others. They see these writers as human beings plying the writing craft in patterns typically their own, and they begin to use the ways of forming words into sentences that these professionals use. Writing is, after all, an art. Knowledge of patterns carries the writer only so far. Then artistic sense takes over as the writer makes words flow rhythmically across a page and interweaves one pattern creatively into another. This fine sense can hardly be taught! We can only hope that a child can catch it by brushing against the writings of those who have a unique flare with words.

SOME SUMMARY THOUGHTS

Chapter 6 has proposed that one of the most fundamental skills a child must acquire in learning to write is the ability to compose complete sentences that adhere to the established noun phrase/verb phrase structure. A related skill is the ability to combine sentences by joining and embedding. The chapter has also presented research evidence suggesting that direct attention to sentencing in classrooms leads to increased ability to handle sentences as children write. This latter finding represents a major breakthrough. Previous studies have tended to show no significant relationship between learning formal grammar and children's ability to write. These studies gave writing teachers no specific clues as to ways to teach writing skills. Today the work of such researchers as Hunt, Perron, O'Hare, and Mellon is suggesting directions that teachers themselves can explore and tools such as the T-unit for testing the results of instructional experimentation in classrooms. To teachers of writing, these are exciting times!

7

LET CHILDREN BUILD WORD POWER AND CONTROL ◄► playing with words

Words are the dress of thoughts, which should no more be presented in rags, tatters, and dirt than your person should.

Lord Chesterfield, LETTERS

Ultimately writers are faced with the task of selecting words and building them into thought units that communicate with precision. They do not wait to do this until after they have formulated an idea or designed a structure to express it. Rather, writers use words to think about ideas; they may even talk out their ideas to themselves using words. Thus, even as an idea begins to develop, it takes on verbal dimensions.

Selecting the appropriate word is the key to writing if clear expression is to result. In the elementary schools, teachers should give considerable attention to this phase of writing. They should help children widen their word pools, substitute synonyms for overused words, tap the figurative power of language, select words that have a delightful ring, and use the dictionary for both spelling and meaning problems.

WIDENING CHILDREN'S WORD POOLS

A storm had raged almost continually for several days. When it abated, Leslie, a four-year-old, came out to survey the damage. Picking up pieces of bark that the wind had pulled from the trees and scattered over the driveway, Leslie concluded, "The wind pulled the skin from the trees." Leslie wanted to communicate her reaction, but lacking the exact word to express her thoughts, she had extended the meaning of a word she did know (skin) to the one she required (bark).

One of the authors was with Leslie when she discovered the "skin" of trees. The author suggested, "Leslie, let's look at the trees where the bark has been pulled off." Together they peeled off bark loosened by the storm, looked at the new surface, compared it to the still bark-covered surface, and picked up more pieces of bark from the lawn. During the entire experience, they talked about bark, what it looks like, how it feels to the touch, and what purpose it serves.

Leslie, a child who likes to collect paraphernalia, made a collection of different kinds of bark. A short time later, she called out to a little friend who had come to play, "Look at all my pieces of bark!" Leslie had acquired another building block of communication; she had acquired a verbal label through which to talk about experience.

As with Leslie, talking is the bridge to vocabulary development. To build word power, children need numerous encounters with words they are beginning to use so that they can broaden their concepts and refine their understanding of word meanings and usage. This means hearing words in many different and meaningful contexts. It also means having opportunity to try them out in speaking and writing and seeing these same words in print. Here are some examples.

Talking about Real Experiences

Youngsters in a kindergarten class were learning about the colors and learning to attach color labels to objects in their immediate environment. Toward this end, the teacher had hung various colored balloons around the room and from each she had suspended a labeling card—*orange, blue, yellow*, and so forth. One day youngsters went on an orange hunt, locating other objects in the room that were the same color as the orange balloon. They finger painted all of them in orange. They dictated about things they liked that were orange. They even drank orange juice in the afternoon and talked about why it was probably called *orange juice* and why an orange was called *an orange*. Successive days were blue ones, yellow ones, red ones. Children thus gradually refined their understanding of colors through meaningful contacts that allowed them to discover and explore meanings for themselves and to use the color words that the teacher was modeling in her own oral usage.

At the first-grade level, similar types of vocabulary work are possible through a variety of firsthand experiences. Children visiting an aquarium can talk about fins and gills, scales and barbs. They can describe the fish as streamlined, shiny, or slim; and they can assign inventive names to the fish that they like: Finny, Sword, Tiger. Similarly, at the third-grade level, youngsters who have experienced a particularly happy activity—a party, an outing in the woods, a puppet play—can be encouraged to talk about happy-feeling words. Teachers should also interject their own happy-feeling words, which the children can appropriate on the spot to talk about their feelings. When a sad event occurs, children can talk about sad-feeling words, and into the talk teachers can again interject words that children obviously need. In the sixth grade, youngsters carrying on a plant growth experiment can be asked, "What do you guess will be the outcome?" As the youngsters propose educated guesses, the teacher can ask them, "What hypothesis can we make?" Hence, the word *hypothesis* will begin to appear as youngsters model their use after the teacher's.

Opportunities for such vocabulary building talk and exploration are almost limitless. Observing fast-moving vehicles on a busy city street can be the trigger for using action words. Touching different types of materials, such as cotton, silk, and sandpaper, can be the trigger for using texture words. An accidental fall in the playground and the skinning of a knee can lead to talk about pain. Watching different chemicals burn can lead to use of expressive color words. Fighting with a friend can lead to use of mad words. It is the teacher who must uncover the language development potential of the experiences children encounter every day in classrooms.

Talking About Vicarious Experiences

Vicarious experiences can also lead to vocabulary building. One of the authors observed a kindergarten teacher discussing with a group a picture of a person rolling out cookie dough. Many of the children had never seen dough in its uncooked state and did not know what it was. Several children who had had the experience explained it to the others. As the group made plans to make dough the next day, children among those not originally knowing about dough were using the word in a natural way.

In the same way, upper-grade boys and girls add words to their speaking and writing vocabularies through study of the content areas. A fifth-grade class was observed discussing geologic changes after a six-week period during which they had studied geologic processes. Words such as *erupt, submerge, crater, fissure*, and *alpine* were used naturally by the youngsters as they talked about the experiences they had had within their unit. The teacher of this class had as one of his unit objectives that the children assimilate these basic words into their functional vocabularies. The culminating discussion—the evaluation of the objective, so to speak—indicated that Mr. Dee had achieved his objective.

As youngsters encounter rather complex concepts that are relatively abstract or that children have never had opportunity to handle firsthand, it is most essential that vocabulary-building activity initially be oral. Looking up a list of technical words in a dictionary, checking the statement of meaning found there, and then writing five sentences using each word are not necessarily steps in the progress of students toward word power. If those words are to show up in children's inner and socialized speech and eventually in their writing, youngsters must see the need for the words in talking about their experiences, whether firsthand or vicarious. They must have opportunity to explore meanings by hearing their teacher rely on specific words to communicate thought. They must have opportunity to use those same words as they discuss ideas together. Memorization of a definition and creation of one or two sentences based on that definition do not supply that opportunity.

Moving from Talking to Writing

Beginning with relevant words can be a useful bridge between using words in talking and using them on paper. This is especially so with youngsters who have a limited writing vocabulary. For example, a group of seventh graders from a city school participated in a science experiment. This was followed with talk about words to use to express what they had done. During the discussion the teacher also informally mentioned words that the students might need later in writing. The students kept pencils in hands during the talk-time and jotted down words to use in the writing period to follow. If students did not know how to spell a word, they put down an approximation. During the actual writing period, the teacher circulated from student to student to correct the spelling of words on students' lists. By the time youngsters wanted to use a word, they could copy it from their own corrected vocabulary list.

This type of bridge between talking about and writing down is particularly significant with youngsters who speak a nonstandard dialect of English or whose first language is not English. These boys and girls need to encounter words in numerous situations that have meaning to them if English words are to be assimilated into their speaking and eventually their writing vocabularies. Experiencing words through hearing, speaking, and writing should be an integral part of their daily school programs, so that youngsters will be able to use language both for thinking and communicating.

Seeing Words Around

Still another bridge between talking about and writing down is seeing words one is beginning to use in speaking. To this end, many teachers fill the walls of their classrooms with charts containing words that are important in the content area units in progress. Word cards are suspended from lighting fixtures, are taped to the floor, and are posted on doors, windows, and bulletin boards. For example, as youngsters meet various landforms as part of a geographical study, they produce illustrated charts of plateaus, deltas, foothills, mesas, and so forth, adding appropriate word labels to their colored drawings. The result is an illustrated landforms atlas, the pages of which are posted around the room. As youngsters go on to write as part of their social studies investigation, they need only glance up at their atlas charts to find the technical term they need. The importance of such prewriting vocabulary-building activity in informational-type writing is just beginning to be realized by specialists in the content areas of the curriculum. As Barry Beyer wrote in an issue of *Social Education* that focused on "Writing to Learn in the Social Studies" ("Pre-writing and Rewriting to Learn," *Social Education* 43:187–89, 197, March 1979), "Teachers must engage students systematically with subject matter about which they are to write *before* the students put pen to paper."

One way to help children master technical terms that are part of subject units is through development of individual dictionary or glossary cards or pages. Encountering a new term, each youngster can create an illustrated index card that provides some visualization of the term, a definition, and diacritical marks showing pronunciation. He or she slips all the cards for a unit on a shower curtain ring in alphabetical order and refers to items during writing-down and even during talking-about times. This strategy has been used successfully by young people even at the junior high school level.

USING WORDS WITH FLAIR

In writing, it is not enough to use an approximate word in a mundane way. To write with style, one must be able to single out the particular synonym that communicates meaning with greatest clarity and does it tunefully. One must be able to add color by interjecting a simile, a metaphor, an appropriate colloquialism, or even in some cases a bit of slang. One must be able to hear the music of words and create combinations that dance across the page. In short, a writer must be able to use words with a creative flair.

Singling Out the Appropriate Synonym

Children can begin to realize the power that words have by working with synonyms. Synonyms usually do not have exactly the same meaning; fine distinctions exist. Take, for example, the simple sentence, "I hate him." It is a perfectly acceptable sentence that follows a typical kernel pattern:

Subject	*Verb*	*Object*
I	hate	him.

However, there are other ways of constructing the same sentence by substituting synonyms:

1. I detest him.
2. I abhor him.
3. I dislike him.
4. I abominate him.
5. I loathe him.

Each communicates a slightly different shade of meaning. *Webster's New Collegiate Dictionary* clarifies these differences:

> *Hate* implies aversion often coupled with enmity or malice; *detest*, violent antipathy; *abhor*, profound, often shuddering repugnance; *abominate*, strong detestation, as of something ill-omened or shameful; *loathe*, utter disgust and intolerance

Compared with any of these, *dislike* represents a much lesser feeling.

To come to a more concrete and functional understanding of synonym sets, children can play with a simple sentence: "The man walked down the street." Children can volunteer to pantomime the sentence, keeping in mind another verb that tells more precisely how the man walked. Children will stagger, limp, hobble, saunter, stumble. Others will guess the verb that describes the activity and record it on cards that they hang up on their bulletin board of words to use. Here are other examples for pantomiming:

1. The teacher *looked* at the boy.
2. The woman *got out* of the car.

3. The horse *trotted* down the street.
4. The man *ran* into the house.
5. He *drove* his automobile through town.

Youngsters can also be encouraged to keep lists of possible substitutes for words they typically overuse. What word can we substitute for *make*? for *do*? for *say*? for *pretty*? for *nice*? for *interesting*? Answers may result in a class thesaurus, which children construct together. As they compose, junior high school youngsters can refer to *Roget's International Thesaurus*, a volume that many professional writers find more valuable than a dictionary. Younger children can refer to *In Other Words: A Beginning Thesaurus* and *In Other Words: A Junior Thesaurus* by W. Cabell Greet, William Jenkins, and Andrew Schiller (Scott, Foresman, 1968, 1969). In a sense, when we expect children to write without such an aid, we are expecting them to do better than the professional.

For older elementary youngsters, a thesaurus can actually become a fun book to take along on an excursion as a means of expanding word power. A group of sixth graders got carried away with words after they had listened to the sounds at a busy intersection. The thesaurus supplied them with words like *whiz*, *buzz*, *zip*, *screak*, *screech*, *crump*, *jangle*, *clash*, *clatter*, *rattle*, *clank*, *whoop*, *squeal*, *whine*, *wail*, *whistle*, *blare*, *rasp*, and *hiss*, which appealed to the children because of the onomatopoeic sounds. When the children returned to their classroom, they concocted sounds, by voice and by rubbing objects together, that were actual examples of the words from the thesaurus. They made a tape in which words and sounds were juxtaposed. Through their own activity, the words became meaningful symbols for actual events.

Adding Color Through Creative Expressions

Certain word combinations add color to a written piece. These combinations include colloquialisms, dialect, slang, figures of speech, play on words, and informal language usage.

Colloquialisms. In American English we can "fly off the handle," "dress a turkey," and "face the music," and when we do, we add another dimension to our language. Children delight in looking at the idiosyncracies of our language if they are presented as colorfully as in Peggy Parish's *Amelia Bedelia* (Harper & Row, 1963) or Eth Clifford's *A Bear Before Breakfast* (Putnam, 1962, out of print). Based on material supplied in such books, children can make their own dictionaries of favorite idioms and add to them day by day. They can keep these homemade dictionaries as ready references when they write creatively.

Starting about third grade, youngsters are tickled by the task of sketching pictures that show the literal meaning of a colloquialism and its more figurative one. Imagine a drawing that literally shows the meaning of these familiar expressions:

> He jumped from the frying pan into the fire.
> She wore her heart on her sleeve.
> Every day you must eat at least one square meal.
> Don't spill the beans.
> He has butterfingers.
> The whole time I was on pins and needles.

For a lengthy listing of other idioms of this kind as well as other ideas for expanding children's word pools, see Dorothy Hennings's *Words, Sounds, and Thoughts: More Activities to Enrich Children's Communication Skills* (Scholastic/Citation, 1977).

Dialect and Slang.   When writing, we sometimes convey a mood, develop a character, or describe an occurrence by employing dialects, slang, or the jargon associated with a particular pursuit. For instance C. S. Forester relies on the distinctive jargon of the sailor and of the sea in this passage from *Captain Horatio Hornblower*:

> "Hard-a-starboard," he rasped at the quartermaster at the wheel, and then to the hands forward, "Smartly with the braces now!"
> With the rudder hard across the ship came round a trifle. The fore topsail came round. The jibs and fore staysails were set like lightning.

We can and should encourage children to do the same by supplying them with references when they attempt stories that might require slang or jargon. References in this case are books written in the desired style—sometimes novels, sometimes short stories. Second, we can encourage children to write realistically by our own attitude toward slang and even toward swearing. One of the authors vividly remembers being told as a child to write "proper English" when she tried to write a story about the sea. Now sailors do not always use "proper English." Instead of insisting on inappropriate standards of word usage, teachers should help youngsters find material that will give them a rather accurate impression of the speech characteristics of a group of people, remembering that quotation marks around a group of words indicate that these words were spoken by a character in question.

Figures of Speech: The Simile, the Metaphor, and the Hyperbole.   In *The Elements of Style* (Macmillan, 1972), William Strunk and E. B.

White recommend that figures of speech be employed sparingly, as too many can be "more distracting than illuminating." Employed sparingly and in appropriate contexts, however, figures of speech can add a creative flair to writing. For example, Carl Sandburg turned to metaphor when he made fog into a cat in "Fog." Alfred Noyes used it too when he wrote "The road was a ribbon of moonlight." In contrast, Wordsworth turned to simile when he wrote "I wandered lonely as a cloud," as did Coleridge in his line "I pass, like night, from land to land." Most of us have used the hyperbole when we have made such a gross exaggeration as "I was so hungry I could have eaten a horse" or "I was so embarrassed I thought I would die."

In playing with simile, metaphor, and hyperbole, children should not be required to distinguish among them. To know the difference between a simile and a metaphor does not necessarily result in effective use. Emphasis should be on encouraging children to play at writing figures of speech. For instance, we can project beginnings of similes to be completed by children in numerous ways. Suggest "as lonely as . . . ," and children will add "a butterfly," "an undersea diver," "a picked rose," "a discarded banana peel." Suggest "as happy as . . .," "as peaceful as . . .," "as warlike as . . .," "as unhappy as . . .," "as tiny as. . . ." The possibilities are endless as children themselves take over the game to propose similar base phrases for similes. Children can also play with these beginnings:

- The man walked like (as if) . . .
- The girl sang like (as if) . . .
- Her hair looked like . . .
- The man drove like . . .
- The man worked like . . .
- The child ran like . . .

In much the same fashion, children can play with analogies in the form of metaphor. To start, youngsters identify a product or cbject with which they are familiar—for instance, a compact car, a 747 jet, the Concorde, a big Mac. They devise a string of equations for the chosen material:

A compact car = a turtle on wheels = a bunny with its tail
   clipped off = a gas-sipper = a four-wheeled bicycle
A 747 jet = an overweight whale = a flying boat = an oversized sardine can

Here the rule is anything goes, with children competing with one another to devise the most farfetched combination that still retains an element of sense.

Hyperboles are equally fun to devise. Phrases such as "He was so tall that . . . ," "She was so cold that . . . ," "The horse was so strong that . . . ," or "The car was so fast that . . . " are written at the tops of individual sheets of paper. Youngsters in groups react to a phrase by writing down the most outlandish exaggeration that completes it. Each group adds its hyperbole to the one written by a previous group, until papers carry the products of several groups' efforts. The resulting hyperbole series are striking when read aloud. This type of work is especially suitable as youngsters read tall tales, for exaggeration is the essence in this form of story, which youngsters can go on to write on their own.

Play on Words.   We can all remember one type of riddle that we especially appreciated as children—the riddle that is essentially a play on words. The reader probably remembers these old-timers:

Why does an elephant have a trunk?
Answer: Because it couldn't carry a suitcase.
What is green and goes ding-dong?
Answer: A green ding-dong.
What is black and white and red all over?
Old answer: A newspaper. *New answer:* A skunk with diaper rash.
What has four wheels and flies?
Answer: A garbage truck.

These riddles base their humor on the double meanings that some words have.

Children are a storehouse of play-on-word-riddles. The riddles they know can be recorded in a class riddle book and can stimulate the invention of original ones. The riddles children invent can be shared with others during a riddle-upmanship contest, and the best can be carried to other classes. Such plays with words encourage children to manipulate words in humorous ways that also are important in writing, particularly in the writing of satire.

Older elementary youngsters delight in usages that incorporate word plays. One of the authors vividly recalls an incident with an eighth-grade class she was teaching. She began a statement with "Now I grant that. . . ." The children giggled. "What's wrong?" she queried.

"Grant grants," one replied. What had struck the funny bones of these bright students was Miss Grant's use of *grant*. With children like this, we can capitalize on their natural enjoyment of the humor in certain word-sound combinations. We can record "Grant grants" on a Pun Board to which students add puns that they find in reading, that they themselves invent, or that they hear television comedians present. The current crop of television programs is a gold mine of examples of the playful use of words that upper-grade children can borrow as a base for creating similar word plays. Classroom humor can be compiled in the mode of the old TV program, "Laugh-In," in which jokes, plays on words, satire, changing facial expressions, and flashes of color and motion are juxtaposed in rapid-fire succession.

Oral play with the humorous relationships found in certain word combinations pays secondary dividends. Young people not only learn the pleasure to be had in creative manipulation of words but they also are quicker to pick up such plays in reading. Often higher-level reading, inclusive of "reading between and above the lines," requires one to glean the hidden meanings a writer is communicating through use of creative word-sound combinations. In teaching creative word usage, the teacher is getting at both writing and reading skill.

Informal Usage.   Given the two sentences "I wish that I *was* rich" and "I wish that I *were* rich," which usage is "correct"? According to *A Dictionary of Contemporary American Usage*, *was* is very acceptable even in formal writing. The same is true of dangling prepositions, split infinitives, and use of *me* in "It's me." Actually, modern-day linguists no longer think of a particular usage as correct; rather they distinguish levels of acceptability: formal, standard, and nonstandard. Then too, some usage previously considered nonstandard is today categorized as standard because of its general use in conversation.

Why insist on outmoded levels of usage in writing by children? Too often we put ourselves in the position of Rat in the following short sequence from Kenneth Grahame's *The Wind in the Willows*, originally written in 1908:

> The Toad, having finished his breakfast, picked up a stout stick and swung it vigorously, belabouring imaginary animals. "I'll learn 'em to steal my house!" he cried. "I'll learn 'em, I'll learn 'em."
> "Don't say 'learn 'em!' Toad," said the Rat, greatly shocked. "It's not good English."

Teachers should be familiar with what is considered standard usage in informal writing to avoid such unnecessary controversies as that between "Does everyone have his book?" and "Does everyone have their book?" and between "Let's put our best foot forward" and "Let's put our better foot forward." We must remember that most people generally split infinitives, dangle prepositions, use *like* as a conjunction, and say "different than."

This point relates particularly to the written expression of youngsters who come to school speaking a nonstandard dialect of American English. This dialect differs from standard American English in several basic respects. First, the vocabulary includes words and expressions not found in a standard dictionary or words used in ways other than a dictionary suggests. Second, the dialect has structural patterns that differ from those typically employed in standard informal usage. To insist that speakers of nonstandard dialects speak and write in only standard English patterns and with standard vocabulary is to ask the impossible and is, in essence, to reject an element of the child's culture. Walter Loban's words are relevant here ("A Sustained Program of Language Learning" in *Language Programs for the Disadvantaged*, NCTE, 1965).

> Pupils need to learn standard English in addition to the social class dialect they know, Cajun, Appalachian, or whatever it may be. (We are not here concerned with *regional variations* of English but with *social class variations*.) If such pupils do not learn a second kind of dialect, standard English, they will be forever prevented access to economic opportunity and social acceptance. We can learn to grant full dignity to the child and to the language spoken in the home. At the same time, we must help him or her to acquire the established standard language so he or she can operate in society as fully as he or she may wish. He or she would, of course, be free to make the choice of not using the second dialect. . . .

Loban, however, proposes:

> In the kindergarten and in the earliest years of school, the emphasis should be upon the child's using *whatever dialect of the language he or she already speaks* as the means of thinking and exploring and imagining. Language is also more than a tool of thought. It is a way of expressing emotions and feelings. It is a way of adjusting to other people. . . . If the child speaks a dialect and says, "Them magnet's pickin' up the nails," we do not need to worry about "them magnet's" at this point. Let him or her say, "them magnet's." That usage will not interfere with the crucial cognitive processes. If we do not first encourage the child to use his or her own language in its full range, we may diminish the desire to use language in school.

Dialectally different youngsters in upper-elementary grades should be systematically introduced to standard vocabulary and sentence patterns through interaction with the teacher. Children begin to distinguish between what Gladney and Leaverton call "Everyday Talk" and "School Talk." They listen to school talk, imitate it, distinguish the elements of school talk from everyday talk, and begin to differentiate the situations in which school talk can be used and those in which everyday talk is acceptable. What children basically do is learn standard English as a second language.

The characteristics of children's talk—their vocabulary and sentence structure—will be reflected in their writing, of course. To start, children in the primary grades may write in their native dialect; but as they become more familiar with standard English and situations in which it tends to be used, they must decide whether it is appropriate to use the native or standard dialect and function in terms of this decision.

Getting a Feel for the Sounds of Words

Although selecting the precise word to convey meaning is important, a sense of sound is also vital in the construction process. Rhythm and rhyme can be used to heighten an effect an author is attempting to create. Alfred Tennyson rhythmically creates the effect of galloping horses in this selection from "The Charge of the Light Brigade":

> Half a league, half a league,
> Half a league, onward,
> All in the valley of Death
> Rode the six hundred.

In a similar way, Robert Burns repeats words and phrases in "My Heart's in the Highlands"; by placing the same words at the beginning of successive lines, the poet helps the reader make the transition from one line of verse to the next and creates a musical rhythm at the same time. In these lines, Robert Burns repeats sounds by selecting words that begin in the same way; this is alliteration. The poet uses rhyming as well in eight lines that appeal to the ear much in the manner of a song:

> MY HEART'S IN THE HIGHLANDS
> Farewell to the mountains high-covered with snow,
> Farewell to the straths and green valleys below,
> Farewell to the forests and wild-hanging woods,
> Farewell to the torrents and loud-pouring floods!
> > My heart's in the Highlands, my heart is not here;
> > My heart's in the Highlands a-chasing the deer,
> > A-chasing the wild deer and following the roe—
> > My heart's in the Highlands, wherever I go!

Writers rely on rhythm, repetition, rhyme, and alliteration to make words sound melodious to the ear; they also use onomatopoeia, a device in which a word is chosen because its sounds communicate part of the message. For example, penning "the burning wood *crackled* and *hissed*!" or the "bee *buzzed* through the flowers," a writer may have selected *crackled* and *hissed* because the sounds of those words are the sounds of fire; he or she may have selected *buzzed* because it imitates the sound the bee makes.

At times writers use their knowledge of phonics to create special sound effects. Knowing that some sounds are hard and others soft, a writer may select words with harder sounds to convey a message—the message of galloping hoofs, for example. Words such as *gate, galleon*, and *gusty* more effectively create this impression than the softer sound of *g* in *gem, gist*, and *gypsy*. Likewise, words with the hard sound of *c* may be more strident. Doubtlessly, Alfred Noyes was keenly aware of sounds when he wrote "The Highwayman," who came riding, riding, riding. Listen to how he played with hard sounds in these repetitive lines:

> The moon was a torrent of darkness among the gusty trees,
> The moon was a ghostly galleon tossed upon cloudy seas.

As we read poetry and prose to children, we can help them begin to hear the sounds of language by encouraging creative play with words. Children can chant a poem together, beating out the rhythm with clip-clops of their feet, "conducting" with their arms, or catching the beat with bongo drums or castanets. They can draw a rhythm as Langston Hughes does in his little book *The First Book of Rhythms* (Franklin Watts, 1954). Sentences from some prose selections can be handled in the same way.

Children can also play with alliterative effects. Tongue twisters like "Peter Piper" and "The Woodchuck" are simple beginnings. Children follow up oral chanting of these with creative composing of twisters of their own. Having participated in such oral plays, children very often can discover alliterative effects in pieces they hear. Ask children to listen to the sounds as you read a poem by a child, then one by a famous poet, both of which employ alliteration. The listening activity may help children comprehend the kinds of effects possible with words in writing.

For children to attempt rhyme can be more of a liability than an asset at times. To achieve rhyme, children may select inappropriate words and settle for awkwardness of expression that destroys an otherwise pleasurable image as Mark did in this little piece:

SPRING
Spring is a feeling
inside you. It
brings love and joy
to the cold land.
To me Spring
is very grand.

Mark

For this reason, we should be hesitant about requiring children to write rhymed poetry or about stressing rhyming in selections we share. Instead, we can introduce children to rhyme in Mother Goose, Dorothy Aldis, Aileen Fisher, and Dr. Seuss. We can also encourage children to play with rhyming sounds, searching through their minds to find words that rhyme with a given one such as *know*, *quick*, *dash*, or *way*. Writers who have brainstormed rhyming words can go on to create a sentence— not a poem—that includes an artful use of two or three "rhymers."

In each instance, whether it be play with onomatopoeia, alliteration, repeating words and phrases, rhyme, or rhythm, the beginning is an oral one. Youngsters must hear the sounds of language spoken aloud before they can develop awareness of the sounds of language they hear in their heads as part of inner speech used to facilitate writing.

BUILDING SPELLING FACILITY

To write in an acceptable way requires some ability to spell words being used. Just how to build spelling facility that carries over to actual use in writing continues to be a moot question. Currently, however, emphasis in most spelling programs is on helping youngsters develop control over sound-symbol relationships and over the structural units of which words are comprised. Emphasis too is on systematic use of the dictionary as a spelling tool.

Sound-Symbol Relationships

It is helpful for a writer attempting to encode to understand the relationship between sounds and symbols in the English language. Teaching children to spell linguistically, what we fundamentally do is to teach children different ways in which speech sounds (what are called *phonemes*) are represented on paper. The representations of speech sounds are known as *graphemes*. In recording words on paper, young people must be able to handle the different graphemes through which a phoneme is represented.

Learning to spell, children encounter specific situations in which certain graphemes tend to be used. Moving from specific examples, children discover generalizations for themselves: the sound /f/ is represented with the letter *f* or the letters *ph* when it occurs at the beginning of words, but never with *gh*; /f/ at the end of a word is more likely to be represented by a double *f* than by a single *f* if the preceding vowel is short. Or /k/ followed by an *i* is represented by the letter *k*, whereas /k/ followed by an *a* is represented by the letter *c*.

The older child who has not acquired a rudimentary ability to manipulate such phoneme-grapheme relationships is severely handicapped in recording thoughts on paper. Essentially he or she is language-disadvantaged. For instance, Gayle, a girl in the third grade, wrote, "I Kope you cowld canem to my birtday waday 7, 1980 an Maine 200." Tommie, a boy in the same grade, recorded "I hop yue come to oue pony. We well have a pig kake and we well have somd fize."

How can teachers help children like Gayle and Tommie? First, both of these children need experience with the full range of phonemes employed in the English language so that they themselves can produce the sounds. They would benefit from listening-speaking lessons in which they encounter the speech sounds and reproduce them orally. One lesson for Tommie would involve distinguishing the two consonant sounds, /p/ and /b/, as in *pig* and *big*. He could listen to words beginning with /p/ and /b/ and sort them into two groups. Later he would write down a *p* when he heard a word beginning with the sound represented by that grapheme, a *b* when he heard a word beginning with the sound represented by it.

Granted, activities like those suggested for Tommie are typically conducted in kindergarten and first grade. They are not "third-grade" activities. Yet Tommie is not functioning at a theoretical level called third grade. He is language-disadvantaged through no fault of his own; he probably had limited exposure to the full range of American English phonemes and as a result has not acquired skill in encoding. He still cannot differentiate among speech sounds. Much of his writing activity, therefore, must still be oral; he records via tape or via dictation. Simultaneously, he must be developing encoding skills in a systematic program geared by his teacher to remediate his personal deficiencies.

On the other hand, children who have acquired some basic knowledge of linguistic relationships can apply their understanding to the encoding of words that they are writing down for the first time. Uncertain how to spell a word, they write it in the most logical way they can, drawing on their understanding acquired in inductive spelling lessons. When they have finished recording their thoughts, writers reconsider the letters they have written, checking the dictionary to assure accuracy. Of course, to be overly concerned with using the correctly spelled word can be a handicap as youngsters begin to compose a written piece. Stopping midthought to go to a dictionary can cause loss of the thought altogether. To write down an approximation, or even leave a blank to be filled in later, appears to be a more productive option.

Having children acquire skill in handling graphemic representations of speech sounds aids in final dictionary checking. Children often raise the question, "How can we look up a word in the dictionary if we can't spell it?" Working with phoneme-grapheme relationships, children have a *modus operandi*: they write down as many graphemic representations adhering to generalizations as they know; then they check the possible representations in the dictionary, looking up each in turn.

Structurally Related Words and Word Units

Understanding some of the patterns that exist within English words can also aid the writer in encoding words during composition. Some of these understandings can be acquired much in the manner of a game. For instance, children in fourth grade can be given these two sets of words:

Pattern A	Pattern B
days	flies
buys	cries

They must determine in which of the two patterns other related words belong: *journeys, blueberries, plays, armies, ladies, monkeys, valleys, alleys, assemblies.* Then they must add *s* or change the *y* to *i* and add *es* to the following words: *dry, lay, boy, joy, alloy, injury, jury, strawberry.* The word puzzle to be solved in this case is, "In what instances do we change the *y* to *i* and add *es*?" The children can apply this understanding later as they check words about which they are uncertain during rewriting.

Children's vocabulary and spelling are also improved if they have some grasp on the internal structure of words, the meaningful units or morphemes of which words are composed. For example, children who know what happens to the meaning of a word when *un-* is affixed in the initial position may be able to add other words to their functional word repertoire with little difficulty—words they also may be able to spell with ease. In middle elementary grades, children can play with *un-* opposites: happy-unhappy, pleasant-unpleasant, able-unable, and cooperative-uncooperative. The teacher can begin the word game by printing the *un-* opposites on cards, mounting the cards on a bulletin board, and asking children to figure out how the second word was made out of the first. A stack of empty cards can be made available so that over a period of a week or so they can search for other *un-* opposites to print on the cards and add to the board. If the game is played team-style, a team gets a point for each *un-*opposite uncovered by a member. A team has a right to challenge any words added by the other side.

A similar word game can be played with other structural units, such as *dis-, con-, in-, -ment, -tion, -ance, -ness,* and *-ful.* In each case the children start with words they already know. In searching the dictionary for others to add to their listings, they increase the number of words on which they can rely as they speak and write, and they increase their understanding of structural spelling relationships—how these morphemes are added to other morphemes. The latter understanding can be applied as children attempt to use words in their writing, especially if lists of new word discoveries are posted about the classroom. Such listings serve as crutches to encourage young writers to use words that they have not used before to record thoughts on paper.

Structurally similar words can also be encountered in groups. Playing orally with relationships within such words, youngsters incorporate the words into their functional vocabularies. One fun example is the words in which /ey/ is represented by et because of a common French origin. Children can begin with words like *buffet* and *bouquet* supplied by the teacher. Their job is to uncover structurally related words, and to get the job done, it is permissible to go to the dictionary. The search continues for several days as young word sleuths search and add related words to a bulletin board chart. Similar game-search activities can take place with words that contain units like *photo*, *phono*, *therm*, or *graph*; with contractions like *it's*, *don't*, and *shouldn't*; with hyphenated words; with words of similar foreign origins. The objective is more than just having the youngsters develop an understanding of the structural relationships among words within their language. The objective is having youngsters begin to use these words in writing and when they do to spell them correctly.

To achieve this goal, some teachers at times ask children to write based on a set of given words. One set for writing might be *their*, *there*, *they're*, *motorcyclist's*, *motorcyclists'*. Youngsters must write a paragraph that includes each of these words. The results often are not what teachers typically call creative; however, creativity is not the purpose here. The purpose is to get children to use certain words accurately spelled in their writing. Sets of words assigned for use in this way include contractions, homonyms, words often confused (*affect*, *effect*; *desert*, *dessert*), and possessives.

SOME SUMMARY THOUGHTS

To write is to build words into sentences and paragraphs by selecting those words that communicate most precisely and attractively. In making this statement, the authors of this book hasten to add that learning to write is not merely the study of vocabulary lists. If it becomes this in the classroom, then we are not really involved in writing at all. We must remember that words are merely a vehicle to be used. Children must learn how to use their growing word pools to play with ideas and capture them on paper. This is the function of word study as it relates to written expression in the language arts and in the content areas.

8

LET CHILDREN REWRITE, EDIT, AND EVALUATE ◄► puttying up the holes

Blot out, correct, insert, refine,
Enlarge, diminish, interline
Be mindful, when invention fails,
To scratch your head and bite your nails.
Jonathan Swift, ON POETRY

In *Poetry and Poets* (Houghton Mifflin, 1930), speaking of the process of making poetry, Amy Lowell asserted that—

> a poet must be both born and made. He must be born with a sub-conscious factory always working for him or he never can be a poet at all, and he must have knowledge and talent enough to "putty" up his holes—to use Mr. Graves's expression. Let no one undervalue this process of puttying; it is a condition of good poetry. Of the many first manuscript drafts of great poets that have passed through my hands in the last twenty-five years, I have seen none without its share of putty.

Samuel Johnson talked too of the effort of writing: "What is written without effort is in general read without pleasure" (*Miscellanies*, vol. 2). Boileau in *L'Art Poetique* suggested continued revision as part of writing: "Hasten slowly; without losing heart. Twenty times upon the anvil place your work." Ovid proposed discarding unsuccessful attempts: "Much have I written, but what I thought defective I have myself given to the flames for their revision" (*Tristia*, Book 4). Some of these writers were concerned with poetry, some with prose. Yet there seems to be general agreement among them that revision is a necessary part of writing. The writer cannot do without "putty."

RESEARCH ON WRITING AND REVISION

Rewriting and editing words already committed to paper are integral parts of composing. These twin processes, with the self-evaluation necessary to achieve a more polished piece, should be a part of classroom writing activity. Research studies, which are helpful to the teacher who is assisting children in puttying their own writing, are beginning to supply some understanding of what is involved in improving writing. These are of three kinds:

- Statistical analyses of a broad sample of children's papers to determine the kinds of revisions children of different ages typically make.
- Case studies that focus on how individual children at given stages in their development approach revision tasks.
- Analyses of the effects of certain instructional strategies on children's developing skill.

How Children Generally View and Approach Revision Tasks

One of the most comprehensive studies of children's writing ability is that carried out over the last ten years or so by the National Assessment of Educational Progress. Researchers in this instance studied samples of writing from 2,500 children age nine, 2,000 young people age thirteen, and 2,000 young people age seventeen. Although faulted because only one writing sample from each participant was analyzed, an important phase of the research centered directly on how young people make revisions in their own writing. (See John Mellon, "Round Two of the National Writing Assessment—Interpreting the Apparent Decline of Writing Ability: A Review," *Research in the Teaching of English*, 10:66–74, Spring 1976.) For purposes of the study, revisions were classified into nine categories, which may be of help to the teacher who must think in terms of programs to assist children in revising. These included—

- cosmetic changes, or changes in the overall appearance of a composition.

- mechanical changes, or changes in spelling, punctuation, underlining, paragraphing, and capitalization.
- grammatical changes, or changes made to conform to grammatical conventions like subject and verb agreement.
- continuational changes, or additions of a word, phrase, sentence, or section to the end of the report.
- transitional changes, or additions, deletions, or substitutions of connecting words or short transitional sections.
- informational changes, or additions or deletions of information.
- stylistic changes, or the substitution of a word, phrase, or sentence where informational content was not altered.
- organizational changes, or the rearrangement of elements within sentences or paragraphs.
- holistic changes, or radical departures from the overall approach of the first draft.

Figure 8.1 is a graphical representation of the nine categories. Taken from the document *Write/Rewrite: An Assessment of Revision Skills* (NAEP, 1977, p. 13), the graph indicates the kinds of changes made by nine- and thirteen-year-olds. It shows that most changes, regardless of a child's age, were stylistic, mechanical, and informational, and that the thirteen-year-olds made more mechanical, grammatical, informational, transitional, stylistic, and organizational changes than their younger counterparts. Specifically, "13-year-olds made twice as many organizational changes and three times as many transitional changes as did the 9-year-olds." In contrast, "the changes made by 9-year-olds seemed to reflect a more superficial perception of revision; 9-year-olds included more cosmetic changes than did 13-year-olds, and when they added information, entered it without concern for logical order" (p. 12). Then, too, the younger writers made slightly more holistic changes than their older counterparts. Since holistic changes involve "starting from scratch," the researchers hypothesized that this indicated a lack of familiarity with what is expected in revision and thus a lesser ability to revise.

Discussing the results of the write/rewrite study, NAEP researchers developed a "working definition" of revision processes as performed by children and youth. Students generally revise by substituting more appropriate words for those in earlier drafts, adding or deleting information, and reviewing capitalization, punctuation, and other mechanical conventions. They seldom revise by improving the overall organization or by clarifying the transitions between ideas.

An obvious question at this point is, "Why?"—Why do students function as they do? Several explanations can be proposed. One possibility is that students are functioning in terms of what they have been

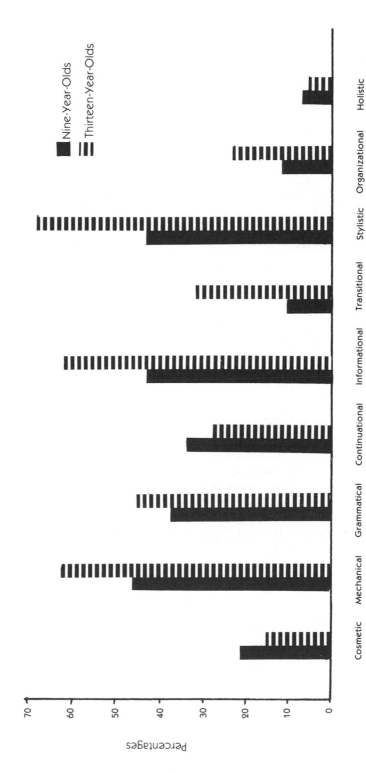

Figure 8.1. Percentages of types of revision for nine- and thirteen-year-olds

taught. If teachers tend to emphasize matters of spelling, capitalization, punctuation, and word changes, is it not likely that youngsters will emphasize these in their revisions? If teachers do little with helping children organize ideas and smooth out transitions, will not children's attempts reflect this lack of attention? Also, organization of ideas into smooth-flowing paragraphs requires higher-level thinking skills than those required to review capitalization or check spelling in a dictionary. If teachers have done little to help children see relationships among ideas, children must acquire this important skill on their own. Perhaps what this research is saying to the teacher is that we ourselves must review our conceptions of revision processes; we must go beyond concern simply with cosmetic, stylistic, and mechanical matters and put greater emphasis on organizational and transitional aspects of writing.

How Individual Children Revise

Instead of studying the compositions of many young writers, some researchers are beginning to observe a few youngsters while they actually write to determine how they function in consigning thoughts to paper. An oft-cited study is one by Janet Emig (*The Composing Processes of Twelfth Graders*, National Council of Teachers of English, 1971) in which the researcher studied the prewriting, planning, starting, stopping, and reformulating behaviors of eight twelfth graders using a case study approach. In her report of the study, Emig describes the reformulating attitude and activity of one young person, Lynn. For Lynn, "rewriting seems to be the act of 'correcting' errors in the accidents of discourse—spelling, punctuation, titling, and the like. Such essences as organization of the whole and tone are, seemingly, left undisturbed. There is only a superficial, a surface realignment or correcting the trivial" (p. 68). Lynn herself explains the reason for her inconsequential use of revision:

> Partly because it seemed to be punishment work we were just said (*sic*), if you have more than so many mistakes, you have to rewrite your composition and it has to be in by Friday . . . maybe she talked to me about my composition I don't remember but I never remember any suggestions which inspired me, to rewrite something, so that there was any change in the, so that it was any better, the only changes seemed to be technical.

Others of the case study subjects in the Emig study do more with revision than Lynn does. Some differentiate aspects of the process. One talks of proofreading, or "seeing if I left anything out" and of revising, or moving "things around." Another talks of proofreading and rearranging:

First I reread, to see if I left out any commas or used the wrong tense. . . . I know a lot of times I don't see better ways to write things and then sometimes I will; I will rearrange a lot (p. 86).

But none actually engages in reformulating pieces he or she wrote as part of Emig's investigation. Emig concludes, "Students do not voluntarily revise school-sponsored writing" (p. 93).

In 1978 Donald Graves began an investigation of the revising behaviors of elementary children. At this writing, the study is still in progress, but, as he proceeds, Graves is reporting his findings in a series of articles in *Language Arts* (see January 1979, March 1979, and October 1979). Using a case-study approach, Graves is focusing on the activity of eight children as they move from grade one through grade two and eight children from grade three through grade four. Through the investigation Graves hopes to find out how children's revision behavior changes over a two-year period, specifically how they change in terms of—

1. Composing: Concept of composing, composing in several media forms, proofreading, precomposing activity, use of overt language while composing, reading habits, use of resources, themes in unassigned writing, use of territory in content areas, semantic and syntactic issues, use of logic, use of adverbs, verbs and verb tense.
2. Spelling: Approach to invented spelling, use of resources for spelling, concept of spelling, child's reading in relation to words used in writing, description of how he/she spells.
3. Handwriting: Use of thumb and forefinger, writing continuity, elbow position and motion, strength, use of space on paper, directional language, use of writing instruments, composing surfaces, imitation of set forms, concept of handwriting. (January 1979, p. 77)

In March 1979 Graves reported on some of his initial findings and provided some blow-by-blow descriptions of children's activities. For example, he described Sarah:

Sarah stops, and with furrowed brow, looks again at the word, *jul* (*jewel*) she has just written, erases it, and over the same thin, blackened spot of lined newsprint paper she sounds and rewrites, *juwul*. Sarah sensed that something was missing when she first wrote. Sounding it through again confirmed that a *w* was needed. Six-year-old Sarah has been writing for a week; this is her first act of revision.

Graves also described eight-year-old Brian who has just begun to change words because he wants more precise meanings and eight-year-old Andrea who runs jagged lines through sentences and draws arrows to indicate changes in word order rather than erasing.

The behavior of these youngsters hints that most early revisions are at the word level and involve adjustments in spelling and that the revisions children attempt are influenced by the teacher's approach to the activity. Brian's teacher asked him to write about personal experience, believing that revision is easiest when it relates to incidents with high personal significance. Brian's teacher also asked him to write three leads, or beginning sentences, and to choose the best from his multiple starts and encouraged rather than discouraged crossing-outs. Andrea's teacher did much the same, helping her overcome the dilemma posed by the wish to adjust problems in writing she perceived and the desire to make it look neat—not to have a messy paper. Between early October when she first faced this problem and learned to handle it and December, Andrea's revisions advanced to the point where she would delete paragraphs, reorder sentences and paragraphs, and insert new information—rewriting activities not that common among the samples of writing examined in the National Assessment of Educational Progress study of revision. To do this, she does not erase, but employs a variety of editing techniques. Graves suggests that such behavior indicates "a changed view toward words. Words for these children, are now temporary, malleable, or claylike. The words can be changed until they evolve toward the right meaning . . ." (*Language Arts*, 56:319, March, 1979).

What does this research tell the teacher of the language arts? At one level, the investigations by Emig and Graves provide evidence of the usefulness of the case-study approach in gathering data about the composing act. The fact that these data are in anecdotal form that makes for delightful reading is an added bonus. But more than this, these studies tell us how important teacher attitude and behavior are if we hope to involve children in revision and if we hope to have students come away with the feeling that to rewrite and edit are integral components of writing. As teachers we must not put such stress on neatness that children are fearful of scrawling lines of a first draft or marking it up with arrows, lines, and additions. Instead, we must show youngsters how to do it and even give assignments such as Graves's "multiple starts" that involve children in revision from the very beginning. In Graves's words "teachers can play a significant role in releasing a child's potential for revision."

How Various Instructional Strategies Affect Children's Writing Behavior

Other researchers supply teachers with evidence of the effectiveness or ineffectiveness of certain instructional strategies in helping youngsters improve in writing ability. These studies are significant in that they debunk numerous myths about just what constitutes good instruction in written expression.

For example, many teachers believe that by teaching children formal grammar they are helping to improve the skills of writing. Research evidence, however, shows otherwise. In 1960 Ingrid Strom analyzed more than fifty studies conducted from 1906 to 1939. Based on this comprehensive analysis, Strom concluded that instructional strategies focusing directly on writing processes are "more effective in improving writing than are grammar drills and diagramming" ("Research in Grammar and Usage and Its Implications for Teaching Writing," *Bulletin of the School of Education, Indiana University,* 36:13–14, September 1960). Summarizing a series of more recent studies, some of which considered the effects of formal study of structural or transformational grammar, Elizabeth Haynes reported similar findings and concluded that "the effectiveness of transformational grammar as an aid in writing seems doubtful" ("Using Research in Preparing to Teach Writing," *English Journal,* 67:82–88, January 1978). In short, rather than spending considerable time in the study of formal grammar, young people need to be involved actively with the actual processes carried on by successful writers—one of which is rewriting.

A second strategy some teachers employ to encourage student revision is teacher correction. Reading a youngster's paper, they revise for the child—reorganizing, editing for punctuation, capitalization, and usage, rewriting awkward sentences, and making deletions. Receiving a teacher-edited paper, the child makes a final draft by copying the composition with the teacher's changes. Studies by Buxton, Clarke, and Adams summarized by Elizabeth Haynes in the January 1978 issue of *English Journal* show that intensive marking by the teacher does not necessarily result in heightened writing skill. More important than intensive teacher corrections were positive comments; a study by Gee in 1972 suggests that such comments resulted in greater sentence maturity than negative comments or no comments at all. In Haynes's words "intensive correction of errors is futile" (p. 85).

Haynes also concludes that just letting children write more and more is not that productive. Numerous studies have been undertaken that have compared groups given extensive opportunity to write with groups given much less opportunity. Summarizing these investigations, Haynes comments, "It seems safe to conclude at present that although some of the studies relating to frequency of writing are inconsistent, most of them point to the contention that mere writing does not improve writing." In short, grammar learning, teacher correction of errors, and frequent writing—all strategies on which elementary teachers have relied in the past to improve children's writing skills—have been proved ineffective. Other forms of direct teacher intervention in children's writing activity must be designed.

MAKING REVISION A PART OF CLASSROOM WRITING

Clearly, if children and youth are to perceive revision as an integral aspect of writing and are to function on their perceptions, revision must be structured directly into programs in ways that are not odious. Unfortunately, although research indicates what strategies are ineffective in building and refining skills, teachers have almost no definitive data suggesting successful practices. For that reason, we must start with a premise: instruction in revision should involve children directly in the process so that children learn revision skills as they write. Let us next look at ways to achieve direct involvement.

Revising Together

February second—Groundhog Day! Roxanne Russell, the teacher of a group of middle graders, gathered her class for a talk-listen-write-revise session on groundhogs, woodchucks, and the groundhog legend. Students began by recalling what they knew about this furry little animal and what they knew about groundhog folklore. Not sure exactly how woodchucks were related to groundhogs, they checked the dictionary, listening to definitions read aloud by a classmate. They also listened to a brief section from a trade book that their teacher shared orally with them and to the poem "Groundhog Day" by Marnie Pomeroy. Then they summarized their understanding through writing. Functioning as a group, students took turns dictating sentences that Ms. Russell recorded on the board. This is their summary first draft:

> THE GROUNDHOG
> A groundhog is a small, furry animal. He looks for his shadow once a year. Woodchuck is another name for groundhog. The day he comes out is February 2. If he sees his shadow there are six more weeks of winter. A groundhog lives in a burrow. A groundhog sleeps all winter.

As was her custom, Ms. Russell returned immediately with her students to recast what they had written in a better form. The teacher asked, "What sentences belong up here with our first sentence about the groundhog?"

Students saw the problem they had created. The sentence *He looks for his shadow once a year* was written down too soon. It belonged not with the first sentence but with the two about Groundhog Day. Dividing their sentences into two kinds—those dealing with groundhogs in general and those telling about Groundhog Day—the youngsters redrafted their sentences to form this description:

THE GROUNDHOG AND HIS DAY
A groundhog is a small, furry animal. A groundhog lives in a burrow. A groundhog sleeps all winter. Woodchuck is another name for groundhog. He looks for his shadow once a year. The day he comes out is February 2. If he sees his shadow there are six more weeks of winter.

Once children had grouped related sentences together, Ms. Russell inquired, "We have a number of very short sentences here about the groundhog. Is there any way we could build one longer sentence out of two?"

One participant suggested combining the second and third sentences to form *He lives in a burrow and sleeps all winter.* Another suggested making one sentence from the two remaining ones: *A groundhog is a small, furry animal that sleeps in a burrow all winter.* And when Ms. Russell asked the students if they could add more information to this "million dollar" sentence, one youngster proposed *A groundhog is a small, furry, brown animal that sleeps in a burrow all winter.* This became the first sentence in the class-revised summary.

Ms. Russell guided her students to consider successive sentences in a similar way. They combined ideas into more complex sentences, added more information, and then checked punctuation. The dictionary sleuth for the week double-checked the spelling of burrow and of groundhog to see if indeed it was a compound word as written in their story. The final product, replete with arrows to show changes and with cross-outs to show deletions, went like this:

THE GROUNDHOG AND HIS SHADOW
A groundhog is a small, furry, brown animal that sleeps in a burrow all winter. Woodchuck is another name for groundhog.
This little animal comes out of his burrow on February 2. If he sees his shadow, there are six more weeks of winter. If he doesn't see it, it is time for spring.

Ms. Russell's fourth grade

In much the same way, as part of a study of Greek myths, Janet Neu led her third-grade class to compose and revise their own Greek myth. Having listened to and read many myths, the youngsters cooperatively dictated this piece, which the teacher wrote on charting paper for them.

THE GREEK PARTY

After the Troyan War the Greeks brought lots of food and popcorn and peanuts. Crayolaus brought beer. Alphyus got drunk. He poured beer on Gigi's head. Gigi threw Alphyus down the stairs. This started a war between themselves. All of a sudden guards came in and stopped the fighting and Crayolaus attacked one of the guards and Prumie took on the other three. Then the god Zeus heard the fighting and decided to punish them. Zeus' punishment for Gigi was falling through a hole and Alphyus was put in a bag and thrown in the river. Which just goes to show, two wars are not healthy.

Working sentence by sentence with the third graders, Ms. Neu guided children as they applied "putty" to their cooperative story; she asked specific questions such as "What word might we substitute here? What word or words in this sentence are unnecessary and could be crossed out? Instead of stringing these three sentences together with *ands*, how could we change them? What word could we add here to combine these two sentences and show the relationship between the ideas? Where do we need a new paragraph? Why there? Why did I put an apostrophe here when I recorded for you? Did I do it correctly?" Youngsters volunteered to come forward to add arrows, cross-outs, circles, additions to the class story until everyone was satisfied with it. So satisfied were the children that a group got together to record the story on tape; a second group drew a series of illustrative pictures to go along with the tape in the manner of a sound filmstrip. Here is their finished product:

THE GREEK PARTY

After the Troyan War, the Greeks decided to have a party. Everyone brought lots of food, including popcorn and peanuts. Crayolaus brought beer, and Alphyus who got drunk poured beer on Gigi's head. Gigi threw Alphyus down the stairs and started another war. All of a sudden, four guards came in and stopped the fighting. Crayolaus attacked one of the guards, and Prumie took on the other three.

The god Zeus heard the fighting and punished Alphyus and Gigi. Zeus' punishment for Gigi was falling through a hole forever, and Alphyus was put into a sack and thrown in the river. Which just goes to show, too many wars aren't healthy!

The Advantages of Teacher-Guided Group Editing and Rewriting

As these two examples demonstrate, through teacher-guided group editing and rewriting, students are encouraged to reformulate sentences and paragraphs they have composed together. Guided by a teacher's focused questions, children begin to acquire the powers of self-evaluation. They see that no first writing is perfect, that all must be "puttied" if the results are worth sharing with others.

Equally important, through participation in group-editing sessions children learn to handle basic language conventions associated with writing. For children to revise what they have written independently, they must have some understanding of the way in which the English language is manipulated and some skill in handling these manipulations. For instance, when children write stories containing dialogue, they must be able to handle quotation marks as well as place other punctuation markers in reference to the quotation marks. Basically, recording direct quotations is a rather simple process, but unless children have some idea of how speech is written down, they will be unable to record verbal interactions between story characters in the conventional way.

As part of teacher-guided group revision sessions, children can distinguish the words their story characters speak from other narrative-type lines. Beginning to handle quotation marks, they must at first follow the teacher's lead, who may have to show the children just where quotation marks are placed by having them check stories in their reading books. The books in this case serve as models as to how authors use punctuation in recording their thoughts. Cooperatively children and teacher apply punctuation in the same way as book authors do. In later group sessions children and teacher decide together just how to place punctuation marks as they revise stories they are writing together.

Not only can children acquire first-level understandings of language conventions as part of teacher-guided group editing and rewriting, but they can also acquire editorial skills. Children must know how to "putty" if they are to proceed eventually as independent revisionists. To demonstrate to children just how to add "putty," some teachers record first drafts of cooperative compositions on charts with black flopens and have children make changes they suggest with green or some other color. In addition, changes are made not by erasing but by marking over. Children scratch out unwanted words, draw arrows to relocate sentences and paragraphs, add new words by inserting them above the line. Some basic proofreading symbols are helpful here. Instead of rewriting, students insert on the first draft the standard signs shown on page 220.

By participating in group rewriting in this way, youngsters like Andrea in Donald Graves's study learn that a first draft need not be neat and that it is perfectly acceptable and even essential to put notes on the draft to show where "putty" is to be applied.

Clearly, however, if these advantages are to accrue from group revision sessions, the teacher must be firmly in control of the situation, for the questions that he or she asks about the composition in first draft lead youngsters to consider possible avenues for editing and rewriting. If the teacher does not see the possibilities for revision and for instruction in related language conventions inherent in a particular piece being dictated by children, little or no learning can go on. In group revision the teacher is key!

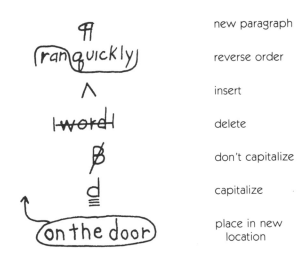

new paragraph

reverse order

insert

delete

don't capitalize

capitalize

place in new location

Moving from Group Revision to Individual Revision— Some Strategies

Eventually students must work as independent editors, going back to putty their own pieces. Group activity as just detailed lays the foundation for independent work. In addition, teachers can facilitate the transition in several rather specific ways. Here are just a few.

Writing with Eventual Revision in Mind. Youngsters should write knowing that a revision will take place. They begin by writing on every other line with ample margins so that they can add or cross out later on without problems of space. Unable to think of a precise word, youngsters are encouraged to leave a blank to be filled in later with the aid of a thesaurus, another student, or the teacher. Uncertain of how to spell a word, they make an interpretable attempt, noting *sp* over the word as a reminder to make a later dictionary check. If uncertainty is with a technical problem of usage—whether to capitalize, indent, use a possessive form—they indicate the site with a predetermined mark such as *u*. These items are the first to be checked as writers return to polish their writing.

Listening to What One Has Written. Another technique that some successful writers employ is listening to what they have written, using the sound of sentences, words, phrases, and punctuation markers as a guide for making changes. (See Charles Cooper and Lee Odell, "Considerations of Sound in the Composing Process of Published Writers," *Research in the Teaching of English*, 10:103–15, Fall 1976.) Children should be encouraged to read orally what they have written and to listen to identify sentence boundaries and the kinds of punctuation necessary. Through oral reading and listening, students can identify words omitted unintentionally from a sentence or letters simply left out of a word. One second-grade child had written *The boys are in the street* as *The boys a in the street*. Reading the sentence aloud to her teacher, the child promptly perceived her omission and said, "Oh, I forgot to finish the word." Without prompting, she made the correction.

Similarly, listening to what one has written helps in identifying words placed inappropriately in a sentence and jerky repetitive sentence patterns. Especially with rhythmic poetry, listening makes evident the interplay of sounds and the flowing rhythm of the lines. As writers hear their own poems, they can extend the listening process, conducting the lines with the hands or beating the rhythm with the feet. When editing prose selections, writers simply mouth the words to themselves, listen while another youngster reads the words to them, or listen while a tape recorder plays back words previously recorded.

Obviously, children gain much from reading compositions aloud to their teacher, who then helps them listen for problems. However, because teacher time is limited, at some point children can work together in listen-and-revise-teams. Two youngsters who have just written independently can orally share their compositions with each other. Together they listen to each piece to make revision decisions.

By fourth grade, children can function as independent and team editors rather successfully if they have had gradual introduction to procedures through teacher-guided sessions. In contrast, primary youngsters need greater teacher guidance; some editing and rewriting have to occur in conference with the teacher so that children acquire the skills they need to improve their writing.

Creating Alternative Lines. Asking youngsters to create several alternative lines to use in a particular instance is another way to help them see that there is not just one way to express a thought on paper. A good beginning is in titling a piece. The teacher urges, "Let's brainstorm as many different titles to our poem, or summary, or story as we possibly can." Following up, the teacher queries, "Which one shall we use? Why?" Similarly, children can be asked to write a line that could substitute for one already contained within a composition, create several different beginning lines to use in starting a story, or create several different possible endings from which to choose. Having written a descriptive word into a sentence such as *small, light, funny*, children can be asked to identify several alternates and then select one from the group to use in a final sentence. Such activity can occur as part of teacher-guided writing, small group writing, and independent writing.

Applying Putty in Color.   Proofreading techniques applied in group sessions can be carried over to independent writing. Charts outlining editorial symbols as given on page 220 can be hung in the writing center; children can use colored pens in editing and rewriting. Both first and follow-up drafts of revised compositions can be mounted on the bulletin board to show the development of ideas.

Writing It Again for a Different Audience.   In writing, a sense of audience is important. Since a piece of writing is intended to communicate an idea to a particular group of people—the audience—just who that audience is should be considered in writing. Upper graders can be asked to rewrite a paper, written initially to communicate with one audience, to communicate with a different group. Or upper graders can write two versions of the same piece as part of one assignment: Let's write a thank you note to a friend who has just given you a skateboard for your birthday. Then let's write a note to a friend of your father's who has given you the skateboard. How would you vary the letter to communicate to each of these people?

Revising and Editing with a Word Processor.   Some microcomputers have text editing capabilities. This means that a writer types on a keyboard, that his or her words appear on a television-like monitor rather than on paper, and that the writer can then tell the computer to make changes in what has appeared simply by feeding in a series of commands. Having arrived at a revised draft the writer commands the machine to print out a copy.

As Seymour Papert of MIT explains, "The computer is rapidly becoming the standard writing instrument. Most journalists use word processors, as do increasingly many offices. . . . A well-designed text editor makes editing—substitution and deletion of words, shifting of sentences or paragraphs, and so on—an easy and aesthetically acceptable process. Compare the situation of a child attempting such a process with paper and pencil: the mess of multiple erasures and labor of rewriting means that the first draft is almost always the final copy.''

Although the use of microcomputers with word-processing capabilities has not infiltrated the schools to any extent today, they could conceivably change the way children in school writing programs approach individual writing and rewriting. Youngsters would go to a writing center to type thoughts into a computer, rewrite by feeding in commands, and then call for a clean copy to be produced by the printer-component. How this approach would affect children's attitudes toward writing is still an unknown. Papert, however, tells us, "I have seen children who hated writing become avid writers when they have a text editor at their disposal" (*Byte Publications*, September 1980, p. 238).

Reviewing Language Usage Conventions— Some Strategies

Even as they encounter conventions associated with writing down as part of group writing and rewriting activity, youngsters may need some related work with the conventions. The standard ways in which language is manipulated on paper can be taught inductively by having children analyze examples of a specific usage and discover for themselves the generalizations that describe the way the language works. For example, to help children who are writing conversation stories, the teacher might sequence in some work with the way conversation is handled in writing. Teaching inductively, the instructor would present a group with a series of model sentences. These can be ones that youngsters have just dictated and that have been recorded on an experience chart:

> THE DOUGHNUT STORE
> Mara said, "I liked the doughnut store best."
> Jack asked, "Why did you like the doughnut store?"
> Mara answered, "I liked the smell of the doughnuts. They smelled so good."
> Tom added, "I liked the smell too."

Following the dictation, the teacher suggests, "Let's read the words Mara said, the words Jackie said, the next words Mara said, and Tommie's words." He or she then helps the youngsters analyze: "On paper what marks show the words each child spoke? What kind of pause marker do we use just before the spoken words? Where do we put our end punctuation?" To see if children can apply their understanding, the teacher can ask them to finish sentences using their own words:

- Marty asked, _____
- José answered, _____
- Keith said, _____
- Marcia replied, _____
- Laurel wrote, _____

Working in editing pairs, children compare sentences they have written to the models.

The second lesson in an inductive series involves analysis of sentences of slightly greater complexity:

> "I like the doughnut store best," said Mara.
> "Why did you like it?" asked Jack.
> "I liked the smell of the doughnuts. They smelled so good," Mara answered.

The initial focus is on how these sentences differ from the models studied before. When children have identified the differences, they can consider how they know which words were spoken, what kinds of pause markers are used at the ends of a speaker's words, and what kinds of pause markers are found at the ends of sentences. Their next task is to rewrite sentences composed previously so that each patterns in this new way. Later, perhaps working in sentence-writing teams, they create other sentences that adhere to the pattern. Later still, they create stories in which characters talk to one another.

Helpful in applying understanding in follow-up editing and rewriting sessions are editing guides against which individuals can evaluate their own productions. An editing guide would include such questions as these: Have I put quotation marks around all the words spoken? Have I used a comma after such words as *John said*, *Sylvia remarked*, *Kim asked*, when these words come before the spoken words? Have I put a period, question mark, or exclamation point inside the quotation marks depending on whether the words make a statement, ask a question, or exclaim, if those words come at the end of the sentence? Questions of these kinds are raised after children have written their stories when they are in the process of revising their own work.

Teachers can develop similarly structured sequences when they find that children's writing indicates an inability to handle a specific language convention. As children write, at some point they will probably require instruction in economical and precise word use, standard usage patterns, punctuation and capitalization conventions, sentence and paragraph construction, handwriting, and forms considered appropriate for final drafts. Here is a brief discussion that suggests areas for consideration as youngsters write and return to polish what they have composed.

Using Words with Precision. Children generally need some dictionary work so that they can use this tool to check word meaning, usage, and spelling as part of revision activity. Of course, young writers must know how to locate entries in the dictionary. Additionally, they need to realize the importance of checking words with silent letters (*pneumonia, knight*), vowel sounds that may be represented by one of several graphemes (*although, beau, doe, owing*), consonant sounds that may be represented by more than one grapheme (*phone, fox*), foreign origins that may not abide by generalizations learned (*buffet, apropos*), and two vowels coming together that might be reversed (*conceit, believe*). Young writers may also need work with commonly encountered homonym sets, contractions, and words the meaning of which are sometimes confused as *affect* and *effect, desert* and *dessert, further* and *farther.*

Standard Usage Patterns. Many dictionaries and style manuals enumerate specific points of usage that are helpful to the teacher. William Strunk and E. B. White's *The Elements of Style* (Macmillan, 1979), Porter Perrin and Wilma Ebbitt's *Writer's Guide and Index to English* (Scott, Foresman, 1972), and Robert Graves and Alan Hodge's *The Reader Over Your Shoulder* (Vintage, 1979) should be part of every writing teacher's personal library so that he or she can answer student queries. Still, the average elementary student will probably encounter only limited aspects of usage in composing: agreement of subject and verb, use of past and future forms of verbs, use of the appropriate participle form, and use of negative forms.

Punctuation and Capitalization. Closely related to standards of word usage are accepted notions regarding capitalization and punctuation in writing. As they write children in elementary school will probably need some specific work with these punctuation patterns—

- selecting appropriate end punctuation as in *Help! Where are you? I am here.*
- using comma in compound constructions as in *I will bring pie, cake, and doughnuts. The clouds formed, the rain came, and rivers ran in the streets.*
- using comma in direct address as in *Bruce, come here.*
- using comma and quotation marks in direct quotations as in *Coach Thompson asked, "How many boys can play?"*
- using period after abbreviations.
- using comma in subordinating ideas at the beginning of sentences as in *If you are happy, your face glows.* Nonuse of comma in subordinating ideas at the end of sentences as in *Your face glows when you are happy.*

- using comma in nonrestrictive adjective clauses and appositives as in *Ms. Alvarez, who is our fifth-grade teacher, is home today. Merv, the star of the team, broke his leg.*
- using comma in parenthetical expressions as in *Tim, on the other hand, decided not to go.*
- using semicolon in coordinating clauses as in *The flood waters rose; the people evacuated their homes.*

Children also need some attention to capitalization conventions, specifically the capitalization of first words of sentences, titles, countries, continents, states, cities, towns, and languages, all proper names, major words in titles.

Economy in Word Usage.   To edit their work, children need to consider how to avoid wordiness in writing. Specific duplications for which a writer/self-editor may look are—

- needless duplication of adjectives, adverbs, or verbs as in *The big, enormous building towers over Chicago. Jose stared and gaped. She did it quickly and speedily.*
- unwarranted use of determiners and intensifiers as in *She was very contented in the spring.*
- use of two or more words where one suffices as in *I ascended up to the fifth floor.*

Sentencing.   In checking clarity of sentence construction, the self-editor looks for—

- run-on sentences as in *Mary bought some candy, her favorite was chocolate-covered almonds*, which should be punctuated as two sentences.
- incomplete sentences as in *Running into a big, stone wall*, which requires a verb structure to make it complete.

In addition, to prepare for rewriting activity, children will need work with sentence joining and embedding as described in chapter 6.

Paragraphing.   When rewriting, writers focus not only on words and sentence patterns but also on larger thought units—the paragraph, the stanza, the material included under major and minor subtitles. The reader may wish to review chapter 5 that details specific instructional strategies. Once children have gained some understanding of how to handle these larger thought units, they may use a guide for self-analysis similar to the one given in figure 8.2.

Figure 8.2. A guide for analyzing paragraph structures

HOW I AM DOING WITH MY PARAGRAPHS			
	Always	Sometimes	Never
1. Does each paragraph have a main idea that holds it together?			
2. Are there any sentences in a paragraph that do not belong there?			
3. Is the same idea developed in more than one paragraph? Should some paragraphs be combined?			
4. Are related paragraphs grouped together?			
5. Does the order of my paragraphs seem natural?			

Handwriting and Form. Clear handwriting is important, but the writing of a first draft is *not* the time to perfect one's skills. Preparing a final draft for "publication"—that is, for mounting on the bulletin board, for inclusion in a class book, for sharing with parents and other students—is another matter. At that point, clarity in handwriting becomes significant. Perhaps one of the most meaningful contexts in which to take particular care with penmanship is in recording a final

Figure 8.3. A checklist that focuses on handwriting and form

HOW MY PUBLISHED PIECE LOOKS												
	Paper 1			Paper 2			Paper 3			Paper 4		
	G	OK	P	G	OK	P	G	OK	P	G	OK	P
1. Do all my letters sit on the line?												
2. Is my spacing uniform throughout?												
3. Are my letters clearly written?												
4. Is my title centered on the top line?												
5. Are my margins even?												
6. Is my paper attractive?												
Code: G = great; OK = average; P = poor, or needs improvement												

draft; the activity is not an academic exercise but a necessity if others are to enjoy what one has written. The same is true in regards to the form of that draft, specifically location of title, evenness of margins, and overall neatness. Having created a "published piece," youngsters can go back to evaluate it by asking themselves the kinds of questions given in figure 8.3.

ORGANIZING A WRITING PROGRAM FOR REVISION

Some readers who have had considerable experience teaching elementary school children by now may be saying, "But I must correct children's work for them; they could never do it by themselves." In one respect, this is true. Children on their own probably will not have the skill as self-editors to go back to putty their work unless the teacher has prepared them for the task and has organized writing activity to encourage revisions. Let us talk for a moment about how to build revision into the writing program.

The Writing Folder and the Editing Guide

Time is a factor in an author's ability to revise a manuscript. Only after time has passed can an author look at his or her own work with the eye of an impartial outsider, deleting words and phrases that only several days before seemed pure inspiration. Children, too, should wait to revise; they should write today, revise tomorrow, and even revise again the next day. In the words of Quintilian, "Let our literary compositions be laid aside for some time, that we may after a reasonable period return to their perusal, and find them, as it were, altogether new to us." (*De Institutione Oratoria*, book Y).

As a way of encouraging children to return to a piece "after a reasonable time," the teacher can have all youngsters keep a writing folder of work in progress. Beginning a piece, a young writer marks it *first draft* and adds it to his or her personal file folder. In the folder are pieces going through second and third revisions, as well as final drafts.

The individual writing file brings certain advantages. The folder makes it possible for youngsters to work at their own pace; all need not be working on the same "assignment." One child may decide to revise something in which she may be deeply involved today while another may begin a poem with which he has been toying subconsciously. Also the folder system makes it easy for children to go to the file during seatwork periods, locate his or her folder, and edit materials not yet in final draft.

Finally the file folder works well from a practical standpoint. After a period of revision, a paper may begin to look like a patchwork quilt—a sheet stapled here, half a sheet clipped there. Of course, no intermediary draft should be judged on neatness, for a paper under revision can hardly be kept neat as lines and paragraphs are added, deleted, and changed. Under these conditions, a folder helps maintain order.

Still another way to encourage revision is the individualized editing guide, a list of specific points to look for in revision. Usually, each youngster has specific writing weaknesses that are unique to him or her. One may not differentiate between *there* and *their*, tend to write run-on or incomplete sentences, and overwork the word *nice*. After the teacher has worked with this child on these points, they become items on the personal editing guide to be used during revision. The child posts the guide on the inside of the personal writing folder to use in editing. Initially, the teacher, who is "senior editor," helps the youngster construct a guide, but as writing progresses both the writer and the "senior editor" add further items. The writer can even acquire a "house editor," another child with whom he or she pairs for cross-editing.

It is impossible, of course, to include all the points of construction and usage a youngster is encountering on his or her personal guide. In revising, emphasis must be on two or three items in primary grades and four or five items in upper grades. Items relate specifically to major problems recurring in writing. Each guide, therefore, should be simple, reflecting most serious problems in construction. Some constructions and usages are employed only in formal pieces. This level is hardly applicable in elementary school communication, and such conventions should not be stressed in the development of writing and editing guides.

Functional Selection

All of children's written work need not be revised. If students are given opportunity to write every day, they will produce much more than they have time to rewrite and more than any teacher has time to read. The key here is functional selection: after children have written a number of pieces, they select the ones they wish to share with others. They may decide to edit a news story, a report, an editorial, or a puzzle to submit to the class newspaper; to revise a story for the school magazine; to rewrite a poem for mounting on the bulletin board; or to revise a letter to send to a manufacturing concern. Or, they may decide to reconsider a story to be shown to classmates via the overhead projector; to rewrite a letter to send to a sick friend; to edit a verse that will be printed on a valentine card. The teacher's job here is to supply meaningful "publications" that encourage revision—the writing bulletin board, the school paper, the class magazine, the letter actually sent—making these integral aspects of class activity.

In expecting children to revise, teachers must change their philosophy if they believe that only "perfect" copy is to be displayed, posted, or included in a classroom publication. While youngsters are learning to revise their own work and are doing so in terms of four or five major concerns listed in their personal guides, other weaknesses will remain. But the question to be asked here is, "Who will benefit from the existence of such perfect copy?" Certainly not youngsters who simply copy teacher's corrections to produce the paper. Of course, principals and parents must understand this philosophy so that they too agree that the process is as significant as the product.

The Conference and Group Instruction

The keystone of a writing program in which children revise their own work is the teacher-pupil conference. As Donald Graves describes it, "The conference, depending on the developmental level of the child, may be as often as every five days, or every ten days." (See "Let's Get Rid of the Welfare Mess in the Teaching of Writing," *Language Arts*, 53:649, September 1976.) Some writers need more frequent interviews and are "often helped best while they are actually engaged in the first two phases of the writing process. Sometimes the teacher may be able to be of assistance when the child has just finished writing, through questions and reactions during the postcomposing phase."

It is in the conference setting that the teacher can draw out youngsters to talk about their writing decisions. Identifying areas of weakness and strength, the teacher asks questions that require young writers to think through what they have written. According to Graves, a teacher should ask questions where appropriate that make writers identify more specifics needed to express the idea fully, consider the language and organization they have used, evaluate their own progress and changes in their development, and decide the audience that would best appreciate what they have composed. For example, playing with language and organization, the teacher might ask, "Which word do you like best?" or "Do you think this sentence ought to come after this one? Read it aloud and tell me what you think." or "You have two thoughts in this sentence. Read it out loud and tell me where the first one ends." Handling a child's progress and change, Graves (p. 650) suggests that the teacher instead might ask, "Let's look in your folder here. Do you see any changes between this paper you wrote last December and the one you have just completed?'' Questions asked are determined by each child's unique combination of strengths and weaknesses.

Of course, even as teachers build reading skills in small groups, they can gather together children who exhibit similar writing problems to build specific language and editorial skills. For instance, children who are just beginning to write in complex patterns can work in a group on embedding sentences by adding *when*, *if*, *because*, *who*, *that*, and *which* clauses to a kernel sentence. Children who have difficulty sequencing thoughts can order ''scrambled paragraphs'' in small groups, while children who are having trouble with possessive forms or contractions in writing can be grouped for instructional purposes. Only rarely does an entire class reach the point where each member's weakness is common to the total class. Therefore, much skill development activity that parallels children's writing must be pursued in the conference or small group setting.

To handle a conference productively, teachers must be able to diagnose children's strengths and weaknesses as writers. Teachers must be able to perceive problems in word usage, paragraph organization, or sentence structuring if they are to ask questions that go beyond matters of spelling, handwriting, and neatness. The difficulty posed by a teacher's lack of understanding of writing is evidenced by an actual example observed in one teacher-pupil conference. A little girl had written ''Bonnie was awake in bed. She heard a thud.'' Her teacher led her to revise the story by converting the period to a comma and marking the capital *S* as a lowercase *s*. The teacher had created a run-on sentence for the girl. How could this teacher possibly help children develop sentence sense until she had investigated sentences more thoroughly herself?

SOME SUMMARY THOUGHTS

Although teachers must accept some instructional proposals on faith, revision research is beginning to offer some answers about what is effective and ineffective. This chapter has detailed some of these investigations and described specific applications based on conclusions reached. Applications include personalized revision guides, the individual teacher-pupil conference, small group instruction in related and needed skills, and group writing and revision in which skill development is a part. These strategies should take the place of intensive teacher correction of children's products and study of formal grammar, both of which have been shown to result in no improvement in children's writing.

If structured well, these strategies through which youngsters can be involved directly in the revision phase of writing can be both a challenge and fun. For those attuned to it, writing is far from a chore. As Isaac Asimov—who during one 96-month period wrote 96 books—explains his obsession with writing, "Writing fascinates me. I love it. And I'm a very lucky man. I spend all my time doing what I love."

Even as we teach children how to putty their writing, we need to instill this love for words on paper. Writing and revising together can be a delight in classrooms. Teachers who have tried it attest to children's enjoyment and interest. In this context, let us end with one caveat! Writing and revision must never be made a punishment. The child kept after school to write a two-page composition in neat handwriting on "Why I Should Raise My Hand Before Talking" will more than likely come away with a dislike for writing, an association that writing is punishment. Writing is a joy. Let us make it that!

Part III

IDEAS AND SKILLS

There is a sound made of all human
  speech,
And numerous as the concourse of all
  songs.

Richard Dixon, "Humanity"

9

LET CHILDREN ENTER
THE REALM OF POETRY ◄►
the magic and beauty
of words

The forms of things unknown, the poet's pen
Turns them to shapes, and gives to airy nothing
A local habitation and a name.
Shakespeare, A MIDSUMMER NIGHT'S DREAM

What is it that we ask children to do when we ask them to create within the realm of poetry? Carl Sandburg begins an answer in two of his definitions of poetry: "Poetry is the opening and closing of a door, leaving those who look through to guess about what is seen during a moment," and "Poetry is a series of explanations of life fading off into horizons too swift for explanations." For Christopher Morley, "Poetry comes with anger, hunger, and dismay," whereas to Percy Shelley, "Poetry is the record of the best and happiest moments." Voltaire adds, "Poetry is the music of the soul; and above all, of great and feeling souls." To William Hazlitt, "Poetry is the fine particle within us that expands, refines, raises our whole being," and to Thomas Chivers, "A perfect poem (is) the crystalline revelation of the devine Idea."

Poetry, then, begins with music in the soul, a feeling, an expansion, of our being, an explanation of life too swift for explanation, but it is music, a feeling, an expansion, an explanation clothed in the beauty of words. Edgar Allen Poe writes that "I would define, in brief, the Poetry of Words as the Rhythmical Creation of Beauty." Matthew Arnold echoes this view: "Poetry is simply the most beautiful, impressive and widely effective mode of saying things." Whereas painting is "silent poetry" to Plutarch, poetry is "speaking painting." In essence, poets paint their ideas with a radiance of words that sing, shout, bubble, and burst forth upon the ear.

CREATING POETRY

Plying their craft, poets take rather ordinary events and feelings and add a new dimension to them. They build images by looking at events from their own individual perspectives, by combining words in music-like patterns, and by laying out their words on paper in a distinctive architectural design that heightens the impact. Recall for just a moment the familiar nursery rhyme of childhood days:

HEY, DIDDLE DIDDLE
Hey, diddle, diddle,
The cat and the fiddle,
The cow jumped over the moon!
The little boy laughed to see such sport,
And the dish ran away with the spoon.

What a mind-boggling way to describe an ordinary barnyard ruckus—cows jumping over moons, cats playing with fiddles, dishes and spoons running together. The resulting picture is fantastic. But so is the sound of such words as *hey, diddle, diddle*, and *little* and *laugh* when juxtaposed. The words tease the ear and tickle the tongue. Through this creative blend of image and sound, a mundane occurrence has become a dancing, delightful time.

The Images of Poetry

Good poetry is filled with unique images, or ways of viewing the world. Take, for example, this familiar little piece attributed to Christina Rossetti:

WHITE SHEEP, WHITE SHEEP
White sheep, white sheep,
On a blue hill,
When the wind stops
You all stand still.
When the wind blows
You walk away slow.
White sheep, white sheep,
Where do you go?

In it, the poet presents an image for the reader that is actually a riddle, for the white sheep on the blue hill are not really sheep at all but clouds driven by the wind.

A bit more outrageous is the image painted by Edward Lear of an owl and a pussycat setting sail together on life's great adventure:

THE OWL AND THE PUSSY-CAT

The Owl and the Pussy-Cat went to sea
In a beautiful pea-green boat,
They took some honey, and plenty of money
Wrapped up in a five-pound note.
The Owl looked up to the stars above,
And sang to a small guitar,
"O lovely Pussy, O Pussy, my love,
What a beautiful Pussy, you are,
You are,
You are!
What a beautiful Pussy you are!"

Lear's picture is one that "blows the mind" by its complete unexpectedness just as does Lewis Carroll's picture of a lobster quadrille in this piece of fluff:

THE LOBSTER QUADRILLE

"Will you walk a little faster?" said a whiting to a snail,
"There's a porpoise close behind us, and he's treading on my tail.
See how eagerly the lobsters and the turtles all advance!
They are waiting on the shingle—will you come and join the dance?"

In a more serious vein are pieces such as "Birches," by Robert Frost, in which the poet explores new relationships:

When I see birches bend to left and right . . . ,
I like to think some boy's been swinging them.

Here birches bent down from the weight of snow and the force of wind are juxtaposed with the notion of boys swinging on tree branches. The result is a thought with obvious simplicity and striking beauty. This same simplicity and beauty are found in the image that Emily Dickinson created:

To make a prairie it takes a clover and one bee—
And revery.
The revery alone will do
If bees are few.

Here out of simplicity leaps a profoundness of thought that overwhelms.
Christina Rossetti, Edward Lear, Lewis Carroll, Robert Frost, Emily Dickinson are just a sampling of the poets who have extended our

awareness of the world around us by creating images that strike us to our core. Sheep in the sky, an owl and a pussycat in a pea-green boat, whitings dancing with snails, swinging boys and birches, reveries and prairies—these are the images that young poets can discover too as they create within the realm of poetry.

The Sounds of Poetry

The images of poetry fascinate the mind; the sounds fascinate the ear and tongue. Words flow, dance, and tumble, making listener or reader believe that those particular words were especially created to go together in just that way. It is sound—more than anything else—that accounts for the enduring qualities of Mother Goose. "Hey, Diddle, Diddle" builds on the recurring sound of *d*, giving a sharp staccato sound to the piece. It accounts too for the continuing popularity of Christina Rossetti's poems in language arts. "White Sheep" gains warmth and intimacy from the alliterative use of *w*—a use that almost simulates the wind whistling through trees. "The Owl and The Pussy-Cat" has a musical lilt that comes from its songlike rhythm, the rhyming of words within lines—*honey* and *money*—and the repetitive use of a refrain—*you are, you are!*

Pieces from the past that have survived the passing of time very often are those in which sound patterns interweave. Take, for example, Longfellow's opening lines to "Hiawatha":

> By the shores of Gitche Gumee,
> By the shining Big-Sea-Water,
> Stood the wigwam of Nokomis,
> Daughter of the Moon, Nokomis.
> Dark behind it rose the forest,
> Rose the black and gloomy pine-trees,
> Rose the firs with cones upon them;

The beat of these lines is the beat of Indian tom-toms; they echo and reecho from line to line. The same is true of the rhythmic beat of Robert Louis Stevenson's "From a Railway Carriage," in which the sound of the train wheels echoes through each line:

> Faster than fairies, faster than witches,
> Bridges and houses, hedges and ditches;
> And charging along like troops in a battle
> All through the meadows the horses and cattle.

The cacophony of harsh syllables placed in juxtaposition can be the basis of a poem's ear appeal. The repeated croak of the frogs, "brekekekex-koax-koax," echoes through Aristophanes' "The Frogs." *Chimborazo, Cotopaxi, Popocatepetl* are the exotic-sounding names that clang upon the ear in W. J. Turner's "Romance." Strange-sounding names add the magic of faraway to the poetry of Rudyard Kipling. He gives glimpses of the Moulmein Pagoda on the Road to Mandalay, and he introduces us to the steadfastness of Gunga Din in India. Lewis Carroll's magic is of jabberwockies, "slithy" toves, and "frumious" bandersnatches. His art is inventing words by combining adjectives: *lithe* and *slimy* into *slithy*; *fuming* and *furious* into *frumious*. The result is a portmanteau—one word that carries the meaning of the two originals—that is often jarring and strident, bringing a distinctive dimension to the poetry.

Some poets employ rhythmical patterns to build beauty into their poetic images. There is a lilt to Robert Burns's "A Man's a Man for A' That":

> Then let us pray that come it may,
> As come it will for a' that,
> That sense and worth, o'er a' the earth,
> May bear the gree, an' a' that.
> For a' that, an' a' that,
>   It's coming yet for a' that,
> That man to man, the world o'er,
> Shall brothers be for a' that.

This same musical quality is found in a myriad of poems, such as "The Green Grass Growing All Around" (author unknown), John Masefield's "Sea Fever," A. E. Housman's "When I Was One-and-Twenty," and Robert Burns's "Flow Gently, Sweet Afton."

The Visual Appeal of Poetry

Poetry has a distinctive architectural form and shape that some poets play with to add beauty to their poetry. Italics, capitalization, short line/long line combinations, indentation, and punctuation may all contribute to the image being communicated. Similarly, the overall arrangement of words into artistic patterns on a page may be an integral element of the piece. Spaces can take the place of punctuation, supplying the pauses that allow the ventilation of thought.

Most readers are familiar with Lewis Carroll's "The Tail of a Mouse" in *Alice in Wonderland*: in that verse, words are placed on the page to resemble the mouse's tail. Readers are familiar too with the way e. e. cummings designs with words, spaces, and letters, breaking lines of verse into visual units, ignoring the conventions of punctuation and using space instead, and placing words with artistry upon the page. On a lesser scale, young people can create word-sound arrangements that are heightened visually. One group designed this:

TORNADO
The wind is a whirling dragon
Leaving destruction in
Its wake as it
Whips
Its
Tail
Across
The
L
A
N
D.

Diane, Stephanie, and Tom

ENCOURAGING POETRY

This chapter began by asking, "What is it that we ask children to do when we ask them to create within the realm of poetry?" Certainly we are not asking them to produce at the level of a Carroll, a Dickinson, a Burns, or a Rossetti. But if poetry is image and word beauty wrapped in one, then we *are* asking children to search for unique images through which to express their thoughts, emotions, and explanations of life; we *are* asking them to play with words that communicate with the beauty of "smouldering radiance," becoming aware of the sounds, rhythms, and architectural shapes of words and spaces.

As a way of encouraging children to experiment within the realm of poetry, a teacher can have children create images, sounds, and visual elements without expecting them to produce fully crystallized poems. Children toy with words, word pairs, phrases, and clauses in what may be termed *prepoetry writing sessions*, their only task being to play with the sounds of words, to concoct visual patterns out of words and spaces, and to play with images that may express their ideas and emotions with simplicity and beauty. How does the teacher begin? The following sections give specific suggestions for fostering prepoetry experiences. Each suggestion can be expanded by a teacher into an actual teaching-learning activity—a mini-lesson—for use in a classroom.

Creating Images

Image Brainstorming.   With children working either as a class or in smaller groups, toss out a question: What is summer? Have the children respond with as many words or word combinations as they can concoct. Tell the children this is a no-limit fun game—their wildest thoughts are to be expressed. Record on the chalkboard if this is a class activity; otherwise have each child record his or her "storm of ideas" anonymously on a slip of paper, collect the papers, and have a group of compositors select ideas from the slips to design into a poem.

In response to this activity, a sixth grade produced the following "idea storm":

> School's over. It's mischief time. Forget everything you learned in school. Hot, dragged out time of swimming and sunbathing. Glad to get back to school. The sun shining on the sandy beaches. Watching the sky changing color. Summer is too much when your in love very much. Endless summer is never having to end. Happiness with guess who at the boardwalk bench. The school is done and over with. Its time to have that summer fun.

Several youngsters combined these random images into a poem. It was entitled "Endless Summer."

ENDLESS SUMMER
Forget everything you learn in school.
School is over and
Done till September.
Summer is just too much when you're in
Love—
Endless swimming in cool lukewarm water,
Dragged out time for swimming and sunbathing,
Sun setting on the sandy beaches,
Watching the sky change its colors.
Endless summer
Is
Never having to
End.

Other questions that can be used to motivate similar image brainstorming sessions are What is a/an fish? friend? cloud? mountain peak? mother? brother? elephant? day? What does vacation mean? snow? wintertime? friendship? Halloween? war? peace? loneliness?

In a similar way, ask youngsters to identify the creative relationships that are the essence of metaphors and similes. Begin by suggesting, "I could say that the wind is a mighty giant. In what way are the wind

and a giant similar?'' Children proffer a chartful of suggestions and go
on to write ''The Wind is a Mighty Giant'' poems. Having had this
preliminary experience, children can create even more dynamic relationships: ''What else might we say the wind is?'' the teacher asks now.
Youngsters may proffer ''a giant vacuum cleaner,'' ''a powerful earth-
moving machine,'' ''a gentle powder puff,'' ''a magic carpet.'' In one
class, a brainstormer proposed the wind to be a ''whirling dragon.'' The
poem on page 240 of this book was one group's product after the class
had brainstormed all manner of ways in which wind and whirling
dragons are the same.

Image Listening. Read children poems that derive their appeal
from the images painted with words. Below are examples of collections
that contain image-filled pieces to share aloud with children:

> Arnold Adoff, *Where Wild Willie* (Harper, 1978) and *Tornado*
> (Delacorte, 1977).
> May Hill Arbuthnot and Sheldon Root, *Time for Poetry*, 3rd ed.
> (Scott, Foresman, 1968).
> Aileen Fisher, *My Cat Has Eyes of Sapphire* (Crowell, 1973).
> Lee Bennett Hopkins and Misha Arenstein, *Thread One to a Star*
> (Four Winds, 1976).
> Langston Hughes, *Don't You Turn Back*, ed. L. B. Hopkins
> (Knopf, 1969).
> Nancy Larrick, *Room for Me and a Mountain Lion* (Evans, 1974).
> Richard Lewis, *The Moment of Wonder, In a Spring Garden*, and *Of
> This World* (Dial, 1964, 1965, and 1968).
> Myra Cohn Livingston, *Listen, Children, Listen* (Harcourt Brace
> Jovanovich, 1972).
> Valerie Worth, *Small Poems, More Small Poems*, and *Still More
> Small Poems* (Farrar, 1972, 1976, and 1978).

Image Experiencing. So that they can experience an image in a
physical way—

- have children imagine what a giant spider web would be like by
  building one with twine laced from tree to tree out-of-doors;
  follow up with brainstorming about the feel of being caught
  in a web.
- have children imagine they are lost by following a maze while
  blindfolded; follow up with brainstorming about lost sensations.
- have young children pretend to be a leaf buffeted in the wind, a
  jellyfish carried on the tide, a bird flying for the first time, a
  banana being peeled; this activity can be done to a musical
  accompaniment.

Image Fantasizing. Give children the opportunity to imagine the fantastic. Build a lesson on what it would be like to—

- be one-inch tall looking at the world.
- be ten-feet tall looking at the world.
- sit on a cloud.
- be all alone in a rowboat at sea.
- be a bee, sitting on a flower petal.
- climb the side of a skyscraper.
- push the earth with a giant bulldozer.
- tunnel down an anthill.

Either record each child's image on the board, or have him or her do it anonymously on a slip of paper. Later, two or three youngsters write a brief piece by combining suggested images.

Constructing Visual Effects

Seeing Poems. Construct poetry broadside charts in which poems printed in manuscript on large sheets of oaktag are displayed, or project poems using the overhead or opaque projector. For this purpose, select poems that draw their special effect from a variety of visual devices. Good sources include:

Robert Froman, *Seeing Things: A Book of Poems* (Crowell, 1974).
Robert Froman, *Street Poems* (Dutton, 1971).
Ruth Gross, *The Laugh Book* (Scholastic Book Service, 1972).
Lee Bennett Hopkins, *This Street's For Me!* (Crown, 1970).
Eve Merriam, *Out Loud* (Atheneum, 1973).

Seeing Pictures in Words. Give children the fun of concocting visual pictures with single words. Show them some examples as in figure 9.1.

Let children select words that they can picture. The following are highly workable for this purpose:

hippopotamus	flat	dot
endless	circle	motorcycle
ladder	snake	climb
zigzag	column	fall
candle	monument	reverse
electric	thin	upside-down
pyramid	fat	lean

Figure 9.1. Words communicating visually

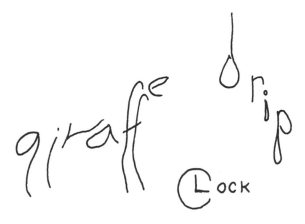

Children can also try to produce visual effects using the letters of the words in phrases: *giant step*; *waves, waves, waves*; *fir tree*; *apartment house*; *climbing up a tree*; *tiny ant*; *walking in circles*; *railroad train*; *head-on collisions*; *automobile tires*; *running downhill*; and *up, periscope*. Figure 9.2 provides some examples to get children started.

Building Visual Effects into Poems.   Structure class activity so that there is time for writing experience-poetry charts in which young children dictate images in groups and the teacher records. When recording, the teacher should keep in mind that the way he or she capitalizes, punc-

Figure 9.2. Phrases communicating visually

tuates, and positions words on paper may heighten the effect, and that, through it, children intuitively pick up some of the architectural shapes and forms of poetry.

Older children can be encouraged to write the words of poems they have created on individual word cards. These can be laid out on large brown paper sheets much in the fashion of advertising layouts. Cards can be moved around and tried in various patterns to achieve different spatial relationships; even the letters of a word can be cut apart to try for unique spatial effects. Once a final pattern has been determined, the youngsters paste or staple their cards to the paper and use watercolor or felt pen to add color to the written poem. The same technique can be employed with a magnet or flannel board. Word cards bearing the words of a poem written by a child or a group can be juggled on the board until poets decide they have the space-word relationships that best fit their message.

Building Sound-Word Relationships

Writing Noises into Poetry. Some of the sound effects of poetry can be derived from noises that are not typically expressed in words. Take, for instance, the way Vachel Lindsay uses lion noise in "Daniel Jazz." Lindsay incorporates two lines of lion roar—Grrrrrrrrrrrrrrrrrrrrrrrrrrrrrrrrrr—into the body of his poem. The fact that these lions also speak "We want Daniel, Daniel, Daniel" adds to the effect.

Children can experiment in much the same way, working with the sounds of—

a dentist's drill	leaves in motion on a tree
a scream	a foot coming down on a leaf
the cry of a bird	ocean waves
a coin dropping on concrete	a horse's trot
a horn	a motorcycle
radio static	pneumatic drills

Selecting any one of these noises, children listen to the real sound or the sound on record. Verbally, they attempt to mimic it. Then they write a representation of the noise in letters, drawing on their phonics understanding to assist them. This activity works well with small groups of youngsters, each working with a different sound.

Playing with Repetitive Words and Phrases. Encourage youngsters to play with some of the repetitive word patterns of poetry by repeating one word or a few over and over, perhaps changing it slightly with each repetition and then adding four or five other message-sending words. For instance, children could play with *red*, repeating it as many times as they want in whatever visual pattern seems right. They add an image-creating phrase at the end as in—

red red red
Red Red Red Red
RED RED RED RED RED
BURNING UP THE
SKY

Words that work here are color words, such as *black*, *yellow*, and *green*, and words like *fear*, *stop*, *fire*, *wind*, *up*, *never*, and *forever*. Figure 9.3 is

Figure 9.3. A sound-filled poem by a fourth grader

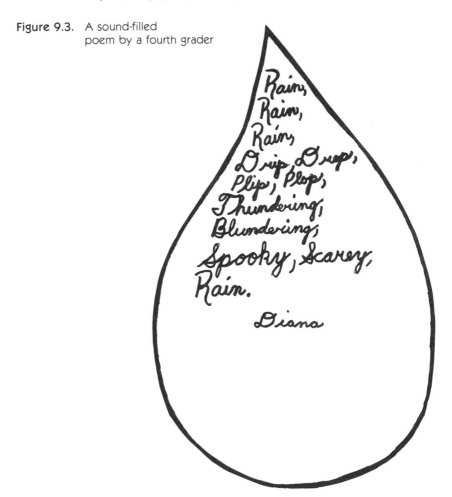

Rain,
Rain,
Rain
Drip Drop,
Plip, Plop,
Thundering,
Blundering,
Spooky, Scarey,
Rain.

Diana

an example of a piece by a fourth grader that derives its appeal from this effect.

A related approach is to begin with a word such as *drippity, swishy, diddily, doodolly, tickity, flippity,* or one that a child invents and that has a "nice" ring to it. In composing orally together, children repeat the word in patterns they devise, adding only a small number of other words to achieve a musical sound effect as in this piece:

Drippity, drippity, drippity—

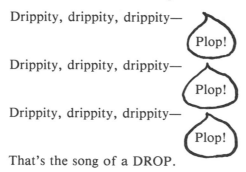

Plop!

Drippity, drippity, drippity—

Plop!

Drippity, drippity, drippity—

Plop!

That's the song of a DROP.

Similarly, give children a phrase: "At the end of a day . . . ," "School means . . . ," "Love means . . . ," "In the spring . . . ," "Suppose that . . . ," or have youngsters devise their own introductory repetitive phrase. Then suggest that everyone write a number of lines that begin with that phrase. If all children begin with the same introductory phrase, a poetry-writing team can later select several lines and build a poem based on the repeated element. Using this technique, a sixth grade began with "Another day . . . ." Initial prepoetry lines included:

Another day to work again for someone else.
Another day is waking up for school.
Another day—tomorrow.
Another day, another bad time.
Another day—a day to come or a day to follow.
Another day, Another hour, with the freshness of a shower.

A poetry-writing team, working with the teacher, later organized the lines into a little poem:

Another day—
    a day to come or a day to follow.
Another day—
    to wake again for school.
Another day—
    to work again for someone else.
Another day—
    Tomorrow.

Inventing Words. Following the example of Lewis Carroll, involve youngsters in word-inventing sessions in which they build words that have no meaning but are pronounceable in English. Such a session can be motivated by Sandburg's "Phizzog"—"This face you got,/This here phizzog you carry around," by Carroll's "Jabberwocky," or by Mother Goose rhymes—"A dillar, a dollar" and "Diddle, diddle, dumpling, my son John." A bulletin board displaying invented words such as *flatter-cocky*, *fiddlebob*, and *crumbledeblah* is another way to prompt young people to concoct words that sound pleasant to the ear and feel nice on the tongue. Children can build their invented words into repetitive patterns in later sessions.

Playing with Exotic-Sounding Names. Have children conduct an atlas search for place names that titillate the ear. This activity can be carried on by a group of youngsters who can then compile a bulletin board that displays the exotic-sounding place names. Individually, in groups, or as a class, children then select a word or words from the board to play with in repetitive, visual patterns.

Building Alliterative and Rhyming Sequences. Working with the whole class, start with a word like *wind* and encourage students to think of verbs starting with *w* that could follow. They may suggest *whistles*, *waltzes*, *whines*, *whips*, *wrestles*, *waits*, *wants*, *works*, *wanders*, *washes*, which, if set down within an architectural design, almost make a poem with space substituting for punctuation:

> Wind . . . whistles and whines
>   waits
>   wants
>   waltzes
>   wrestles . . . Wind

Starting with "The tree," children can look for *t* verbs, for instance, *trembled* and *trailed*, *touched* and *tossed*. Starting with "The fly," they can look for *f* verbs: *floated*, *flew*, *fluttered*, *freed*. A dictionary and a thesaurus are helpful tools to have at fingertips during this activity.

A similar type of activity can be carried out with rhyming words. Children attempt to build a rhyming sequence on a word such as *crash*: *trash*, *flash*, *mash*, *dash*, *lash*, *ash*, *clash*. Again, written down with some attention to visual dimensions but without too much concern with meaning, the words are almost a poem:

> CRASH:
> Dash
> Flash

>Mash
>Trash
>Now mostly ash!

Children can build similar word plays on words that rhyme with *thick*, *go*, *side*, *guess*, *worm*, *bell*, *breeze*, *steam*, *sleep*, *cheer*, or *feel*. A rhyming dictionary is helpful here.

Listening to the Sounds of Words in Poems. Select poems to read to youngsters that derive special effects from sound/word relationships. Below are some examples of collections teachers are finding useful:

Lee Hopkins and Misha Arenstein, *Thread One to a Star*, with poems by many writers (Four Winds Press, 1976).
Eve Merriam, *It Doesn't Always Have to Rhyme* (Atheneum, 1968).
Eve Merriam, *There Is No Rhyme for Silver* (Atheneum, 1962).
Mary O'Neill, *Hailstones and Halibut Bones* (Doubleday, 1961).
Mary O'Neill, *Words, Words, Words* (Doubleday, 1966).
Robert Louis Stevenson, *A Child's Garden of Verses*, ill. Brian Wildsmith (Franklin Watts, 1966).
Jay Zweigler, *Man in the Poetic Mood* (McDougal, Littel, 1971).

WRITING POETRY OF MANY KINDS

The imagery, sounds, and visual effects of poetry are expressed in numerous verse forms: free verse, haiku, cinquain, picture or concrete poetry, rhymed couplets, series of rhymed couplets, and limericks, to name a few of the genres popular in elementary schools. Youngsters can inductively discover the characteristics of a verse form by hearing, seeing, and studying poems written in a particular form. Teachers themselves should experiment with the forms so that some of the examples children study inductively are those teachers have written. A related technique is to share samples written by students in previous years. Youngsters may perceive that poetry writing is something they themselves may enjoy; it is not an activity restricted to professionals.

Of course, children should not be required to replicate precisely the structural characteristics of a type of poetry. Creating a haiku, a limerick, or a couplet can lead youngsters to modify the form into a structure that is uniquely theirs. Perhaps the pinnacle of poetic pleasure is the invention of a new form in which a child can effectively communicate. Thus a child may invent a form to which he or she has not previously been introduced, a form like a pyramid, in which the number of syllables per line follows the scheme of 1-2-3-4-5 as in the lines:

Wait!
Stand Still!
Listen,   Man
To   the   Crashing
Of   Worlds   Colliding

Or children may change a 1-2-3-4-5 pyramid introduced to them by their teacher into 1-3-5-7-9 as in these lines:

The
Silver Star
Showered Stardust Beams
Across   the   Shimmering   Sky
Asking   Me   the   Question—"Who   Are   You?"

As teachers, we should not consider a particular form of poetry so perfect or so sacred that a child cannot play with the form itself, modify it, and create something new in the process. In this respect, work with the traditional forms of poetic expression in the elementary grades should be considered a springboard to carrying the mind into original areas rather than merely replicating what is.

Let us turn briefly to some of the traditional forms that can serve as creative springboards to invention.

Free Verse

Free or blank verse is unrhymed poetry in which the poet has no restrictions of total length, number of syllables to the line, or rhythmic pattern. The images and the sounds determine the overall product. The poet must sense or feel the point at which to break lines, the point at which a new stanza should begin, the point at which an image is complete.

To start, children can build images around such topics as love, pain, fear, subways, snow, beach, people, being little, being lost, and being unhappy. In motivating free-verse writing, the teacher must start with talk about ideas and brainstorming of random thoughts. Later youngsters individually or in groups build their ideas into verse, experimenting with different arrangements. One group of second graders did this and cooperatively produced—

SPRINGTIME
Spring is a time—
      for eating ice-cream cones.
Spring is a time—
      for riding bikes and jumping rope.

Spring is a time—
for picnics.
Spring is a time—
for happiness.

Joyce Hash, an eleven-year-old, began image-building around the phrase "A mother is a person who . . . ."

A MOTHER IS—

A mother is a person who says she loves you even though she
doesn't act like it, who calls you
in the house just when you're having
fun,
who makes you wear a coat in June,
who makes you go to bed early even though you
tell her that you
will get up in the morning.
A mother is a person who washes clothes but makes
you iron them and who is very nice when she makes
nice clothes for you.

Concrete Poetry and Acrostics

When a poem's image is derived primarily from its visual elements or when it is the way letters and words are arranged on a page that communicates the message most strikingly, the poem is concrete or picture poetry. There are several forms picture poetry can take. First, the initial letters of a line can in themselves relate to the image or create the effect. This is the case in an acrostic or ABC poetry. After the letter of the alphabet that will be the beginning point has been chosen, each successive line or word must begin with the letter next in alphabetical sequence as in these pieces:

Donuts   Jumping Kangaroos—
Enter   Landing Merrily Near—
Fat   Open Pouches. Quickly
Gaily   Run
Hopping.   Some Tiny
                              Jumping Kangaroos!

Related to ABC poetry is poetry in which the first letters of lines spell out the title as in this star-centered poem:

Sparkling spot of light
Trailing in the sky,
After night is over,
Runs away and hides.

Or in—

> The tube spews light
> Entwining thought in threads—
> Like hypnotist—
> Entices minds to
> Vacant hollowness.
> In desperation
> Should I not ask, "Am
> I a person or a puppet
> On a string?"
> No, do not ask.

Because it is necessary to find a word beginning with a specific letter to start a line, this is rather difficult poetry to write. However, the form can be used in elementary grades, if short specific words as *sun, wind, fog, cat, dog, home, sky, me, tree, bug, bee,* or *worm* are used. Children begin by brainstorming words that begin with each letter in the title word as in: **S**—*scorching, shining, solar, silver, still, sweltering, some, so;* **U**—*up, under, umbrella, universe, us;* and **N**—*noon, 'neath, now, never, night, no one.* In creating short verses, young poets help themselves to these words listed on chart or board, remembering that words may flow across lines and that thoughts need not end at line's end. This is the principle of enjambment discussed earlier in chapter 5.

A second, more common type of concrete poetry is that in which some part of the message is communicated visually as well as verbally. One way to achieve such a visualization is to arrange the letters on the page to suggest word meanings as in figure 9.4. Another way is to build pictures directly into the poem. In the poem "Grasshopper Race" given in figure 9.5, for example, the words *Race Cancelled Today* are blocked to form a sign like those posted when a race is actually cancelled.

Figure 9.4.   A SHORT TRIP, a concrete poem using graphic placement of words

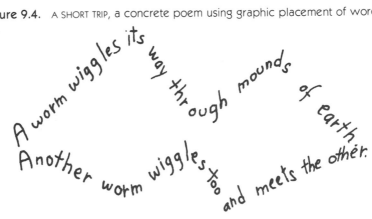

Figure 9.5. An example of a concrete poem

GRASSHOPPER RACE

L
I
N
E

U
P
      our grasshoppers
      for a grasshopper race.
Start!
Jump! Faster!
Stay on the Track!
But off the raceway the grasshoppers
Leap.

Obviously the medium of concrete poetry does not allow the sophisticated development of imagery possible in free verse because the form is limited by the strictures of visualization. However, because there is a puzzlelike nature to the construction of concrete poetry, the form may appeal to youngsters who usually turn off to poetry based on more abstract images.

Haiku, Senryū, Tanka, Cinquain

Here are two poems by John, a sixth grader.

Shiny blue water
ripples as the boy throws stones
into the still sea.

It is raining now!
Blossoms falling from the trees
fade in the puddles.

John's poems are haikus that turn to nature for subject matter, are unrhymed, and adhere to the syllabic scheme 5-7-5. A Japanese form, haiku is a brief interlude of imagery, a glimpse that children can handle with amazing ease and beauty. Haikus can be stimulated by excursions into nature and by parcels of nature brought into classrooms—an opening bud, a gnarled branch, a cactus, a water lily, a hermit crab—by touch, smell and taste experiences, and by abstract art—finger painting, ink blobs, metal sculpture. Again, ideas can germinate in image-brainstorming sessions. And again, the pattern 5-7-5 does not have exclusive rights on perfection: the child who builds a delicate image adding two or three more syllables or using two or three fewer has manipulated the form to meet the unique requirement of his or her image. The result is a modification of the haiku, or what the Japanese call senryu. Paul did this when he created—

> Dandelion flowers
>   blowing in the breeze . . . little airplanes
> flying round and round.

It is possible to carry haiku a step further to embrace larger interludes of imagery that cannot be expressed in the seventeen syllables of haiku. The result can be a tanka, in which the poet begins with the syllabic scheme of a haiku (5-7-5) and adds two more lines (7-7). A piece so constructed has a total of five lines and thirty-one syllables: 5-7-5-7-7. It too is unrhymed, and its stress is on the image expressed.

A second way of varying and expanding the haiku is to juxtapose several sets of 5-7-5 lines to form a series of verses on one theme. The first haiku in a set may talk about the daffodil, the second about the crocus, the third about the dandelion—all signals of spring. This approach to the haiku is particularly applicable when a group of children are composing within an umbrellalike topic such as a winter storm, a summer seashore, a forest walk. If each youngster reads his or her piece aloud in sequence, the result will be a string of haikus that can later be printed on a chart as one large poem comprised of a number of individual parts. Here is an example composed by an older group:

> SNOW DAY
> A white snow sweater
> covers all the sleeping land
> with cold winterness.
>
> A snowflake falls and
> catches on a barren twig—
> so soft and fragile.

Bright and blue, the sky
outlines stark and leafless trees,
weighted low with snow.

Tiny footprints cut
trails of life across the snow
as nature wakens.

Although the cinquain does not have Oriental origins, youngsters work within the form in much the same way as they create haikus, senryūs, tankas, and verse haikus. As with the syllabic forms already considered, cinquains are small interludes of imagery. They are constructed within five lines and typically follow a syllabic scheme of 2-4-6-8-2.

Candles—
flickering flames
that fill the dark with light—
cast hope where once there lay despair.
Candles.

Traffic:
An endless stream
Of autos, buses, trucks.
Start, stop, start, stop, start, stop, start, stop.
Hours late!

Some cinquainists also adhere to the additional stipulations that the—

- first line is composed of only one word.
- the second of two words.
- the third of three words.
- the fourth of four words.
- the fifth of only one word.

Another poetry form that children enjoy is the diamante. (See fig. 9.6.) Chapter 2, page 54, gives an explanation of this form.

Rhyming Poetry

One of the basic building blocks of rhyming poetry is the couplet—at its simplest just two lines of verse each ending with the same sound or sounds:

A flower shifting in the breeze
Scatters pollen to make me sneeze.

Pete, grade 6

Figure 9.6. A diamante

March
Windy, rough,
Swaying, whistling, blowing,
Wind, puddles. Dew, rainbows.
Brightning, blooming, warming,
Calm, beautiful,
March
Nancy

Requiring only two rhyming words, the couplet can be an easy introduction to rhyming-word patterns. With the aid of a rhyming dictionary or lists of rhyming words, children can play with numerous word pairs, building them into couplets.

Once children have handled the couplet, they can try writing a series in sequence as these two fifth-grade girls did:

WHAT IS WINTER?
Winter is snow and ice
    And everything nice:
Skis and skates
    And holiday dates,
Snowball fights
    And very cold nights.
Christmas vacation
    Is a sensation.
THAT'S WHAT WINTER IS.

Sue H. and Babs K.

A step beyond the couplet is the limerick, five lines of verse with a humorous tone and with two sets of rhymes—the first, second, and fifth lines rhyming together, the third and fourth lines rhyming. Since limericks sometimes start with "There once was," for children to begin with that phrase can prove as helpful as it was for Bobby, an eleven-year-old who wrote:

There once was a stupid cat
Who got hit by a flying bat,
    Soared high in the sky
    She flew like a fly,
And got caught by Officer Fat.

Since a limerick is essentially a rhyming, rhythmic word play, short phrases with a list of accompanying rhyming words can motivate limerick writing:

Base Phrase	*Rhyming Words*
a plain Jane from Maine	rain, attain, champagne, complain, Spain, train, drain, cocaine, domain, abstain, hurricane, vain
some merry mice	slice, dice, twice, ice, rice, precise, spice, sacrifice, suffice, nice, advice, lice

Base Phrase	*Rhyming Words*
a mixed-up chick	brick, sick, lick, trick, hick, quick, kick, slick, stick, thick
a Lady of Kent	bent, gent, scent, circumvent, vent, cement, descent, invent, lent, rent, spent, went
a man called Jake	bake, ache, shake, mistake, sweepstake, awake, brake, cake, lake, flake, make
a musketeer	fear, insincere, volunteer, severe, steer, beer, cheer, clear, dear, queer, spear, leer

Of course, rhyming in free style with no limitations on syllables, no prescribed rhyming scheme, and no strictures on overall length is easier to conquer than a tighter form. Karin Hennings, a fifth grader, used an unstructured approach when she wrote this poem:

SNOW
Snow is light and very bright.
Snow is green; snow is white.
Snow is the kind of thing I like.
Snow is red; snow is blue.
Snow is for—more than two.

SOME SUMMARY THOUGHTS

The majority of youngsters in elementary schools today will not be the great poets of tomorrow. As a matter of fact, it is a rather unique adult who spends leisure or professional time writing poetry. What then is the purpose of taking children into the realm of poetry? We hypothesize that as children play with word-image, word-sound, and word-picture relationships, they become more able to formulate the ideas that are the essence of all written communication. They learn to handle the English language in patterns valuable even in work with other forms of writing; thus, they are learning to express their ideas more effectively.

From this point of view, prepoetry writing experiences are a most important element within language arts programs, for in prepoetry children are involved with the building blocks of communication—ideas, words, sounds, and visual elements. This involvement is more essential than the production of perfect, fully crystallized poems by all youngsters in a class, which is—after all—an objective beyond the teacher's grasp. It is an involvement that may also contribute to children's appreciation of poetry with young people coming to like it and seeking it out to read on their own. If we achieve that end, then instructional time has been well spent.

10

LET CHILDREN ENTER THE REALM OF PROSE ◄► writing one's mind

I'll call for pen and ink and write
my mind.
Shakespeare, HENRY VI

Joan Ryan called for a pencil and wrote her mind:

HOW THE WIND BLEW

Long ago there lived a cloud and a wind. But the wind did not know how to blow. And so not a single person or animal could breathe. Then one day while having tea the cloud died and wind was very sad and lonely cause wind wished to stay with his friend.

Then cloud began to rise and wind followed. And soon they touched the sky. Wind began to sing like this. O O O O O O O O O O O! and that made air. The cloud woke up and began to breathe.

Joan, second grade

To write his mind, Joseph told a tall tale:

THE LONE STRETCHER

Once upon a time, there was a boy who thought he wasn't important. He set out to think.

After a while, he said, "I'm going to stretch myself! I'll be the tallest man in the world! I have it all planned out! I'll be famous!"

Indeed he did. He got a job after school. He worked every day after school and didn't come home till 10:00 every night. When he felt he had enough money, he bought two swing sets and put them ten feet apart in his yard.

He climbed one of them and tried to stretch himself to the other one. When he tried, he fell and got a giant bump on his head. Then he grew muscles in his bump and made his bump reach the other set. He hooked on and cried, "I did it!"

He said "I did it" so many times that one of the neighbors called the police. The police locked him up. Can you guess what he did? He stretched out and escaped.

THE END!

Joe, third grade

Prose writing offers many opportunities to children. It offers them, as it did Joan and Joseph, the opportunity to play with the inventive content of story and to let fancy soar up there with wind and clouds. It offers

Figure 10.1. Joan's drawing of the wind and the cloud

too the opportunity to play with more realistic forms of expression, expository forms such as letters, reactions, and reports. Unquestionably, from very earliest group writing activity in kindergarten, children should be welcomed into the realm of prose and urged to take pencil in hand and write their minds.

THE WORLD OF STORY

In creating stories, writers are not concerned with the actual; their concern is with the invention of descriptions, speeches, characters, and plots that go beyond actual occurrences. Story writers create characters who do not precisely resemble any living persons, settings in which action is to occur, and sequences of actions that may not have happened in that precise way in real life. Writers devise words and sentences that they put into the mouths of their characters, endowing inanimate objects and animals at times with the gift of human speech. The art of story is blending setting, plot, characters, and dialogue into a believable whole to which a reader can relate.

Encountering the Elements of Story in the Real World

One way of welcoming children into the world of story is through the world of reality. Children should be encouraged to see opportunities for invention in real life situations; they should invent action, dialogue, and characters based on real people they have observed and real events they have experienced. To help young writers jump from the real into the fanciful, the teacher can take students on short observation walks in the park, along a city street, or through a nature preserve and ask them to look for interesting or unique people and phenomena to work into a story. Suggestions that lead to inventive thinking include these:

Action
Imagine what scrape that boy is going to get into.
Imagine what could happen here at night.
Imagine what happens here in winter.
Imagine what would happen here if this spot were transported to outer space.
Imagine what would happen if those two people bumped into each other.

Dialogue
Imagine what those two people who are talking are saying.

Imagine what that boy's mother will say to him when he gets home.

Imagine that the birds (or the fish in the pond) are talking. What are they saying?

Imagine that the grass is talking to the wind. What is it saying?

Imagine that Mama Monkey is actually talking to Mike, the baby monkey. What is she saying? How will he answer?

Character

Imagine what kind of person that man is. Let's think of adjectives to describe his appearance, to describe the way he is inside.

Imagine what he does, what he enjoys doing, where he lives, how he talks, and how he acts.

Create a name for the person or animal you are observing.

Setting

Describe this place as it would look at night, in the summer, in the winter. Let's use good, clear adjectives.

Describe this place as you imagine it will look next year.

Describe what this place would look like during a storm, on a hot day, filled with hundreds of people, or inhabited only by animals.

Brainstorming, youngsters can pursue this activity from an observation site: sitting on a grassy plot by a popular park path, on a bench in the outdoor zoo, or on an old log in a wooded area; standing discreetly by a supermarket entrance or a busy street corner; or even looking out of the classroom window. Observing can be assigned as an individual activity: "During the next week, 'people-watch.' See if you can find a real person who would make a good story character. Develop a list of descriptive phrases about the person and draw a sketch if possible."

Encountering the Elements of Story Through Literature

One of the best introductions to setting, plot, character, and dialogue is through the finest of stories already written. During daily story sharing times in primary and intermediate grades, characters come alive, moving and talking on a stage created by a writer who in a sense manipulates the strings, or story events, much in the manner of a puppeteer.

In a story each character has distinctive qualities and contributes in some special way. Reacting to a story they have heard or read, children can identify qualities of contrasting characters; they can brainstorm words that describe each major character or group of characters. Joy Moss did this with her students at the Harley School ("Using the 'Focus Unit' to Enhance Children's Response to Literature," *Language Arts*, 55:482–88, April 1978). Developing a unit for six- and seven-year-olds around the topic of bears, Ms. Moss shared a series of bear stories including Lynd Ward's *The Biggest Bear* (Houghton Mifflin, 1952), Brian Wildsmith's *The Lazy Bear* (Watts, 1974), and Mirra Ginsburg's *Two Greedy Bears* (Macmillan, 1976). In response children developed charts of "Bear Facts" and "Bear Tales"; and because emphasis was to be on characterization in writing, children went on to brainstorm possible types of bear characters they might create. They also listed "descriptive words which could be used in their stories to portray their bear characters." Summarizing the children's creative writing activity that was an outgrowth, Joy Moss wrote, "This brainstorming session combined with all the previous experiences listening to and discussing bear stories and working on related projects provided a rich soil for the growth of ideas from which to create a story independently" (p. 487).

Brainstorming and the development of character charts work equally well in upper grades as either a group or independent pursuit. Students who have read or heard chapters from E. B. White's *Charlotte's Web* (Harper & Row, 1952), which Charlotte Huck has called one of the most popular children's books to be published in the past twenty-five years, can brainstorm and chart words they associate with Charlotte, Wilbur, and/or Templeton, returning to study their character-word charts to figure out the characters who function as heroes, protagonists, villains, or antagonists. Later they can brainstorm words to describe characters who will star in their own stories. Other stories with strong characters to chart are James and Christopher Collier's *My Brother Sam Is Dead* (Four Winds, 1974), Laurence Yep's *Dragonwings* (Harper & Row, 1975), and Mildred Taylor's *Roll of Thunder, Hear My Cry* (Dial, 1976), all of which are Newbery Medal or Honor Books. With these books, children can again identify protagonists and antagonists and brainstorm words to describe major characters.

Even as they refine their understanding of characterization, children can acquire a sense of plot development through continued contact with stories. Having listened to or read a story, youngsters can plot key story events on a time line, adding illustrative sketches to the line if they wish. As upper graders encounter more complex plots, story lines can begin to resemble river patterns with systems of tributaries (or subplots) feeding into the main stream of events and in turn flowing into distributaries (or other subplots). The advantage of this kind of story interpretation is that children can plot out events in a similar fashion even as they invent stories of their own.

First encounters with plotting out story time lines can be through simple tales in which events build rather systematically one upon the other. Good for this purpose in lower grades are wordless storybooks such as Peter Spier's *Noah's Ark* (Doubleday, 1977) in which action is clearly discernible but which require children to find words to summarize the action. Equally good are picture story versions of traditional folk and fairy tales such as Verna Aardema's telling of *Who's in Rabbit's House?* (Dial, 1977) and Margot Zemach's telling of *It Could Always Be Worse* (Farrar, Straus, 1977). Upper graders can use the story time line as a way of reporting on books they have read independently.

Children can become more aware of the importance of setting in a story by creating visual and verbal maps to accompany stories they have heard or read. To make a visual map, children simply plot key story locations on paper much in the manner of an actual map, adding illustrative sketches to provide detail. To get children started in this endeavor, a teacher can share a book containing a setting map, for example, Virginia Burton's *Katy and the Big Snow* (Houghton Mifflin, 1943, paper 1974) for primaries or Kenneth Grahame's *Wind in the Willows* (Scribner's, 1933) for intermediate youngsters. Later creating their own stories, children can draw maps to accompany them. To make verbal maps, children brainstorm words that describe story locations. These can be added to visual maps made in response to stories read or ones that children are writing.

Dramatization can help children see the importance of dialogue in stories. Having read a story to themselves, children can assume roles and speak the parts of specific story characters. Such activity can occur as part of regular reading sessions with on-the-spot dramatizations also supplying a check on children's reading comprehension.

From everyday encounters with stories comes the realization that the world of story is not like the world of reality. Kindergarten children soon realize that the world of Maurice Sendak's *Where the Wild Things Are* (Harper & Row, 1963) is different from that in which they themselves exist, that events happen differently in the make-believe world, and that people and animals may even behave differently in books. By middle elementary school, children are fully aware that Pippi Longstocking's experiences in Astrid Lindgren's classic (Viking, 1950) are not exactly real and that life does not go on like that. From numerous encounters with books, children know that when they write stories, they too can depart from reality.

Encountering a Variety of Story Forms

There is no reason to restrict children's writing of inventive content to what is typically called a short story. Although children can be motivated to write delightful stories by the types of activities described in chapter 4, they can also experiment with other story forms: the picture storybook, the fable, the tall tale, mystery and adventure stories, comic strips, and plays. In working with any of these forms, children are assisted by hearing numerous samples in preparation and in some cases modeling their own productions after those they have heard.

Picture Storybooks. Young people who have listened to and read picture storybooks during their early years can be encouraged to write their own picture storybooks. (See fig. 10.2.) This is not as immense a task as it first appears. Children who have read extensively know this form of literature better than any other. Children can also collaborate with one serving as writer, another as illustrator.

Children can adapt the recurring patterns found in picture storybooks for use in writing. As Jon Stott ("Running Away to Home—A Story Pattern in Children's Literature," *Language Arts*,

Figure 10.2. Two pages from an "I Like" book by a first grader

55:473–77, April 1978) explains, "Stories are based on patterns and these patterns are generally based on the patterns of other stories." According to Stott, the most common pattern in stories for younger children is the linear journey of wish fulfillment to "a perfect place where life is lived happily ever after." Another common pattern is the circular journey, which brings the major character back to the place where he or she began. A variation on this latter pattern is the "running away to home" story seen in such tales as Marjorie Flack and Kurt Wiese's *The Story About Ping* (Viking, 1933) and Maurice Sendak's *Where the Wild Things Are*. Children who have listened to one of these can brainstorm a character and the adventures he or she can have in running away to home. They can decide why the character decided to leave home and why he or she decided to return. Early story-writing activity of this kind can be teacher-guided in a group setting, with the teacher asking questions and recording children's stories for them on board or chart. Later, children can create their own individual stories that follow the same pattern.

Other patterns children know from their story listening and reading experiences include:

- ABC-books in which each page describes something that begins with a successive letter of the alphabet.
- Day-of-the-week-books in which each page recounts something that happens on a successive day of the week.
- Down-the-rabbit-hole-books in which some magical device such as a looking glass, a toll booth, a swing, a time machine, or a cupboard becomes the entry into fantasy land.
- Magical-transformation-books in which donkeys are transformed into pebbles, princes into beasts, princesses into swans.
- Long-sleep-books (or Rip Van Winkle books) in which a hero returns after an extended sleep of many years.
- Three-tasks-to-overcome-books in which a hero must surmount three impossible hurdles before claiming a desired reward.
- Three-wishes-to-make-books in which a hero is granted three wishes and typically flubs his or her chance by wishing for a sausage or two.

Any one of these patterns can be discovered by children who have read several books that follow a specific development. Searching for similarities, listeners and readers can also note differences that make each story unique. The result can be an appreciation of literature that carries over to children's own writing.

Book writing brings with it still another advantage—participation in Young Authors Conferences that are being held across the country.

Many organizations are sponsoring conferences where youngsters who have written books can come to share their own productions and listen to illustrators, writers, book publishers, and book binders explain their crafts. Participation in this kind of event can be the highlight of young authors' elementary years.

Fables. If a teacher wants to try a book-writing activity on a smaller scale, all members of a class can become involved in writing a class book to which each youngster contributes a short piece and an accompanying illustration. Writing fables—short prose pieces building toward a moral—lends itself particularly well to this activity. Having heard a series of fables and perhaps having dramatized favorites both verbally and nonverbally, children select a moral and write original fables based on it. Fables created in this way are compiled as a class book by a team of compositors. Here is Patty Coombs's fable as it appeared in "Fables by Sixes," a sixth-grade class book:

A CHICKEN WHO SPOKE A FOREIGN LANGUAGE
Once there was a chicken who could speak a foreign language. The language that he could speak was Spanish. Every morning he went to all his friends' homes to play with them. But they would never play with him because he couldn't speak English.
One day when the chickens were playing, that is all except Puncho, a wolf was hiding in the bushes. Puncho saw him and didn't know how to warn his friends.
Suddenly, Puncho ran right out in front of the wolf to attract his attention. The wolf ran after-him and the other chickens were safe.
Later they saw Puncho pass their house. The next morning when Puncho came to their house, the chickens were happy to see him and they played with him all day.
Moral: ACTIONS SPEAK LOUDER THAN WORDS.

Tall tales. Some children are delighted by the exaggerations and impossibilities inherent in tall tales. After meeting Paul Bunyan and Babe the Blue Ox, children can write and illustrate their own books of tall tales on an individual basis, in collaboration, or as a whole class with each youngster contributing a tale to a class book. Vicky Giambra's story was entitled simply "Worms" in her sixth grade's "Tall Tales of Nature":

WORMS
Did you know that a long time ago when Mother Nature was setting up housekeeping, worms played a very important part in helping her?
The Tape Worm would furnish the tape measure so that the Inch Worm could measure the right lengths on their projects. Their

projects ran anywhere from making flowers to making honey-suckle vines.

Then the Angle Worm would make sure the angles were correct. After that, the Cut Worm would cut out whatever pattern or design every other worm was making. When that was finished, the Pin Worm would pin on the leaves to the bushes.

At mealtime the Grub Worm would furnish the "grub" for all the worms to eat. While the worms were eating, the Book Worm would read to them about people. When it got dark, the Glow Worm would provide light so the worms could continue their work.

When they had completed their work in one place, they would call on the Skip Worms to furnish transportation along the "Route" Worm to another place where they could do more work and start their tasks over again.

Mystery or Adventure Stories. By upper elementary grades, youngsters begin to enjoy a good mystery or adventure story. This accounts in part for the success of the Nancy Drew books despite the fact that each book replicates others in the series in terms of plot and character development. A teacher can share aloud a short mystery-type story with a group—a story in which exciting, puzzling events occur and must be solved by a young detective. When children have listened to or read several stories that are filled with adventure, a teacher can help youngsters begin to write by supplying introductory paragraphs such as these:

- It was almost dark as Tara and I started down the lonely country road. Suddenly, she grabbed my arm and whispered, "Do you see what I see?"

- No one was in sight! I looked down through the cracks in the grating. There was a _____ that started to _____.

- We were just sitting there in the kitchen the morning it all started. My mother had just said, "Nothing ever happens around here," when suddenly _____.

- I was lying in bed. The house was quiet. Lying there, staring at the ceiling, I thought I heard a noise. It was a noise that sounded like. . . .

Story starters of this type can be placed in an Adventure–Mystery Corner, set apart from the rest of the classroom. Children go there to create stories that excite or frighten. Here too can be a collection of books of the same genre, which students can read. As writers complete original tales of adventure, they add these to the collection for others to read.

Figure 10.3. Children's comic strips

Comic Strips. Youngsters also enjoy comic strips. (See fig. 10.3.) For this reason, a let's-read-the-comics session in which teacher and children share some of their favorite *Peanuts, Henry, Nancy,* and *Blondie* strips can be a prelude to writing. Having shared and listened, children can work cooperatively to add dialogue to strips from which the words have been blacked out. This group activity focuses children's attention on the contribution of dialogue to story. Individuals can later create dialogue for strips of their own creation. From individual pieces, a class publication can be made by stapling the children's strips on large pieces of brown paper in the style of the funnies.

Plays. Writing plays brings students into direct contact with the key elements of story. A group of youngsters working together to write a play that they will eventually perform must decide what characters they will write into their play, what things will happen, and, of course, what lines each character will speak. In addition, they must consider what props they will use and what kinds of costumes, if any, they will wear. In dramatizations involving puppets, they must paint scenery on the sides and back of the puppet stage to communicate a sense of setting, and they must construct puppets whose shape, form, dress, and coloring communicate some dimensions of character. They must use dialogue and movement to carry the plot forward.

Play-writing activity perhaps has a beginning in the creative play of young children. For example, as children play with plastic dolls representing make-believe characters who dwell in the swamp with Pogo—the owl, the alligator, the turtle—they may pretend that the owl is talking to the alligator and may carry on an imaginary conversation, or they may load all the plastic animals into a dump truck and pretend that they are going for a ride through the swamp. What children do with their toys during creative playtimes carries them into the world of invention. It can be a first step toward eventual writing of prose.

A next step is when children put on a long green sock puppet—an alligator—and improvise with it. Now players are no longer Tommie and Laurie. They are Albert, the alligator who lives in the swamp with Pogo. Now they must act and talk the way they think Albert acts and talks; they must create conversation and action. Older children can go a step further: they can take a character met in a storybook or TV cartoon and compose a playlet, a scene in which the familiar character meets a lonely bear, a friendly hippo, or perhaps a giant whale. Later, children can use as their major characters a strange man met in the park, a little bird who could not fly, or the friendly fellow who sells ice cream on the corner by the school. When several children work together on play-writing projects such as these, the results can be exciting. The youngsters can both write and perform their playlets, even recording them on audio or videotape.

THE WORLD OF REPORTING

A reporter covers an event or topic by describing or telling about it as accurately as possible. Of course, a written report cannot have the completeness obtained by recording on tape or film; neither does it reproduce word-by-word all the sources used in a reference. Essentially, the reporter's job is to select the facts and the data that communicate a clear picture. In this respect, reporting has subjective elements. The way a writer originally defines the dimensions of the topic, his or her own conception of what is relevant, and the reporter's point of view color—or even bias—the selection of data.

The reporter must also organize his or her data into a framework for communicating. Sometimes that framework is a chronological ordering that parallels the event itself. At other times when events or topics are more complex, the development of a framework for reporting is as creative an endeavor as is the invention of plot or character. A biographer may employ flashbacks to add interest. A scientist may use graphs and tables to present findings succinctly. A Rachel Carson may clothe her facts in an introductory fable. A historian may build suspense by holding back facts until a climactic point. A Nobel prize winner may add stories of infighting among scientists to make a technical account of discovery appeal to a broader audience. These writers know that facts alone may be unattractive and that the appeal of nonfiction is as dependent on style and organization as is the appeal of fiction.

Numerous skills are involved in writing accurate accounts. Obviously all reports are not cut from the same fabric. Some reports tell about events or things the writer has directly observed. In this context, observational skills are primary. Others tell about events or topics in which writers were not directly involved so that they must rely on their skills to search a topic through reading, listening, and interviewing. Still other reports attempt an analysis of data; in these instances, reporters must be able to identify relationships, perceive reasons, and make hypotheses. Because written reports can be so varied, let's focus on specific kinds of reports and consider ways in which teachers can help children acquire reporting skills.

Reporting on Observed Events

The teacher can supply opportunities for reporting by structuring activities that specifically lend themselves to direct observation. As suggested in chapter 1, observational sites set up in the classroom—incubating eggs, germinating seeds, growing crystals, feeding fish—can trigger the reporting act. Observation walks taken by the teacher and children, who all carry notebooks in hand, have a similar potential. Children can also be encouraged to participate in community activities and report back to the class. Activities associated with the Scouts, Four-H Clubs, or hobby clubs are appropriate here. Books are useful too. See, for example, Ann Grifalconi's *City Rhythms* (Bobbs-Merrill, 1965) and Florence Heide's *Sound of Sunshine, Sound of Rain* (Parents' Magazine Press, 1970). Both of these make young reporters more aware of the significance of things around them.

Observation Guides.   To aid in systematic recording, a teacher can help children develop a checklist of questions to consider when reporting on an event. An observation guide can include such items as these:

What happened?
When did it happen?
Where did it happen?
Who was involved?

How did it start?
How did it end?
How long did it last?
Why did it happen?
What were people's reactions to the happening?

Each child uses the questions as a guide, recording answers to the items that are relevant to a specific happening being investigated. These answers are notes on which young writers base their written reports.

Class Reporters.   One way of encouraging children to write reports is to assign the position of class reporter to several students each week. Class reporters take notes and report on classroom happenings: movies seen by the class; an assembly program; accidents occurring in the class; projects; visits by principals, community leaders, or parents to the class; class trips; or a sports event or contest in which the class participated. At the end of the week, the reporters write headlines for their class news stories and compile them into the weekly class newspaper, which is posted on the bulletin board. The results of this endeavor may be surprising in terms of physical size. When children's stories are printed by hand and mounted on paper, the size of the project may be comparable in overall dimensions to a real newspaper.

Observation Journals.   Another way to encourage children to write about events they have observed is to develop the recording habit by having them keep a daily journal. (See fig. 10.4.) Time each day can be set aside, perhaps as part of individual study periods, for students to write in their journals about things that happened to them the previous day. Youngsters can describe things that happened on the way to school, at home the night before, or in the playground or classroom. The teacher, of course, cannot and need not read all that children write in their journals. Children select one or two reports to share with the teacher during an individual conference scheduled every week. Children's writing problems that are noted during the conference time are listed on the individual child's editing guide. Later, inductive lessons in how to handle certain English structures are developed by the teacher in response to similar weaknesses in the writing of several children.

Reports in the Content Areas.   Scientific investigations in the classroom lend themselves well to reporting based on direct observation. The teacher can demonstrate a scientific phenomenon—for example, expansion of colored water in a narrow tube when heated, combustion of a magnesium strip, the action of a siphon or a pendulum. Children watch

Figure 10.4. An illustrated page from a second grader's daily journal

and record what was done and what resulted. As follow-up they talk about what happened, hypothesizing why. Figure 10.5 depicts a workable observational recording guide based on this sequence. Its format parallels the more complex system of laboratory reports—procedure, results, discussion—that students will use as they move into high school science courses. In this sense, the activity prepares them for more advanced writing experiences.

Scientific observations, of course, need not be restricted to teacher

Figure 10.5. A guide for recording scientific observations

What We Did	What Happened
What We Think about What Happened	

demonstrations. Children can themselves compare and contrast leaves from a single tree to find out about variety in nature, study the runoff of water from different land areas, or grow seedlings under varying conditions. Again, children record what they did and what happened, moving on to propose explanations. If children investigate in this way in groups, each group can collect data, pool its findings with other groups, and cooperate in the writing of a class report.

Reporting on a Topic—The Research Paper

An assignment found at all educational levels from fourth grade to university is what—for lack of a better name—has been called a research paper. In creating a research paper, a writer gathers data on a topic through reading, listening, and interviewing, organizes major facts and concepts into paragraph form, and analyzes them. Although upper elementary students can begin to develop the search and organizational skills necessary to complete this extensive writing task, anyone who has worked with youngsters knows that many are really not ready to handle lengthy and numerous sources. They cannot produce an analysis of data. As a result, to ask youngsters to write research papers is to encourage them to copy material from references line by line.

Teaching Beginning Reportorial Skills.   What can we ask of children in the elementary grades? Beginning about fourth grade, children can look through several sources and compile several paragraphs based on those limited sources. Working within the boundaries of such a realistic assignment, they can gain some basic skills needed when they attack a research paper at higher levels.

One skill is pinpointing a topic. A student announces that he or she is going to write a report about horses. The teacher who wants to help that child build skill in identifying a manageable topic will ask, "What do you want to know and report about horses? Are you interested in the evolution of the horse? Do you want to write about what horses do for people? Do you want to investigate the different kinds of horses and what each one does?" The child can be encouraged to phrase the topic as a question, a strategy that helps a writer to zero in on an actual problem. For instance, a child who begins to think about reporting on cacti and who hears, "What specifically about cacti are you interested in?" may come up with this topic question, "How do cacti survive on the desert?"

As youngsters in upper elementary grades attempt slightly more extended reporting tasks, a teacher continues to ask, "What specifically about this topic are you interested in?" Students identify several problem-type questions in response. For instance, a boy who wants to write about astronauts may narrow his topic to three questions: What kinds of problems does an astronaut meet in space? What training is necessary to prepare astronauts to meet these problems? What kind of person makes the best astronaut? Then the reporter can collect data helpful in answering these questions. If, on the other hand, the boy begins to write without first zeroing in on the topic questions, he has no criterion by which to judge the relevancy of facts uncovered. He has no logical way to decide what to include. As a result, his report may be a potpourri of assorted facts and concepts culled from a variety of sources.

Formats for Reports. At this level a teacher can also introduce youngsters to interesting ways of presenting content. Children reporting on a historical event can write their reports in the form of—

- a TV program: "You Are There!"
- a radio or TV newscast as it might have been recorded at that time in history with modern technology.
- a newspaper story of that day.
- a series of flashbacks recalled by an actual participant.

Children writing about a country as part of geographical study can organize their reports into—

- a travel folder that gives details about the country.
- an itinerary for a tour.
- an article for the travel section of a newspaper.
- a description of travel through part of the country in the style of the *National Geographic*.

Children reporting on the life of a well-known individual can write—

- a TV script for a "This Is Your Life" type program.
- an obituary.
- an award banquet.
- a biography that moves chronologically backward.
- a biography told by a well-known contemporary—for example, Martha Washington talks about George.
- an interview with the person.

Related Search Skills. Another skill that children in grades four, five, and six begin to need is ability to indicate the sources of facts and ideas included in a report. Although complete footnoting and bibliography forms will come in high school, children in the fourth grade can begin to note down the names of the authors and the books from which they took material. They can be taught to underline book titles and alphabetize by author the references they have used. At higher levels, children can add dates to their citations. By sixth grade, especially gifted children can be shown how to footnote a direct quotation from a source and enclose these words in quotation marks. Footnotes at this point are not detailed. Author, book title, and page number suffice. To help sixth graders recall footnote and bibliographic forms, a simple style sheet of examples can be kept in individualized writing folders for ready reference.

A corollary activity relates to library use. Children can be introduced to the card catalog, the Dewey Decimal or Library of Congress system, and indexes. Lessons of this type can be fun when a teacher employs large mock-ups of index listings; of book bindings showing classification number, author, and title; and of author, subject, and title cards. For example, children holding mock-ups of book bindings line up in the order in which books would be found on the shelf. Armed with information from an enlarged subject card, a child attempts to locate the desired book from the lineup of book bindings held by other youngsters.

Now is also the time to teach the search-related skills through which children look for ideas to be expressed in written form. Children should be taught how to summarize, how to identify quotable quotes, and how to search a variety of sources. See chapter 4 for specific suggestions.

THE WORLD OF REACTION

One of the most legitimate writing activities in which students can be involved is the production of what, for lack of a better term, can be called a reaction paper. A reaction is a point of view that is based to some extent on an analysis of related facts. Essentially it is an expression of preference, opinion, or judgment: a reactor proposes, "I prefer this book to that one because . . . ;" he or she states, "The president should . . . because . . . ;" he or she writes, "I judge that action to be unwise because. . . ." Each of these reactions is similar in that reasons are given to support the point of view. They may differ in the number and kinds of reasons given. A judgment presents a highly sophisticated argument in support of a point of view and generally includes some reference to some predetermined criteria. A preference presents a liking or disliking with only a limited set of supporting reasons. An opinion is a belief about the rightness, goodness, or propriety of a course of action and lies somewhere between a judgment and a preference in the amount of substantiation supplied.

Subjectivity is clearly inherent in every kind of reaction. What one person judges to be superb another may judge inferior. Then, too, each person may support his or her judgment about a particular case with different reasons. A case in point is Rachel Carson's classic *Silent Spring*. Some reviews of this book were highly favorable, expressing the view that Miss Carson's work was a notable contribution both to science and society. Others called the book unscientific and myopic. Obviously different reviewers were judging the book in terms of their own knowledge of and attitudes toward pesticides and the environment.

Not only are there subjective elements inherent in reactions but there are analytical elements. A comprehensive reaction separates a whole into its component parts. It focuses on the individual parts, the relationships among the parts, and the relationships between the parts and the other data. These are all steps in analyzing.

Building Reactions into the School Program

First graders can be introduced to the essential steps in reacting by being encouraged to talk about their own reactions toward real events, things, and ideas. The teacher asks questions that ask children to express preferences and opinions: "What part of the movie did you like best? Did you like least? Why? Would you like to see that movie again? Why? Why not?" Eventually the teacher can elicit a general reaction by asking, "Did you like it more than you disliked it? Why?" and by recording reactions in group-chart form for them:

THE MOVIE

We didn't like the movie. It was scary. When the snake grabbed
the frog, we got scared. Sandy said that the music scared her.

The format for such a lesson is simple:

1. *Involvement* with an event, thing, or idea such as watching a movie;
2. *Talk* about the event, thing, or idea;
3. *Formulation* of an opinion about the event, thing, or idea;
4. *Recording* of opinion.

As children advance through the grades and begin to express opinions on complex issues, the search for supporting reasons becomes part of reaction. The talk stage may uncover the fact that children do not have the background on which to formulate an opinion. At this point, children should be encouraged to search books, magazines, newspapers, and pictures for related information, to contact authorities in the field, and to study other people's opinions on the topic. Reacting for them has become Involvement-Talk-Search-Formulation-Recording.

One way to include opinion and judgment in upper elementary grades is to work with a controversial question for which there is more than one answer. Junior high school students who have been studying freedom of the press may formulate opinions as to whether the press should publish reports harmful to the country's standing abroad. Upper graders studying poverty problems may decide whether everyone should be assured a basic living wage.

As students work with controversial issues, talk and search activities can occur in small groups. Each group writes an opinion or judgment following the outline suggested in figure 10.6. This outline parallels the format of a formal resolution and prepares youngsters for more sophisticated writing activity. Having put together two or three paragraphs, each group presents its majority-minority opinion paper for total class consideration. If interest is high, different viewpoints can informally be debated.

Supplying a Variety of Stimuli for Reaction

The events, things, or ideas to which students can react are boundless.

Figure 10.6. Outline for group-reaction paper

OUR REACTIONS
Majority opinion:
Reasons supporting this opinion: 1.   2.
Minority opinion:
Reasons supporting this opinion: 1.   2.

Fashion trends.   Do you like longer or shorter skirts? Why? Why not? Do you like short or long haircuts?

Magazine articles.   Do you react positively or negatively to an article in *Junior Scholastic, Time,* or *Newsweek*? Why? Why not? (Reactions of these types can be written in the form of a letter to the editor.)

TV programs and editorials.   How do you react to a popular TV show? to the news reporting on Channel 2? to the editorials given on television? Why? (A letter to a station is a means for positive action.)

Books.   Would you recommend this book to a friend to read? Why? Do you like the main character in the story? Would you want that character as a friend? Why?

Motion pictures.   Would you recommend this film to a friend? What part of this movie did you like best? What part did you like least? Why? Would you want to see the movie again? Why?

Products.   Do you like this kind of cereal? Why? Is brand X better than brand Y? In what way? Does packaging of the product give false ideas about the content? In what ways?

Situations.   Should the U.S. recognize the new government in Y? Should cigarette smoking be banned in public buildings? Should Community X and Company Z be allowed to dump its wastes into the river? Why? Why not?

To introduce older students to the distinctive style of movie reviews and editorials, it is often most effective to start inductively with actual samples. Children can listen to television movie reviews, collect newspaper editorials, and clip the letters-to-the-editor sections of newspapers and news magazines. These samples can be posted on the Look Here! bulletin board. During independent study periods, children browse through the clippings and go on to create original reviews of books, films, and TV programs and to write editorials on current issues.

THE WORLD OF LETTERS

When we take children into the world of letter writing, concern is no longer with the inventive content of story; rather, concern is with realistic ideas growing out of everyday occurrences in the real world. Letter writers observe and/or participate in a happening and then may use their letters to others to tell about that event, express their opinions about it, or ask recipients to react to it. In letter writing, too, people may question, request, order, or state facts. In all these instances, an accurate mirroring of real events is essential.

Teaching Letter-Writing Forms Inductively

Fundamentally, a letter is written conversation that is either formal or informal in nature. A letter is a traditional form of communication about which numerous social and business conventions exist. A formal business letter typically follows this form:

> 25 Walnut Street
> Lancaster, California 93534
> May 29, 198–

The American Toy Company
16 Friend Street
Toyville, Colorado 80302

Gentlemen or Madam:

Would you send me one mini-racer, catalog number 5984. I am enclosing a money order for $5.30. If there are other shipping charges, would you tell me, and I will send the additional amount immediately.

> Very truly yours,
>
> [signature]
>
> Joseph Anderson

In contrast, a less formal social letter generally is structured like this:

> 25 Walnut Street
> Lancaster, California 93534
> May 29, 198–

Dear Bob,

Will you come to my birthday party? It is at 3:00 PM on Saturday, June 15, at my house.
I hope you can come.

> Your friend,
>
> [signature]

Should the traditional conventions associated with social and business correspondence be taught? We think so. In today's world a correspondent is judged by the way in which his or her letters are written. Whether an applicant gets a job, whether a request is handled with dispatch, or whether a cause being espoused is given adequate consideration may be determined by the form and clarity of the letters a person writes.

How to Organize Lessons for Discovery.   Teaching the conventions of letter writing can be done in lessons organized so that children not only are involved with letter-writing forms but also are gaining skill in fundamental thinking processes. Lessons structured inductively so that children work from specific samples and discover the essentials of letter-writing forms for themselves allow this dual orientation.

To begin in this way, a teacher must have several models of letters available for students to analyze. Teaching a lesson on social forms, the teacher suggests, "Let's study each of these letters. With what kind of information does each letter start? Where is this information placed on the page?" As children respond with different kinds of information, the teacher or a scribe lists items on the board: address of writer, date of writing, and so forth. Later participants together construct a schematic that shows the overall appearance of a letter. This schematic results from students' step-by-step analysis of the information in the model letters. It might look like this:

> street address (of writer)
> town, state   zip code (of writer)
> month   day, year (date of writing)

Dear _____,

_____

_____ · _____ · _____

_____ ·

_____ · _____

_____ ·

Your friend,

[signature]

During the revision phase of letter writing, children can refer to their schematic to check the layout of their letters or to double-check one another's papers against the prescribed form.

Through this technique children not only are learning letter-writing conventions; they are also learning how to design a schematic and how to

Figure 10.7. Model of inductive teaching and learning scheme

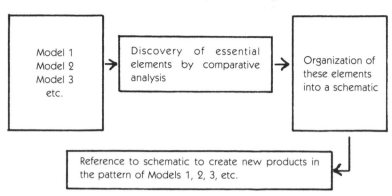

use one to construct their own samples. This is a clear advantage of inductive teaching over an instructional pattern in which the teacher presents the elements and the schematic to be memorized.

Other similarly organized lessons can be structured around the forms of business letters, envelopes for business letters, and envelopes for social letters. In each case, the teacher can begin with numerous models, which the youngsters analyze to determine the key components; in each case too, the students go on to create schematics to use as they write their own pieces. Figure 10.7 outlines the basic steps in an inductive lesson pattern, a pattern that can be applied in such other contexts as teaching punctuation and capitalization conventions, and poetry forms.

Some Points to Consider. Two cautions should be stressed in reference to an inductive system for teaching letter writing. First, models for discovery sessions must be clearly visible to all. One third-grade teacher worked inductively with model envelopes constructed from large sheets of paper and measuring at least a meter across. She mounted her models on the magnetized chalkboards with disc magnets. In the upper grades, models can be handwritten or typed on ditto sheets and reproduced so that every youngster gets a copy to study.

Second, the amount of detail included in the models varies depending on the children's developmental level. In the first grade, children may write social letters that adhere in a general way to this format:

Dear Mother,

　　We are having a party in school on Tuesday, January 10. It will be in our room at two o'clock.

After the party, we will give our play about the frog and the prince. I am the prince. You will like our play. I hope you can come.

Love,

[signature]

Additional detail appears in successive grades.

Taking a Functional Approach to Letter Writing

As children in classrooms converse through letters they should be addressing themselves to real people about real concerns. For this reason, letter writing should be an integral aspect of teaching/learning activity rather than a unit-type experience in which youngsters are exposed to letter writing for a three-week period every year. In short, letters in classrooms should be written as they are called for by the ongoing life of the class. The three facets of classroom activity that supply opportunities for letter writing are—

- content units in science, social studies, language, art, and mathematics.
- events in the world outside the classroom that have direct significance for youngsters.
- the general social life of the classroom.

For instance, business letters of request can be written as part of content units and sent to—

- authors, community leaders, or the principal, requesting that the individual come to speak to the class on a topic under study.
- companies and agencies, such as the American Petroleum Institute, for material and information related to a unit.
- embassies, international organizations, international airlines, or travel agencies, such as Japan Travel Bureau, for material or information about a particular country or region of the world.
- authorities in a subject area, requesting information on a topic. If a single authority in an area is contacted, it is wiser to send only one letter rather than deluging the authority with many letters from different children. Also, write for specific information, not for general points readily available in reference books. One biologist with a leading pharmaceutical firm recalls one request made of him: "Kindly tell me everything you know about the frog."
- airports, industries, and private gardens, requesting permission to visit the sites.

Letters of opinion or protest focusing on events of significance to the children can be written to—

- the school principal, stating a class opinion on a particular school issue.
- the local or school newspaper, stating an opinion on a social issue.
- the governor, representatives, senators, or the president, stating an opinion on a piece of pending legislation or a governmental policy.
- national and state agencies, such as the U.S. Public Health Service, state fish and game commissions, and local consumer agencies, stating an opinion on a problem handled by the agency.

The general social life of the class can call for the writing of letters of invitation to—

- parents, to attend back-to-school night.
- parents, principal, and other classes, to attend a performance, fair, or display being presented by the class.

Letters of thank-you can be sent to—

- another class, for an assembly program or an invitation to attend a performance.
- the principal, a parent, or a community leader, for coming to speak to the class.
- a person or firm that allowed the class to visit his or her business, or that supplied the class with materials or books.

Friendly letters can be sent to—

- a classmate who is at home sick, is away on an extended trip, or has recently moved.
- a pen pal in another state or country.
- relatives, especially cousins who live at a distance.

By using letters to communicate in a variety of real situations such as these, children will gain control over the style and the form of social and business correspondence.

SOME SUMMARY THOUGHTS

To teach writing is to teach children to create ideas to communicate with others. To teach writing is also to teach children ways of organizing their ideas, of building word and sentence patterns, and of revising what they have written. This is a fundamental assumption on which *Written Expression in the Language Arts: Ideas and Skills* has been built. As suggested in this chapter, however, classroom activities related to the ideas of writing merge with those related to skills. Both aspects interweave in an overall program in which children are welcomed into the world of story, reports, reactions, and letters and are encouraged to experiment with each of these forms.

EPILOGUE ◄►
let children feel the
thrill of kingship

A word is dead
When it is said,
Some say.
I say it just
Begins to live
That day.

Emily Dickinson, "1212"

How do teachers organize written activity for children? *Written Expression in the Language Arts: Ideas and Skills* has answered this fundamental question by presenting written expression as part of an integrated, ongoing language arts program. This is in contrast to a more traditional view of writing as an isolated activity in which the teacher motivates a specific writing lesson, children write during the following half-hour, the teacher later corrects their work, and children copy their compositions replete with teacher corrections.

To conceive of written activity as an integral component of the curriculum brings clear advantages. First, children in an ongoing, integrated program are involved in writing as part of everyday classroom activities. They write as they encounter social-science and natural-science content; they write in reaction to life in the world of reality and of fancy; they write when the social needs of the class mandate; they write to share ideas with others. During independent study times, they dictate into tape recorders, edit papers from their file folders, jot ideas into idea books, record in their journals, finish poems begun on the way to school, and work in groups to compile a gag book, a class newsletter, or a book of fables. Organizing this kind of continuing writing is not so difficult as it at first appears. Purposeful writing can be an independent study option or can be structured as a learning center activity. Working on their own or in independent groups, students select the most meaningful options for themselves while the teacher works with other youngsters on guided activities.

An ongoing writing program of this type takes its direction from overall activities within the curriculum. Youngsters write not only stories, letters, and poems but also reports and reaction papers that grow out of subject content and firsthand experiences. In this respect, an ongoing program is a balanced one that gives children opportunities to handle a variety of content and writing forms.

A second advantage of this approach is that writing is not divorced from other communication areas—thinking, listening, speaking, and reading. The teacher organizes speaking experiences not just to help children gain speaking skills but also to encourage ideas to blossom as part of the writing program; conversely, writing may be a prelude to speaking with children sharing their written pieces through creative oral interpretation. Likewise, the teacher supplies a rich experience with literature not just to develop an enjoyment of reading but to encourage the flow of ideas and to build intuitive understanding about the way words go together on the printed page. Within an integrated language arts framework, isolated lessons in writing are rather rare.

Seen as an integral part of the language arts program, written activity must stress both the development of ideas to share and the skills necessary if expression is to serve its purpose. In this respect, a continuous writing program allows encounters with the idea-content of writing to flow into encounters with basic skills. As part of ongoing curricular activity, children are encouraged to think about innumerable things—to reflect, conceptualize, project, feel, and invent. At the same time they play with words, sentences, lines, and paragraphs as they attempt to communicate their emerging ideas on paper.

In a program where youngsters are writing on a continuing basis and developing skills as needed, the notion of evaluation assumes a unique orientation. Children do not write to have their verses and compositions marked as A, B, C, D, or F by the teacher. This approach to evaluation limits the scope of children's writing activity for it leaves out a pivotal step in the writing act—reviewing and rewriting. In contrast, in a continuous program approach, self-analysis and revision take the place of external teacher evaluation. Teacher conferences and individualization of writing experiences take the place of teacher correction.

To structure an integrated, ongoing program of this type, teachers must expand their conception of activities that are part of learning to write. Of course, children must have ample opportunity to write as individuals; but in the development of thinking and language skills, both teacher-guided group writing and independent group writing have roles to play. In the group setting, teachers can help children manipulate ideas so that they blossom fully and can encourage children to revise and edit. Skills developed through cooperative writing are applied as children go on to create ideas and record them on their own.

LAST THOUGHTS

The act of creating ideas and recording them on paper can be tremendously exciting. It is an act through which words "begin to live" not only for a day but perhaps forever. We have seen classrooms in which writing has become the exciting process that it is, classrooms in which children are helped—

> To see a world in a grain of sand
> And a Heaven in a wild flower
> [to] Hold Infinity in the palm of your hand
> And Eternity in an hour.

>   *William Blake, "Auguries of Innocence"*

We have seen classrooms in which the writer is portrayed to children as—

> Nature's real king, to whom the power was given
> To make an ink drop scent the world for ever.

>   *William Davies, "Shakespeare"*

Let us help children feel the thrill of kingship over big ink drops and little ones too, so that as young people leave schoolhouses all over the world, they have the power to express their ideas with clarity and force. To paraphrase Emily Dickinson, words are never dead when people can use them to communicate.

APPENDIX

COMPANIES SUPPLYING LITERATURE-RELATED MATERIALS TO BE USED IN STIMULATING WRITING

CAEDMON
1995 Broadway
New York, N.Y. 10023

A supplier of discs and tapes containing literary selections, some of which are read by well-known personalities or the authors themselves. Examples include Walter de la Mare reading his own poetry, Hans Christian Andersen read by Boris Karloff, Eve Merriam performing her own poems. K-adult levels.

EDUCATIONAL ENRICHMENT MATERIALS (a company of *The New York Times*)
357 Adams Street
Bedford Hills, N.Y. 10507

A source of full-color, sound filmstrips containing favorite stories from children's books, folk tales, fables, legends, and myths. Examples include *The Wind in the Willows*, Kipling's *Jungle Books*, and *Amelia Bedelia*. Primary and intermediate levels.

INTERNATIONAL READING ASSOCIATION
800 Barksdale Road
PO Box 8139
Newark, Del. 19711

A source of taped interviews with successful writers of adolescent literature. Interviewees include Judy Blume, Vera and Bill Cleaver, and Sue Alexander. Intermediate level and up.

MILLER-BRODY PRODUCTIONS, INC.
342 Madison Avenue
New York, N.Y. 10017

A company supplying full-color sound filmstrips and disc or tape recordings of Newbery award winning books and of interviews with Newbery authors.

Examples include *Roll of Thunder, Hear My Cry*, *The Dark Is Rising*, and *Dragonwings*. Intermediate level.

WESTON WOODS STUDIOS
Weston, Ct. 06883

A source of multimedia literature packages (films, filmstrips, tapes, books), many of which are based on Caldecott award-winning books. Examples include *Strega Nonna*, *Chicken Soup with Rice*, *Noah's Ark*, and *Time of Wonder*. Primary and intermediate levels.

MULTIMEDIA PACKAGES AND MATERIALS TO FOSTER WRITING GROWTH

ALLYN AND BACON, INC.
470 Atlantic Avenue
Boston, Mass. 02210

Expository Writing: From Thought to Action and *Creative Writing: From Thought to Action*—a writing program consisting of text, workbook, and teacher's manual for each of the two skill areas. Materials are designed for discussion, debate, and discovery. Grades 6-8.

DEVELOPMENTAL LEARNING MATERIALS
7440 Natchez Avenue
Niles, Ill. 60648

Storytelling Pictures—twelve full-color 12″ X 18″ pictures to use in getting youngsters to write imaginative stories. Discussion questions are on the back of each picture. Grades 3-6.

Storytelling Posters—twelve posters (seven in color and five in black and white) 12″ X 18″ with teacher's pamphlet that includes discussion questions and suggestions. Grades 3-6.

Moving Up in Grammar: Capitalization and Punctuation—a kit designed to provide students with practice in capitalization and punctuation skills. Grades 3-8.

Written Language Cards: General—a set of eight cards to develop language expression by providing youngsters with opportunities to write responses in cartoon-type balloons. Grades 2-6.

GLOBE BOOK COMPANY, INC.
50 West 23rd Street
New York, N.Y. 10010

The Reading Road To Writing—a series of six text-workbooks that integrate three key skills: reading with understanding, using standard American English, and writing effective short compositions. Titles include "Sentences," "Verbs,"

"Adjectives and Adverbs," "Pronouns," "Words Often Confused," and "Mechanics of Writing." Read-along cassettes accompany each book; teacher's guide included. Intermediate and junior high levels.

GUIDANCE ASSOCIATES
41 Washington Avenue
Pleasantville, N.Y. 10570

Write Now Wordshop Series—five programs and ten parts; record or cassette format with accompanying filmstrips. Titles include: "Write Now Wordshop: See It and Write," "Write Now Wordshop: Hear It and Write It," "Write Now Wordshop: Write Lively Language," "Write Now Wordshop: Write in Order," and "Write Now Wordshop: Write a Story." Teacher's guides suggest ideas that encourage creative responses and more effective written communication. Middle and junior high levels.

Writing: From Assignment to Composition—two filmstrips and two cassettes or records with accompanying discussion guide. Considers how to begin and complete a first draft and rewrite to achieve coherent sentence and paragraph design and unity. Grades 5-8.

Let's Write a Poem: A Poetry Workshop—two filmstrips and two cassettes or records with teacher's guide. Enables youngsters to learn to write different poetic forms such as couplet, quatrain, limerick, ballad, and free verse. Grades 4-6.

Writing: From Imagination to Expression—four filmstrips and four cassettes or records with discussion guide. Illustrates ways in which youngsters can create using various sensory and cognitive perceptions and through mood, setting, plot, and theme. Middle and junior high levels.

Speaking of Spelling—two filmstrips and two cassettes or records with discussion guide. Deals with factors contributing to present-day English spellings. Enables youngsters to learn basic patterns and presents devices to help them with irregular spellings. Middle and junior high levels.

What Is Journalism?—two filmstrips and two cassettes or records with discussion guide. Includes interview with Edwin Newman. Analyzes news stories and gives comparison of the functions and problems of print and broadcast journalism. Middle and junior high levels.

Communication Skills: Expository Writing—six filmstrips and six cassettes or records with teacher's guide. The program consists of visual and verbal materials and exercises to enable students to develop skill in use of the elements of expository writing. Middle and junior high levels.

The Research Paper Made Easy: From Assignment to Completion—six filmstrips and six tape cassettes or records with teacher's guide. Enables youngsters to select a subject, narrow it down, make a statement of objectives, prepare a working bibliography, use the library, make an outline, write a draft, and prepare the final paper. Middle and junior high levels.

HOUGHTON MIFFLIN COMPANY
1 Beacon Street
Boston, Mass. 02107

The Write Thing—a multimedia program that provides thought-provoking material that encourages students to write a journal, produce advertisements, write editorials, and so forth. Each level consists of eight units dealing with a variety of themes, issues, and topics. Included in each package are a teacher's manual, sixteen wall-size posters, write-in booklet for each student, and twelve 8 " X 10 " prints for additional topics. Grades 6–8.

The Writing Improvement Series—two workbooks designed to improve sentence and paragraph writing. *Sentence Improvement* reviews basic sentence patterns and then aspects of style and usage in connection with phrases, clauses, parallel structure, and modifiers. *Paragraph Improvement* enables students to group sentences together to form paragraphs. Grades 6–8.

MILTON BRADLEY COMPANY
Springfield, Mass. 01101

Spelling Games—five games to provide experiences for students in the areas of sounds, word structure through affixes, syllables, visual letter sequence, and auditory memory letter sequence. Grades 3–8.

Wordfacts Games—a set of five games that extend and reinforce language skills in the areas of plurals and possessives, silent letters, word endings, and stressed syllables. Grades 3–8.

NEWSWEEK LANGUAGE ARTS PROGRAM
444 Madison Avenue
New York, N.Y. 10022

Writing Descriptions—a program of worksheets. Titles include: "Selecting Details," "Sensory Language," "Exact Language," and "Action Words." Follow-up activities are suggested. Middle grades or junior high school.

Pre-writing Composing Editing: A Complete Essay Writing Program—a series of worksheets designed to help students select topics for essays, approach subjects from a personal point of view, compose precise thesis statements, develop outlines for essays, build arguments that defend the thesis of an essay, write effective conclusions, edit rough drafts, and proofread final drafts. A teacher's guide related to each area is included. Middle grades or junior high school.

The Editor's Story—a program of worksheets and teacher's guides that offer students insight into the structure of a *Newsweek* article. The four sections of a story—lead, billboard, development, kicker—are introduced and explained. Through a series of exercises, follow-up activities, and assignments, students learn how to write a news magazine story. Duplicating masters are provided for each of the following topics: "The Newsweek Formula," "Action Leads," "Then and Now Leads," "Scene-Setting," "Anecdotal Leads," "General Leads," "The Billboards," "The Development," "The Kicker," "Show, Don't

Tell! Writing Style I and II,'' and "Evaluation.'' Middle and junior high school youngsters.

RANDOM HOUSE, INC.
400 Hahn Road
Westminster, Md. 21157

Aware—a multimedia program to increase a child's awareness so that he or she can respond to the poetry of others and begin to write poetry himself or herself. Grades 4-6.

The Writing Bug—an individualized, multimedia writing program designed to get children writing jokes, ghost stories, plays, scripts for filmstrips, directions, diaries, and articles. Grades 4-6.

The Mag Bag—a kit that uses ten popular magazines to teach critical reading and writing skills. Upper elementary through high school levels.

English Writing Patterns—a series of work-textbooks by Helen E. Lefevre and Carl A. Lefevre. Grades 2-12.

SCHOLASTIC BOOK SERVICES
904 Sylvan Avenue
Englewood Cliffs, N.J. 07632

Doing Research and Writing Reports Workbooks—a series of three booklets geared to teach such skills as choosing a topic, taking notes, making an outline, writing paragraphs, and working with references. Grades 4-6.

Writing Skills Books—a series of three booklets to teach punctuation, grammar, and descriptive writing skills. Grades 1-6.

TEACHING RESOURCES FILMS (A *New York Times Company*)
Station Plaza
Bedford Hills, N.Y. 10507

Fokes Sentence Builder and *Fokes Sentence Builder Expansion*—a series of cards and boxes that help children acquire sentence sense through oral activity. Primary level.

Categories—sets of cards to develop students' ability to classify objects. Primary level.

Sequence Picture Cards, Level 1 and Level 2—sets of cards that students must logically order; it can be used as the basis for story building. Primary level.

Tell-a-Tale Cards—a set of thirty-six cards that can be combined in a variety of ways as children orally create stories and then write them down. Primary or intermediate level.

Kaleidoscope: Activities in Creative Writing and Drama—a source book of forty drama and writing activities with stated objectives and follow-up suggestions. Grades K-6.

THE TEACHERS MARKET PLACE
16220 Orange Avenue
Paramount, Calif. 90723

Springboards to Creative Writing—a creative writing idea file for writing sessions and class work; it includes charts and individual files. Grades K–6.

Correct Writing Errors Without Dampening Creativity!—"flub stubs" help students to correct errors in writing; a set of sixty-seven 5 " X 8 " cards with indexes. Grades 4–12.

Tasty Recipes for Creative Writing—over 101 cards containing suggestions for writing. Section on evaluation that helps teachers to use student papers to teach the mechanics of writing. Sets for K–grade 3 and grades 4–6.

Motivate Great Writing!—fifty illustrated 5 " X 9 " activity story-starter cards. Intermediate and primary levels.

Story Sparkers—a collection of fifty creative writing ideas including motivational pictures and questions to inspire students to construct a story. Each card is 4 " X 6 "; cards are contained in a sturdy box. Grades 3–8.

Write On!—fifty activity cards 4 " X 6 " to spark students' imaginations and to get them writing. Convenient tab sections that include Writers' Workshop, Motivators, Flair for Fantasy, Word Power, Holiday Happenings, and Potpourri. Grades 3–8.

More Write On!—a collection of fifty cards each containing "quick sparks" and photograph. Grades 3–5.

UNITED LEARNING
6633 W. Howard St.
Niles, Illinois 60648

Situational Language: Activities for Applying Language Arts Skills—a full-color, sound filmstrip program in which students apply writing skills as they become copy editors for a daily newspaper; skills include language usage, contractions, metaphors, spelling, proofreading, and so forth. Intermediate and junior high.

Building Sentences—four-color, sound filmstrips that present writing as "talk written down," and that stress the nature of the sentence. Primary.

Communication Power—a series of twenty sound filmstrips with duplicating masters; topics include "Oral Communication," "Be a Word Detective," "Sentence Power," "Paragraph Power," "Composition Power," and "Basic Punctuation." Intermediate.

English Comes Alive—twenty-four captioned filmstrips on these topics: "Sentence Parts," "Writing and Revision," "Punctuation," "Parts of Speech," "Adventures in Communicating," "Adventure in Words." Intermediate and junior high.

BIBLIOGRAPHY

BOOKS PROVIDING RESEARCH BACKGROUND

Britton, James; Burgess, Tony; Martin, Nancy; McLeod, Alex; Rosen, Harold. *The Development of Writing Abilities.* London: Macmillan Education, 1975.

Clay, Marie. *What Did I Write?* Auckland, New Zealand, and Exeter, N.H.: Heinemann Educational Books, 1975.

Cooper, Charles, and Odell, Lee. *Research on Composing: Points of Departure.* Urbana, Ill.: National Council of Teachers of English, 1978.

Emig, Janet. *The Composing Process of Twelfth Graders.* Urbana, Ill.: National Council of Teachers of English, 1971.

Hunt, Kellogg. *Grammatical Structures Written at Three Grade Levels.* Urbana, Ill.: National Council of Teachers of English, 1965.

Lundsteen, Sara, ed. *Help for the Teacher of Written Composition (K-9): New Directions in Research.* Urbana, Ill.: National Council of Teachers of English, 1976.

Mellon, John. *Transformational Sentence-Combining: A Method for Enhancing the Development of Syntactic Fluency in English Composition.* Urbana, Ill.: National Council of Teachers of English, 1969.

National Assessment of Educational Progress. *Write/Rewrite: An Assessment of Revision Skills.* Denver: National Assessment of Educational Progress, 1977.

———. *Writing Mechanics, 1969–1974: A Capsule Description of Changes in Writing Mechanics.* Report Number 05-W-01. Denver: National Assessment of Educational Progress, 1975.

O'Hare, Frank. *Sentence Combining: Improving Student Writing Without Formal Grammar Instruction.* Urbana, Ill.: National Council of Teachers of English, 1973.

Shane, Harold, and Walden, James. *Classroom-Relevant Research in the Language Arts.* Washington, D.C.: Association of Supervision and Curriculum Development, 1978.

BOOKS GIVING IDEAS FOR TEACHING

Cramer, Ronald. *Children's Writing and Language Growth.* Columbus, Ohio: Charles E. Merrill, 1978.

Day, Robert, and Weaver, Gail, eds. *Creative Writing in the Classroom: An Annotated Bibliography of Selected Resources (K-12).* Urbana, Ill.: National Council of Teachers of English, 1978.

Gerbrandt, Gary. *An Idea Book for Acting Out and Writing Language, K-8.* Urbana, Ill.: National Council of Teachers of English, 1974.

Hillocks, George. *Observing and Writing*. Urbana, Ill.: Eric Clearinghouse of Reading and Communication Skills, 1975.

Jackson, Jacqueline. *Turn Not Pale, Beloved Snail: A Book about Writing and Other Things*. Boston: Little, Brown, 1974.

Koch, Carl, and Brazil, James. *Strategies for Teaching the Composition Process*. Urbana, Ill.: National Council of Teachers of English, 1978.

Koch, Kenneth. *Rose, Where Did You Get That Red?* New York: Random House, 1973.

———. *Wishes, Lies, and Dreams*. New York: Random House, 1970.

Lefevre, Carl A. *Linguistics, English, and the Language Arts*. New York: Teachers College Press, 1974.

Malmstrom, Jean. *Understanding Language*. New York: St. Martin's Press, 1977.

McCracken, Robert; and McCracken, Marlene. *Reading, Writing, and Language*. Winnipeg: Peguis Publishers Ltd., 1979.

Poemmaking: Poets in Classrooms. Massachusetts Council of Teachers of English, 1975; available through NCTE.

Stewig, John Warren. *Read to Write—Using Children's Literature as a Springboard to Writing*. 2d. ed. New York: Holt, Rinehart & Winston, 1980.

Tiedt, Iris. *Individualizing Writing in the Elementary Classroom*. Urbana, Ill.: Eric Clearinghouse on Reading and Communication Skills, 1975.

Tuttle, Frederich. *Composition: A Media Approach*. Washington, D.C.: National Education Association, 1978.

Weehawken Board of Education. *Individualized Language Arts, ESEA Title IV-C Project*. Weehawken, N.J.: Board of Education, 1974.

ARTICLES RELATED TO PRACTICE

Albert, Burton. "Are You Giving Writing Its Due?" *Instructor*, 87:41–48, October 1977.

Beyer, Barry. "Pre-writing and Rewriting to Learn," *Social Education*, 43:187–89, 197, March 1979.

Calkins, Lucy. "Learning to Throw Away," *Language Arts*, 56:747–52, October 1979.

———. "Writers Need Readers, Not Robins," *Language Arts*, 55:704–07, September 1978.

Charnock, James. "Paragraphing Made Simple," *Teacher*, 95:90–92, January 1978.

Copeland, Kathleen. "Share Your Students: Where and How to Publish Children's Work," *Language Arts*, 57:635–37, September 1980.

Cothran, Ann, and Mason, George. "The Typewriter: Time-tested Tool for Teaching Reading and Writing," *Elementary School Journal*, 78:171–73, January 1978.

Cozzins, Judith. "Publishing: Bringing Language to Life," *Language Arts*, 56:232–35, March 1979.

Donham, Jean, and Icken, Mary. "Reading to Write: An Approach to Composition Using Picture Books," *Language Arts*, 54:555–58, May 1977.

Emig, Janet. "Commentary: Learning to Write," *Language Arts*, 54:739–40, October 1977.

Froese, Victor. "Understanding Writing (Beginning Writing)," *Language Arts*, 55:811–15, October 1978.

Gay, Carol. "Reading Aloud and Learning to Write," *Elementary School Journal*, 77:87–93, November 1976.

Gonzales, Dolores. "An Author Center for Children," *Language Arts*, 57:280–84, September 1980.

Graves, Donald. "Let's Get Rid of the Welfare Mess in the Teaching of Writing," *Language Arts*, 53:645-51, September 1976.

Graves, Donald, and Murray, Donald. "Revision in the Writer's Workshop and in the Classroom," *Journal of Education*, 162:38-56, Spring 1980.

Groff, Patrick. "Children's Oral Language and Their Written Composition," *Elementary School Journal*, 78:180-91, January 1978.

Gudauskas, Birute, and Charnock, James. "Letter Writing: Don't Let It Become a Lost Art," *Instructor*, 86:82-85, March 1977.

Haworth, Lorna. "Figuratively Speaking," *Language Arts*, 55:837-40, October 1978.

Hennings, Dorothy. "Input: Enter the Word-Processing Computer," *Language Arts*, 58:18-22, January 1981.

Hillerich, Robert. "Developing Written Expression: How to Raise—Not Raze—Writers," *Language Arts*, 56:769-77, October 1979.

Kohl, Herb. "Writing: Revisions and Corrections," *Teacher*, 95:14-21, March 1978.

McKenzie, Gary. "Data Charts: A Crutch for Helping Pupils Organize Reports," *Language Arts*, 56:784-88, October 1979.

Meisterheim, Matthew. "Rx for Helping Johnny Write Better," *Elementary School Journal*, 78:4-8, September 1977.

Moffett, James. "Integrity in the Teaching of Writing," *Phi Delta Kappan*, 61:276-79, December 1979.

Moss, Joy. "Literary Awareness: A Basis for Composition," *Language Arts*, 55:832-36, October 1978.

———. "Using the 'Focus Unit' to Enhance Children's Response to Literature," *Language Arts*, 55:482-88, April 1978.

"Nose for News; A Handbook for Junior Journalists," *Instructor*, 86:43-50, November 1976.

Noyce, Ruth. "Another Slant on Mastery Writing Instruction," *Language Arts*, 56:251-55, March 1979.

Pakula, Arnold. "Language Arts: A Fifth-Grade Publishing Company," *Teacher*, 93:80-84, January 1976.

Sorensen, Marilou, and Kerstetter, Kristen. "Phonetic Spelling: A Case Study," *Language Arts*, 56:798-803, October 1979.

Turner, Thomas. "Trapping the Wild (and Independent) Writer," *Language Arts*, 55:798-803, October 1978.

Tway, Eileen. "How to Find and Encourage the Nuggets in Children's Writing," *Language Arts*, 57:299-304, March 1980.

———. "Teacher Responses to Children's Writing," *Language Arts*, 57:763-72, October 1980.

Uehara, Betty. "Language Experience—For What Purpose?" *Educational Perspectives*, 17:14-17, March 1978.

Walden, James, ed. "From Zero to Steinbeck: A Study of Children's Composition," *Viewpoints*, 50:1-66, January 1974.

ARTICLES SUPPLYING BACKGROUND ON RESEARCH AND THEORY

Cooper, Charles. "Research Roundup: Oral and Written Composition," *English Journal*, 64:74, December 1975.

Cooper, Charles, and Odell, Lee. "Considerations of Sound in the Composing Process of Published Writers," *Research in the Teaching of English*, 10:103-15, Fall 1976.

Graves, Donald. "An Examination of the Writing Processes of Seven-Year Old Children," *Research in the Teaching of English*, 9:227-41, 1975.

———. "Research Update: A New Look at Writing Research," *Language Arts*, 57:913-19, November/December 1980.

———. "Research Update: Research Doesn't Have to Be Boring," *Language Arts*, 56:76-80, January 1979.

———. "Research Update: What Children Show Us About Revision," *Language Arts*, 56:312-19, March 1979.

Graves, Donald, and Calkins, Lucy. "Research Update: Andrea Learns to Make Writing Hard," *Language Arts*, 56:569-76, May 1979.

Graves, Donald, and Kamler, Barbara. "One Child, One Teacher, One Classroom: The Story of One Piece of Writing," *Language Arts*, 57:680-93, September 1980.

Haynes, Elizabeth. "Using Research in Preparing to Teach Writing," *English Journal*, 67:82-88, January 1978.

Hunt, Kellogg, and O'Donnell, Roy. "An Elementary School Curriculum to Develop Better Writing Skills." U.S. Office of Education Grant. Tallahassee: Florida State University, 1970.

Mellon, John. "Round Two of the National Writing Assessment—Interpreting the Apparent Decline of Writing Ability: A Review," *Research in the Teaching of English*, 10:66-74, Spring 1976.

Miller, Barbara, and Ney, James. "The Effect of Systematic Oral Exercises on the Writing of Fourth-Grade Students," *Research in the Teaching of English*, Fall 1968.

Perron, Jack. "Beginning Writing: It's All in the Mind," *Language Arts*, 53:652-57, September 1976.

Porter, E. J. "Research Reports: L. Ezor and T. Lane. Applied Linguistics: A Discovery Approach to the Teaching of Writing, Grades K-12, Weehawken, N.J.," *Language Arts*, 52:1019-21, October 1975.

Shapiro, Phyllis, and Shapiro, Bernard. "Two Methods of Teaching Poetry Writing in the Fourth Grade," *Elementary English*, 48:225-28, April 1971.

Strom, Ingrid. "Research in Grammar and Usage and Its Implications for Teaching Writing," *Bulletin of the School of Education of Indiana University*, 36:13-14, September 1960.

INDEX